WALTER BENJAMIN

*Cultural Memory*

*in*

*the*

*Present*

*Mieke Bal and Hent de Vries, Editors*

# WALTER BENJAMIN

*Images, the Creaturely, and the Holy*

Sigrid Weigel

*Translated by Chadwick Truscott Smith*

STANFORD UNIVERSITY PRESS

STANFORD, CALIFORNIA

Stanford University Press
Stanford, California

*Walter Benjamin: Images, the Creaturely, and the Holy* was originally published in German under the title *Die Kreatur, das Heilige, die Bilder* © S. Fischer Verlag GmbH, Frankfurt am Main, 2008.

This translation has been made possible by the support of the German Federal Ministry of Education and Research.

Printed in the United States of America on acid-free, archival-quality paper

Library of Congress Cataloging-in-Publication Data

Weigel, Sigrid, author.
 [Walter Benjamin. English]
 Walter Benjamin : images, the creaturely, and the holy / Sigrid Weigel ; translated by Chadwick Truscott Smith.
     pages cm. -- (Cultural memory in the present)
 "Originally published in German under the title Die Kreatur, das Heilige, die Bilder."
 Includes bibliographical references.
 ISBN 978-0-8047-8059-9 (cloth : alk. paper) --
ISBN 978-0-8047-8060-5 (pbk. : alk. paper)
 1. Benjamin, Walter, 1892-1940--Criticism and interpretation.  I. Title. II. Series: Cultural memory in the present.
 PT2603.E455Z9425 2012
 838'.91209--dc23

                        2012029069

Typeset by Bruce Lundquist in 11/13.5 Adobe Garamond

*In Memory of Stéphane Mosès*
*(1931–2007)*

# Table of Contents

# Illustrations

*Explanation of Translation and Citation*

The book has been translated by Chadwick Smith (New York).

In some cases his translation is based on a previous lecture version of the chapter done by other translators: Georgina Paul, Chapters 1, 2, and 4; and Jeremy Gaines, Chapters 3, 7, and 9.

Since a great number of the citations from Walter Benjamin's writings have been modified (for reasons that are explained in detail in several footnotes and at length in Chapter 7), the book would become unreadable if this were explicitly indicated in every case. The manner of citation is therefore indicated within the parenthetical references as follows:

- If only the German source is indicated, it is our own translation.
- Where only the standard English translation is indicated, we follow these translations.
- In cases where both versions are indicated (the German source preceding the English publication), this formatting indicates *translation modified*.

## Abbreviations of Cited Works

Citations from the German editions of Benjamin's collected works (*Gesammelte Schriften*) and collected letters (*Gesammelte Briefe*) are indicated in the text with volume and page numbers alone. In order to differentiate between these editions, volumes of the works are numbered with roman numerals and volumes of the letters are indicated by arabic numerals.

AB = Gretel Adorno, Walter Benjamin, *Briefwechsel 1930–1940* (Frankfurt/M: Suhrkamp, 2005).

BA = Theodor Adorno, Walter Benjamin, *Briefwechsel 1928–1940* (Frankfurt/M: Suhrkamp, 1994).

GB = Walter Benjamin, *Gesammelte Briefe*, Christoph Grödde and Henri Lonitz, eds., in 6 vols (Frankfurt/M: Suhrkamp, 1995–2000).

GS = Walter Benjamin, *Gesammelte Schriften*, Rolf Tiedemann and Hermann Schweppenhäuser, in 7 vols. with 3 supplementary vols. (Frankfurt/M: Suhrkamp, 1972–1999).

SelWr = Walter Benjamin, *Selected Writings*, ed. Michael W. Jennings, Vols. 1–4 (Cambridge: Harvard University Press, 1996–2003).

OWS = *One-Way Street and Other Writings*, trans. Edmund Jephcott and Kingsley Shorter (New York: Verso, 1979).

Corr = *The Correspondence of Walter Benjamin,* E. M. Jacobson, ed. Gershom Scholem and Theodor Adorno (Chicago: University of Chicago Press, 1994).

AP = Walter Benjamin, *The Arcades Project* (Cambridge: Belknap Press of Harvard University, 2002).

Origins = *Walter Benjamin, The Origin of German Tragic Drama* (New York: Verso, 1998).

BS = Walter Benjamin, Gershom Scholem, *Briefwechsel 1993–1940* (Frankfurt/M: Suhrkamp, 1980).

CBS = Walter Benjamin, Gershom Scholem, *The Correspondence of Walter Benjamin and Gershom Scholem, 1932–1940* (Cambridge: Harvard University Press, 1992).

## Acknowledgments

Work on this book, and the efforts to more precisely understand the significant place religion occupies in Benjamin's thought, started immediately after the publication of my first book on Benjamin's theoretical writing, *Body- and Image-Space. Re-Reading Walter Benjamin* (1996, in German: *Entstellte Ähnlichkeit*, 1997). A crucial impetus for this present work comes from conversations with Stéphane Mosès, for which I could no longer offer my thanks after his untimely death in December 2007. This book is thus dedicated to him, also because his expositions of readings of the Torah, which he introduced to the *Dialectics of Secularization* (*Dialektik der Säkularisierung*) research group at the Center for Literary and Cultural Research (ZfL) as a frequent visiting scholar, were especially important. I thank the scholars and researchers of this project—Ernst Müller, Martin Treml, and Daniel Weidner—for their shared work on the concept of secularization, which is present in my re-interpretations of Benjamin's writings. I thank Georges Didi-Huberman and Monika Wagner for the inspiring conversations about art and Benjamin.

Through their curiosity and questions, my students in various courses at the Technical University in Berlin and Princeton University highlighted the need for more precise readings and elucidations of many of the more difficult passages within Benjamin's writings. I have also had the opportunity to further develop my readings and theses on the basis of discussions at numerous conferences and lectures, for which many thanks are due to, among others, Russel Berman, Amir Eshel, Rodolphe Gasché, Helga Geyer-Ryan, Eckart Goebel, Tony Kaes, Albrecht Koschorke, Vivian Liska, Avital Ronell, Samuel Weber, Peter Weibel, and Bernd Witte.

I especially thank Jutta Müller at the ZfL for the attentive critical readings of my German manuscript and Chadwick Smith for untiring work on the translation.

*Foreword*

The Holy, Life, and the Creaturely

A letter Walter Benjamin sent to Gershom Scholem in Jerusalem in June 1938 contains a remark that allows an essential clarification of his attitude toward the *Holy*. It comes in the form of a rhetorical figure, as if it were superfluous to devote a word to it: "Is it necessary to state that holiness is an order reserved for *life* and that artistic *creation* does not belong to it under any circumstances? And does it need to be pointed out that the epithet of holiness is nothing more than a novelist's empty phrase when used outside a traditionally established religious framework?" (6/106; CBS 220; ital. S.W.) This distinction, uttered *en passant*, throws light on a possibly principal misunderstanding in the engagement with Benjamin, as it is found throughout the critical reception of his work.

The dimension of the sacred in his theory was for decades discussed primarily in relation to his handling of writing, literature, and images. Only recently has the significance that the divine holds for his concept of life stepped to the center of the debates about Benjamin's work, particularly in connection with the rediscovery of the concept of mere natural life (*bloßes natürliches Leben*) in the essay "The Critique of Violence" (SelWr 1.236). Although this concept, with which Agamben's *Homo Sacer* begins, stretches back to Benjamin and indeed plays a central role in his writings (far beyond the essay on violence), the current debate seems largely to fail to grasp the very meaning of Benjaminian concepts. To him, it is precisely *not* about the holiness *of* life; on the contrary, he considers the "dogma of the sacredness of bare life" as the "last mistaken attempt of the weakened Western tradition." Thus he sees in it a reaction to the loss of the saint and interprets the proposition that bare life is indeed sacred as being the mythical replacement for the divine that originates in "cosmological impenetrability" (II.I/202; SelWr 1.251). In contrast to this dogma, his assertion that holiness is an order reserved for life means that the concept 'life' refers pre-cisely to that dimension that transcends *mere natural life* to the order of the holy. It is through a reference to the divine order that the concept of life first accrues a meaning that makes it more than bare life. This *super-natu-ral (über-natürliche)* dimension of the concept of life relies on the biblical notion that human life is part of divine Creation. It maintains its particu-lar contours within the idea inherent to this tradition that man was made in the divine image, even when this 'more-than-natural-life' has then been transformed into philosophical, ethical, or other principles after the bible lost its claim to authority and validity (Chapter 3). A world apart, human activity is fundamentally different from Creation: the fruits or products of human production are artifacts, or as Benjamin says, formed structures (*Gebilde*).

Yet as a part of creation, itself a creature (*Geschöpf*), the human has a share in the world of creaturely[1]—so long as humans are situated in the state of Creation. The concept, understanding, and interpretation of hu-mans as creaturely are leitmotifs in the ideas, texts, and images from both the baroque and modernity that are Benjamin's objects of investigation. In his commentary on the topic, he interprets the concept of the creaturely as both an expression and an indication (*Anzeichen*) of a "counter-historical" stance—not a-historic, but rather an attitude in contradiction to a histori-cal understanding. It comes from the wish to return to the state of Cre-ation, and to this end it leads to history's conversion back into a kind of state of nature. The concept of the creature is, in this way, a symptom of a confusion of the state of Creation with the state of nature (Chapter 1).

His remark that the attribute of holiness is but a belletristic cliché certainly does not mean that in Benjamin's view the holy is unimport-

---

1. During the constitution of the German language, when Latin words were translated by inventing new German words, it often happened that the Latin word got integrated into the lexicon as well, with the result a semantic differentiation between the foreign word and its German equivalent. The translation of Latin *creatura* into 'Schöpfung' (Creation) and 'Geschöpf' (creation) is part of Luther's German and refers to a biblical context; its con-notation stems from the expression 'Gottes Geschöpf'(God's creation). In distinction to 'Geschöpf' the word 'Kreatur' has acquired another connotation that is more linked to the natural, bodily, or animallike state of living beings, including humans. Since the difference between the meanings is central for the whole argument of the book, we will use *creation* for 'Geschöpf,' creature/*creaturely* for 'Kreatur,' and *Creation* for 'Schöpfung.'

ant for poetical works (*Dichtung*).[2] Quite the opposite. Benjamin's critique is in fact aimed against programs of art that sacralize poetic creation and thereby attribute a *divine mandate*, as it were, to the poet. Benjamin, rather, sees the poet as a descendant of cultic practices that are lost in history (understood as the distance from Creation) and considers *Dichtung* more as a refuge for concerns that have slipped away from theology. The latter is less due to the poet than it has to do with language, because every language (at least in European history) to some degree stands in the lineage of biblical language, which is the medium of revelation, although this is the case mainly in the mode of loss, translation, and conventionalization, that is, in the mode of distance and disfigurement (*Entstellung*).[3] Benjamin treats the distance from Creation, in which language also partakes in history, as a structural distinction between it and revelation. If, however, poetic engagement with language is reminiscent of the *Heiligung des Namens*, because the words are "called by their names," poetic works become the site of a breach through which meanings that originate in a higher order can enter. Nevertheless, poetic works never become identical with the higher order; nor do they become its secular substitute (Chapter 4).

Taking center stage in this book is Benjamin's recognition of the fact that not the least, but actually the weightiest, concepts and ideas in European thought (such as life, the human, and justice) arise from biblical tradition. Also of primary concern, however, are the consequences that this recognition has for the formation of his theory and his engagement with language and history, and with literature and art. Today, Benjamin's rhetorical question, quoted above in the letter to Scholem, demands a clear and decisive answer: it is necessary. Considering the fact that he actually considered commentary on the holy to be superfluous, it is surprising how heavily the reception of Benjamin troubles itself with his engagement with theology, religion, and the divine (Chapter 1). In this regard, a structural

---

2. Benjamin uses both words 'Dichtung' and 'Literatur,' the latter having a more profane meaning and including all sorts of texts, whereas 'Dichtung' is reserved for art and discussed in respect of its complex relationship to sacred scriptures.

3. The Freudian term for dreamwork *Entstellung* will be translated in this book as 'disfigurement' instead of 'distortion,' which belongs to the repeatedly criticized translated terms in *Standard Edition* of Freud. As *regards the other two terms of dreamwork*, this book follows the *Standard Edition* in taking 'displacement' for *Verschiebung* and 'condensation' for *Verdichtung*.

configuration can be observed, one that pervades his writings (sometimes clearly, sometimes concealed), particularly in his engagement with terminology. Its matrix persists in the ineluctable distinction between the world of *Creation* (there) and the world of *history* (here), which forms a fundamental epistemic function in Benjamin's writings. It literally represents the foundation of his thinking: "history comes into being simultaneously with meaning in human language" (II.1/139). This epistemic figure found one of its first linguistic expressions in the early essay on language in the image of *the Fall of language-mind* (*Sündenfall des Sprachgeistes*). From the biblical scene of man's expulsion from paradise, Benjamin formed the *epistemic distinction* fundamental for his writing and thought. Through the simultaneous emergence (*Gleichursprünglichkeit*) of history and signs, human acting and speaking always already takes place in the interval between creation and revelation. Thus the historical subject is situated in a state of irresolvable disfigurement (*Entstellung*), while at the same time the subject's concepts always remain based on that from which they were differentiated: law is based on and springs up from justice, the word on the name, images on semblance, and art on the cult. In this respect, there is for Benjamin no thought free from some kind of reference back to ideas that originate in the tradition of the history of religion.

## Neither Theological nor Secular

Thus Benjamin's own stance can in no way be called *theological*. It is rather obliged to the questions that were removed from theology, the latter having lost its privileged claim to meaning. Yet it also cannot be described as *secular*, at least not in the terms with which Hans Blumenberg characterized this term in his critique of the paradigms of secularization: as a "*reoccupation* of answer positions that had become vacant and whose corresponding questions could not be eliminated," in whose transmission, however, a "continuing acceptance of the religious sphere in which language originates" can be discerned (1988, 65, 104). When Blumenberg justifiably judges such practice of secularization as the last Theologoumenon, Benjamin's critique is as well directed to such Theologoumena. This becomes especially clear in his engagement with the interpretations of Kafka available to him at the time (Chapter 6). Perhaps Benjamin's manner of thinking and writing can best be described as *postbiblical*, since it arises from a consciousness for biblical language, holy orders, and the idea of salvation without being tied to it through confession. That the terms of the divine order have singular meanings that may not be transferred into the secular order of human action and social communication is a fixed point within his thought. This acceptance of biblical language absent faith may be described as *Jewish thinking in a world without God*, to borrow the wonderful title of the *Festschrift* for Stéphane Mosès (Festschrift 2000). This thinking is not to be confused with *negative theology*, in which the *Deus abscondicus* itself becomes the center of, and point of reference for, a religious comportment. Nor should it be aligned with a variant of negative theology critical of capitalism that makes the bourgeois world in the image of hell into the object of a quasi-religious evocation (Chapter 5).

Blumenberg once remarked that the God of philosophers is unfeeling, while that of the bible is hypersensitive: "therefore the theologians speak in the idiom of philosophy in order to spare *their* God: could he bear the language of the Bible?" (Blumenberg 1998, 19, my trans.) With Benjamin, one must object to this interpretation to the extent that in his view, theo*logy* as speech *about* God has already been differentiated from biblical language, since it always implies a speaking in history after the "Fall of language-mind," at a distance from creation, so that this fact can rather clarify the closeness the theological idiom has to the language of philosophy. Contrarily, Benjamin is adamant that there is an afterlife of biblical language, and indeed in poetic works. *Dichtung* does not inherit the tradition in such a way that it can be possessed as a resource at *Dichtung*'s disposal, but rather in the sense that poetic works provide a site for a breach through which "something beyond the poet interrupts the language of poetry" (Chapter 4). In this way, his engagement with the tradition does not conform to the opposition of theology to philosophy. Benjamin's position beyond theology and philosophy finds expression mainly in his figures of speech, thought-images, and dialectic images. The genuinely Benjaminian use of language systematically disappears in most translations of his writings into other languages. Because the thought-images are translated either as metaphors or as concepts, his theory often loses its specific signature in international reception. Whereas, because of this elision, his reflections appear to be a great deal more easily compatible with current theoretical discourses, it is often the case that the dimension of language that recalls religious quotations is unrecognizable (Chapter 7).

Forgotten Images:
The Significance of Art in Benjamin's Epistemology

On the other hand, the dominance of thought-images in Benjamin's writing has to date obscured the central and irreplaceable significance that aesthetic perception and the visual images have for his mode of thinking. Artworks, paintings, and prints (that is, images from the history of art) in fact occupy an elevated place in his writings, and not only the two icons of his work, Dürer's *Melencolia* and Klee's *Angelus Novus*—without reference to which few books and articles about Benjamin manage to be published. Similarly, not only are the photographic and cinematographic images so important for his cultural theory of modernity central in his works (Chapter 10), but so are images from artists of the most diverse provenances, from the Middle Ages through to the Renaissance and from the baroque to modernity and expressionism, cubism, and surrealism. Although many works have dealt with Benjamin's concept, critique, and theory of art, an investigation into the question as to what epistemological significance corresponds to artworks themselves remains until now absent.

In Benjamin, the images are also related (like *Dichtung*) to the afterlife of religion. Yet even though poetic language is significant and meaningful for the survival of biblical language, with images it concerns the survival of the cultic, sacred, and magical meanings. If religion relocates its divine kingdom into the clouds, as Benjamin once formulated (VII.1/25), then a preview of the "divine kingdom" becomes perceptible in the artists' painted clouds. Benjamin is interested less in motifs from the history of religion, mostly Christian topics, than he is in the colors and materials of art. In them, the sacred appears practically instantaneous and unmediated. In often short, extremely dense passages, the most diverse images from the history of art come to play a central role in Benjamin's writings. Not uncommonly, it is similar to that lightninglike insight followed by the text as the long-rolling thunder described by Benjamin in one of the thought-images from the epistemo-theoretical *convolute* of the *Arcades Project* (Chapter 9). The viewing of paintings or artists' images often functions like a mode of knowledge in which revelation continues to have an effect: the lightninglike perception of a simultaneity that is not translatable into concepts or terminology. The charge (that thought learns from the images' own mode of perception) continues in

Benjamin's style of writing and is expressed primarily in his thought-images. Because of this, Benjamin's epistemology is unthinkable without the experience of art.

In addition to the afterlife of religion in modernity, Benjamin's physiognomic gaze was also interested in physical movements, pathos formulas, and expression of emotions in painting and art history. Yet despite repeated efforts, he failed to convert his latent affinity with the cultural science (*Kulturwissenschaft*) of the Warburg circle into a real exchange with its members, as testified to by the odyssey his *Origin of the German Mourning Play*[4] took through the Kulturwissenschaftlichen Bibliothek Warburg (Chapter 8). The weight of this missed encounter is clear when one considers the fact that he saw the Warburg school as part of a movement that felt at home in boundary zones (*Grenzgebieten*), just as he did in his own work. This type of being at home thus became existential for him the more he was in reality excluded—barred first from the institution of the university (through the rejection of his *Habilitationsschrift*),[5] then from the country (by the start of the Hitler-Reich). He also considered the *neue* Kunstwissenschaft's treatment of art, one that (like Riegl and Linfert) attributes significance to the insignificant, as a part of his imagined virtual movement. He valued it and considered this mode of research a study of images "in the spirit of true philology."

The missed dialogue between Benjamin and the Warburg school stands in the series of failures that characterize Benjamin's own efforts, while at the same time they continue in the reception of his work. This includes not only the failure to take seriously the epistemic importance art has for his thinking, but also a passage from his "Critique of Violence" that is highly significant for the context for his stance toward biblical tradition, until now largely ignored.

---

4. *Ursprung des deutschen Trauerspiels*, often referred to as *Origin of German Tragic Drama*. The latter mistakes an important argument: In two early essays, written in 1916 just before his language theory, Benjamin discussed the contrast between *Tragödie* (tragic drama) and *Trauerspiel* (mourning play) in respect of totally different concepts of time, language, and emotion. There, he already emphasized mourning and the relation of history and nature in *Trauerspiel*, which later on became leitmotifs of his book on the baroque mourning play.

5. Translator's note: The *Habilitationsschrift* is the postdoctoral, professional dissertation required by German universities to obtain the rank of professor and then lecture at a university.

"In Monstrous Cases":
A Largely Ignored Passage from the "Critique of Violence"

Considering present-day instances of war and terrorism on the international scene, a "Critique of Violence," such as the one Walter Benjamin undertakes in his essay (published in August 1921 in the *Archiv für Sozialwissenschaft und Sozialpolitik*), is of pressing urgency in that it attends to the tense relationship between law (*Recht*) and justice (*Gerechtigkeit*). Firstly, such a critique bears on the violence brought out in the conflict between international law and the unilateral claims of sovereignty made by the U.S. empire as part of the Bush administration's policy exercised in Iraq, Guantanamo, and elsewhere. Yet it also touches on the varying forms of nonstate violence that are legitimized through concepts such as justice and human rights, reaching up to the register of a terroristic violence that itself appeals to the principles of 'righteousness' or 'holy war' and thus relies on instances that override national or international law (Chapter 2). It is precisely for the discussion of these nonstate forms of violence that Benjamin's essay is particularly relevant. It is devoted to the question of "whether violence, in a particular case, is a means to a just or unjust end" (SelWr 1.238, transl. mod.). In addition to phenomena such as the right to general strike and martial law, Benjamin grapples with the legitimacy of revolutionary violence in general and brings his argument to a head at the end when he poses the question of tyrannicide literally exemplified in the "monstrous case [ . . . ] exemplified in the revolutionary killing of the oppressor" (201, 250ff.).

Yet however much Benjamin's "Critique of Violence" is again moved into the center of political theory through the present-day debates, it is indeed conspicuous that the readings of this certainly dense and difficult text consistently disregard (when it is not simply avoided) a particular passage, namely, the nearly two pages on "divine violence" in which Benjamin speaks of what it means to disregard the commandment "Thou shall not kill" when "monstrous cases" (200ff., 250) present themselves. The fact that this passage plays no essential role in the intense present-day discussion of Benjamin's contribution to a critique of violence is therefore quite remarkable, as it is the only one in the entire text in which he not only deals with his contemporaries' arguments about the legitimacy or principled rejection of revolutionary murder but also formulates his own response. His response certainly does not take place under the banner of *legitimacy*, but rather of the *responsibility* of acting subjects. Subsequent to the assertion that "[t]hose who base a condemnation of all violent killing of one person by another on the commandment are therefore mistaken," he writes: "it [the prohibition—S.W.] exists not as a criterion of judgment, but as a guideline for acting of persons or communities who have to engage with it in solitude and, in monstrous cases (*in ungeheuren Fällen*), to take on themselves the responsibility to disregard it (*von ihm abzusehen*)" (250, transl. mod.; Chapter 3).

The question will not be addressed here as to from which motives Benjamin's discussion of the aloneness in which one must take the responsibility in disregarding the commandment "Thou shall not kill" is virtually ignored or bypassed in a systematic way. With reference to his famous declaration "detour is method," however, it can be asserted that circumvention also is and has a method. In this case, it seems to be a necessary precondition to be able to position Benjamin's reflections on violence in close proximity to a theory of the *state of exception* and thereby to integrate the "Critique of Violence" within the paradigms of political theology. At present, the author who gives this positioning the greatest weight is Giorgio Agamben. He claims that though Benjamin "does not name the state of exception in the essay," he nevertheless proceeds, retrenching his argument slightly: "though he does use the term *Ernstfall*, which appears in Schmitt as a synonym for *Ausnahmezustand*." In interpreting the appearance of *Ernstfall* as evidence, Agamben adds another indication for the claimed affinity to Schmitt: "But another technical term from Schmitt's vocabulary is present in the text: *Entscheidung*, 'decision.' Law, Benjamin writes, 'acknowledges in the "decision" determined by place and time a metaphysical category'" (Agamben, *State of Exception* 53).

The claim that Benjamin uses Schmitt's terms and concepts is an important cornerstone both for Agamben's reading of an "exoteric debate between Benjamin and Schmitt" (55) and for his interpretation of the relationship between the two theories, which amounts to a distinction of two sides of the law, both on this side and beyond, in dealing with violence in the state of exception: "While Schmitt attempts every time to re-inscribe violence within a juridical context, Benjamin responds to this gesture by seeking every time to assure—as pure violence—an existence outside the law" (Agamben, *State of Exception* 53). Yet in Agamben's summary, not only is Benjamin's argumentation misjudged but the gesture and diction of the entire essay are as well. Benjamin's argument is both far removed from in-suring (*sichern*) pure violence beyond law and absolutely distant from es-tablishing any *security* for a decision about violence at all. Benjamin is only *sure* in his efforts to clarify the terminology taken from the history of phi-losophy that is operative in his analysis of violence in its relationship "to law and justice" (SelWr 1.236): "[t]he critique of violence is the philosophy of its own history" (SelWr 1.251).

In this endeavor, language and terminology gain a central signifi-cance. A close reading of his essay will disallow the assertion that Benjamin used Schmitt's vocabulary, especially in the case of technical terms, that is, of nomenclatures or disciplinary jargon. The epistemo-theoretical point of departure for his critique of violence, in which he yet takes the historical and theoretical preconditions of law making (*Rechtsetzung*) and law pre-serving (*Rechtserhaltung*) into account, consists precisely in the fact that it takes place beyond the disciplinary boundaries of legal or constitutional law (and thus also beyond positive law). Regarding the specific terminol-ogy in Benjamin's essay that Agamben interprets as coming from Schmitt, a close reading will show that Benjamin indeed speaks of "crisis" (*Ernstfall*), yet only in the context of his analysis of martial law. For him, its contradic-tions obtain precisely in the fact legal subjects sanction violence, "whose ends [ . . . ] can therefore in a crisis come into conflict with their own legal or natural ends" (240). *Ernstfall* here thus means the becoming effective of *law* of war through the entrance of the *event* of war—that is, crisis. And if Benjamin talks about decision, the word "decision" is carefully set within quotation marks, when Benjamin explains that through this acknowledged metaphysical category (namely '*Entscheidung*') law gives rise to the "claim to critical evaluation" (243). He thus considers the utilization of the cate-gory of decision in the law to be worthy of critique.

One likewise fails to recognize the significance of "pure violence," an idea central to Benjamin's mode of reflection, when one understands it (as Agamben does) as *terminus technicus* (technical term) in Benjamin's essay (Agamben, *State of Exception* 53). Benjamin rather inscribes the cen-tral terms in the contemporary debate on revolutionary violence in terms of their mythic and religious-historical foundations, which remain embed-ded within them and are thereby used in mediated ways. In particular, the diction of the passage on the commandment quoted above argues outside of any certainty provided by technical language. Instead of a decision made in the state of exception, the vocabulary is rather one of monstrous cases, solitude, responsibility, and disregard of the commandment.

## On the Problem of Double Translation

The subsumption of Benjamin's "Critique of Violence" into a discourse about the state of exception and political theology is naturally not the result of Agamben's interpretation alone but rather is also the effect of, among other things, problems involved in translation, as it is a debate conducted mainly in the English-speaking context. In English translation "ungeheure Fälle" becomes "exceptional cases" (SelWr 1.250), a rendering in which the difference between the Benjaminian formulation "in monstrous cases" and the "state of exception" disappears. The phrase "von ihm absehen" then becomes "ignoring it" in the translation, which really means taking no note or notice of something. Yet "davon abzusehen," rather than indicating ignorance, refers to a conscious omission, that is to say a kind of negative acting that presupposes acknowledgment. If the struggle with the imperative of the commandment is translated with the phrase "to wrestle with it in solitude," then this situation of acting (judged by Benjamin to be one of uncertain responsibility) maintains a tragic element: it becomes the lonely struggle of a person, which makes the scene suitable for political theology's concept of sovereignty, which holds that the sovereign is the one who decides on the state of exception.

For me, it is not a matter of exposing or criticizing "false" translations, but rather a question of the problem of translatability itself. That even in the best translations Benjamin's argumentation, along with the specific linguistic style of his analyses, is often lost and sometimes reversed is an effect of a double assimilation. First, his writing is assimilated into 'understandable' (that is, accepted or conventional) usage through the translations. The second takes place with the approximation of his very singular (*eigensinnig*) use of language to present-day theoretical language, even though Benjamin's specific mode of writing is incompatible with it because it often relies on unusual, older locutions and so-called outdated words. The difference between the language with which we communicate today and the words favored by Benjamin concerns, if nothing else, the difference between sacred or biblical language and modern, secular discourse.

Benjamin's attitude toward Jewish tradition and biblical language, toward religion and secularization, is apparent not only in his explicit assertions about the relation of messianism to history (such as in the "Theological-Political Fragment" and "On the Concept of History"); in his remarks on literature and religion (such as in "Goethe's *Elective Affinities*" and his essay on Franz Kafka); or in reflections on language and revelation (such as in the essay on Karl Kraus and "The Task of the Translator"). Above all, it is operative in his use of language. His postulate "[to call] on the word by its name" literally means to bend the secular use of language back to the biblical (cultic) origin of language.

The origin and descent (and this also implies the derivation) of secular terms from biblical concepts is a main topic of the essay "The Critique of Violence." For example, when Benjamin amends the contemplation of "every conceivable solution to human problems" with the insertion of the clause "not to speak of salvation from the confines (*Bannkreis*) of all the world-historical conditions of existence obtaining hitherto," (247) then the pair of terms *solution* and *salvation* (*Lösung* und *Erlösung*) opens up a horizon for a critique of violence in which 'solution,' as a notion of human action, reflects its descent from the biblical idea of redemption: as the transport of divine terms into the sphere of human politics. Solution comports itself toward redemption just as law does toward justice. Again this specific wordplay of the pair of terms *Lösung-Erlösung* is largely lost when English translations take "Erlösung" as "deliverance." For Benjamin, the critique of violence is inseparable from his stance in dealing with the dialectic of secularization. Its scene is his work on and engagement with concepts and images.

## Dialectic of Secularization

An engagement with secularized theological language runs through Benjamin's writings as a leitmotif. Above all, his criticism is directed against strategies that counter the dwindling legitimacy of theology after the death of God with an investiture of or participation in its orphaned terms. Benjamin mobilizes those theoretical efforts that can be described as work on constellations of a historical dialectic between Creation and history in order to counter this. Whereas political theology inherits theological concepts, Benjamin's work is committed to phenomena and meanings in which vanished religious and cultic practices have an ongoing effect in modernity. The challenge of reading Benjamin, however, lies in the fact that a consistent theory of secularization is never formulated in his writings. Instead, a web of connections among thought-images, figures, and terminology spans his texts. A trail of his reflections on the concept of *life* and the *creaturely*, for instance, reaches from the short text "Fate and Character" (1919), through the "Critique of Violence" (1921), "Goethe's *Elective Affinities*" (1924–25), the *Origin of the German Mourning Play* (1927), and "Karl Kraus" (1931), up to "Franz Kafka" (1935).

In this context, Benjamin again and again rebuffs terms that represent the unreflecting transferal of a *divine mandate* into secular cultural contexts—without however pleading for an absolute purity of religious concepts. Instead, he is concerned (in acknowledgment of the ineluctable difference between revelation and history) with the illumination of threshold constellations. This is apparent when he situates, for example, Karl Kraus's figures and tone on the threshold between the world of Creation and the last judgment, between lament (*Klage*) and accusation (*Anklage*). From his early draft on the theory of language from 1916, in which the "Fall of language-mind" constitutes the line of demarcation that separates pure paradisiacal language from language within the history of human communication; through "The Task of the Translator" (1921), in which translation is understood as a rehearsal (*Probe*) of the distance between the world's many languages and the pure language of revelation; and up to the theses "On the Concept of History" (1940), one can observe an ongoing and continuously reconsidered work on constellations of dialectic of secularization. It is grounded in the philosophies of language and history. With reference to the idea of redemption, which coincides with the end of history, images of history are necessarily distorted or displaced—like dream images.

Above all, Benjamin's critique is concerned with the adoption of religious concepts such as justice (*Gerechtigkeit*) and redemption (*Erlösung*) to political philosophy or historiography. It also touches on a field of rhetoric and metaphorics that profits from the perpetuation of sacred and biblical terminology: precisely all the practices in which theology becomes the small, ugly hunchback who, as the first of the thought-images to appear in "On the Concept of History," "enlists the services" of another sphere and is, through the refined representation in its puppet, invisible. Benjamin's engagement with secularization in his "Theological-Political Fragment" is formulated in condensed form as an epistemo-theoretical configuration, a thought-image that describes the relationship of the profane order to the messianic as a "teaching of the philosophy of history." In it, he rejects the adoption of 'theocracy' as a political term. Instead, he stresses the principle asynchrony between historical events and the alignment of the secular order with the idea of happiness on one hand, and the messianic (which coincides with the end of history) on the other. Only from this fundamental division can one discuss the specific manner in which the pursuit of happiness orients itself toward the messianic within the dynamic of the secular, namely, in the "rhythm of messianic nature" in which the pursuit of happiness and transience come together (Chapter 1).

Benjamin's essay on Goethe's *Elective Affinities* constitutes thus a type of foil to the "Critique of Violence." He recognizes a "Nazarene breach" within the novel: that Eduard praises Ottilie's striving nature as an incomparable martyrdom, describes the dead as 'saints' and then places them in Christ's line of succession. His critique in this text, however, applies more to a modern cult of the poet that, under the provenance of Stefan George and Friedrich Gundolf, ascribes sacred attributes to poetry. According to Benjamin, when poetry is built up to be a quasi-religion it results in a remythologization of art that reaches back before the separation of art and philosophy, a split that came with the end of mythology in Greek antiquity. He sets this remythologization of art, in which it appears as a crypto-religion, up against a strict border between the discourse of art and a "speech of God" and then develops this basic distinction in his reading of Goethe's novel. Benjamin's text makes this contention in the course of a systematic differentiation between the terms of human and divine orders: between 'task' and 'exaction,' between 'formed structure' and 'creature,' and between 'reconciliation' (which occurs among humans), transcendent 'atonement,' and the notion of 'expiation' through a divine element. In the form of the dialectic construed between natural and supernatural life established by these terms, and then the motif of the "the guilt nexus of the living," the essay on Goethe maintains a direct connection to the "Critique of Violence," a text in which Benjamin's efforts concentrate on conceptual and terminological differences between law and justice (Chapter 4).

WALTER BENJAMIN

ON THE THRESHOLD BETWEEN CREATION
AND LAST JUDGMENT

# The Creaturely and the Holy

*Benjamin's Engagement with Secularization*

It is characteristic of Walter Benjamin's simultaneously fascinating and difficult writing that he neither presents his thoughts in a discursive continuity—ordering them in terms of subject matter, themes, and aspects—nor provides his readers with a conceptual résumé. Although the composition of his texts is founded on a conceptual systematic, he rather unfolds his arguments and his work on concepts and theorems by means of readings, quotations, and thought-images. This manner of writing means that even after multiple readings certain passages may always catch one's eye that hitherto have largely escaped the notice of scholars and that launch new and different ways of reading his works. An example of this is a long quotation from Adalbert Stifter, taking up more than half a page in his 1931 essay *Karl Kraus*, which has up to now attracted little attention.[1] It is one of the few places in Benjamin's writings in which he talks overtly about *secularization*. For the purposes of my reading, it is the point of departure for an investigation of his concept of secularization, or rather, his way of dealing with secularization. Benjamin does not so much work with a *theory* of secularization, a term he seldom uses explicitly; instead his approach to language, concepts, and images involves a rhetorical and epistemological practice that presents *scenes* of secularization.

1. This is also the case in my own earlier reading of the Kraus essay as a critique of the paradigm of 'mind versus sex' and as a theory of Eros and language: "Eros and Language. Benjamin's Kraus Essay," in *Benjamin's Ghosts*, ed. Gerhard Richter (Stanford UP 2002). An exception is Alexander Honold's recent article on Karl Kraus for the Benjamin handbook. Honold had already examined the central significance of Benjamin's literary quotations in his study on *Der Leser Walter Benjamin* (Berlin: Vorwerk 8 2000).

## "This insolently secularized thunder and lightning": The Holy, the Law and the Creaturely

The aforementioned passage is a commentary on a lengthy quotation from the preface to Stifter's *Bunte Steine* (*Colored Stones*, 1853) in which Stifter describes natural phenomena as the "effects of far higher laws" and compares the "wonder" felt in relation to them with the reign of the moral law in the "infinite intercourse of human beings." Benjamin comments on this passage as follows:

> Tacitly, in these famous sentences, *the holy* has given place to the modest yet questionable *concept of law*. But this nature of Stifter's and his moral universe are transparent enough to escape any confusion with Kant, and to be still recognizable in their core as *creature*.[2]

Though appearing harmless at first glance, Benjamin singles out the fact that Stifter describes natural phenomena as the effect of "far higher laws" and thus discovers therein a far-from-harmless operation: a tacit substitution of the holy with a concept of law whose origin in religion is to be discerned only in the attribute "higher." He continues:

> This insolently secularized thunder and lightning, storms, surf, and earthquakes—cosmic man has won them back for Creation by making them its answer, like a statement of the Last Judgment, to the criminal existence of men; only that the span between Creation and the Last Judgment finds no redemptive fulfillment here, let alone a historical overcoming. (II.I/340; SelWr 1.437; emphasis S.W.)[3]

2. Our modified translation gives *creature* or *creaturely* instead of *creation* for German *Kreatur*. Benjamin's essay reflects on the relations and tensions between *Kreatur*/creature, *Geschöpf*/creation, and *Schöpfung*/Creation in the sense of Genesis. This leitmotif gets lost in translation since all English translations of the Kraus essay translate *Kreatur* by "creation." For the problem of translations of Benjamin's writings, see here Chapter 7. Benjamin's *Kreatur* emphasizes the relatedness of human beings to animals, i.e., to creaturely life, whereas *Geschöpf* means a product of God's Creation. In addition to this the discussed relationship between Genesis/*Schöpfung*, generation/*Erzeugung*, and procreation/*Zeugung* opens the door to sexual connotations. For this see my earlier article on "Eros and Language" (note 1).

3. Our modified translation gives "like a statement of the Last Judgment" instead of 'world-historical' for the German *weltgerichtlich*, which seemingly has been mistaken as *weltgeschichtlich*. Benjamin's reference to *Weltgericht* in its double meaning of Last Judgment and worldly court is crucial for the whole essay in which he illuminates the biblical legacy in Kraus's references to justice and to worldly courts/laws. What is at stake here is

What instantly catches one's attention here is the word 'insolently' (*schnöde*). It separates Stifter's version of a poetic secularization of natural phenomena both from a secularization that would somehow not be insolent, and from one that would be more than insolent, perhaps contemptible. Notable, too, is the characterization of the concept of law as "modest yet questionable" (*dem bescheidenen, doch bedenklichen Begriff des Gesetzes*). The ambiguity of the attribute *bescheiden*, which means 'moderate' but might also be read as 'scanty' or 'insufficient,' is echoed in the oscillation of *bedenklich* between 'requiring interrogation' and 'dubious,' even 'discreditable.'

Benjamin's commentary on this insolent secularization consists of two arguments. The first is that in speaking of the 'effects of far higher laws,' Stifter replaces the concept of the holy with the concept of law, a substitution that, since it has occurred 'tacitly,' remains concealed. The questionable (*bedenkliche*) character of the concept of law is not least the result of the tacit substitution through which the formulation 'higher laws' can continue to profit from the allusion to the holy even as law seems to have left the sphere of the holy behind. The second argument is initiated with the word 'but' and highlights the transparency of Stifter's concept of nature and of his moral universe, through which their creaturely status remains discernible: this is why they therefore cannot be confused with the Kantian moral universe. Benjamin does not undertake a closer examination of the opposite form, that is, of a form of appearance that would be obscure and not transparent, so that the creatureliness of Stifter's nature would then not be recognizable. At most, such a contrast is hinted at through the reference to the Kantian moral universe, lest it concern Stifter's nature alone. The pathos formula of the "two things" that "fill the mind with ever new and increasing admiration and awe" that we find in the *Critique of Practical Reason* in the form of the much-quoted phrase "the starry heavens above me and the moral law within me"[4] is contradicted in *Bunte Steine* by the way in which Stifter distinguishes between these "two things." Stifter views "conspicuous events" in nature as manifestations of general laws that act silently and incessantly, while "the miracles of the moment when deeds are performed" are for him only small

---

the notion of a Last Judgment that already casts its shadow on all notions of justice within *this* world.

4. Immanuel Kant, *Critique of Practical Reason* (Cambridge: Cambridge University Press, 1999), 161.

signs of a general power. This power is the moral law, which, in Stifter's view, "acts silently, animating the soul through the infinite intercourse of human beings" (SelWr 1.437). Hence admiration in the face of natural laws is distinguished from admiration owing to moral laws. By means of his commentary on Stifter, Benjamin indirectly criticizes Kant's ethics, which, in assuming a life of 'intelligence' independent of the entire world of the senses,[5] fail to recognize the creaturely core of nature—including human nature. Although Benjamin emphasizes the greater transparency in Stifter's differentiation between nature and moral universe, what still troubles him in the text is the use of the concept of law to function as a term projected onto nature that, like a screen, conceals the notion of the holy.

The definition of a form of *non*-insolent secularization remains a void in Benjamin's text, and the task of imagining it is left to his readers. This much is clear, however: the question concerning the possibility of different forms of secularization that is automatically posed by the word 'insolently' points toward the issue of the *cognizability* of the substitutions through which secularizing operations take place. Benjamin's observation that Stifter's substitution has taken place 'tacitly' implies that another linguistic or rhetorical mode would be required if it were to become cognizable. Secularization that does not operate insolently is thus implicitly defined as a reflexive stance in one's dealings with the legacies of religion in the modern age. The argument up to this point may be summarized as follows: in the context of secularization, Benjamin criticizes the concept of the law as a screen term to the extent that it conceals within it the precise relationship between the *holy* and the *creaturely*. Thus the passage gathers together the three central terms—the *law*, the *holy*, and the *creaturely*—that have been the object of widespread interest in recent Benjamin scholarship.

In order to clarify the importance of insolent secularization for the work on Karl Kraus, the context of the passage needs to be explained. The quoted sentences occur in the first part of the essay *Karl Kraus* of 1931, which is composed as a triptych whose three chapters are titled *Allmensch*, *Dämon*, and *Unmensch*. Translated in the English edition as 'Cosmic Man,' 'Demon,' and 'Monster,' the pair of ambiguous words *All-* and *Unmensch* (profiting from the tension between the prefixes *all* and *un*, and literally meaning 'every men' and 'an a-human being') is strongly determined since

5. Kant, 161ff.

'cosmos' (stemming from Greek κόσμος, the order of the world or the state) emphasizes the aspect of order or universe and 'monster' carries a negative connotation. *Unmensch*, on the other hand, personifies the lack of all ordinary human attributes and attitudes; he is less a monster than an a-human being similar to the angel and the envoy (*Bote*).

In Benjamin's essay, Kraus is presented as a polemicist with an attitude that Benjamin characterizes as noblesse in armor. Kraus's criterion for *world-historical* villainy, according to Benjamin, lies beyond any bourgeois respectability, which he sees as only being capable of *plain* (*home-made*) villainy. His criterion is instead described by Benjamin as a 'theological tact.' Tact is thus understood not as a skill that eases social interaction but as "the capacity to treat social relationships, though not departing from them, as natural, even paradisiac, relationships, and so not only to approach the king as if he had been born with the crown on his brow, but the lackey like an Adam in livery" (II.1/339; SelWr 2.436ff.) This means that tact is, far from adherence to a social norm, a means of treating the creature as a divine Creation.

## Kraus "In the temple of the creature"

In order to clarify what the theological means in this context, Benjamin interprets Kraus's concept of the creature as an inheritance from theology. Kraus's "concept of creature contains the *theological inheritance* of speculations that last possessed contemporary validity for the whole of Europe in the seventeenth century" (339, 437; emphasis S.W.). These speculations have not been able to maintain their validity in unchanging form; rather, the theological legacy in the concept of the creature has undergone a transformation in order for it to find expression, for example, in the "ordinary (all)-human (*allmenschlichen*) credo of Austrian worldliness" (339ff., 437).[6] Benjamin expresses this article of faith in a telling image: the fog of incense that occasionally still recalls the rite in church into which Creation has been transformed. Incense and church are here interpreted as the zero degree of rite and Creation. For Benjamin, then, Kraus's concept of creature is a symptom of *theological legacy* in a world in which the idea

---

6. Benjamin's usage of *allmenschlich* connotes not only cosmos (*All*) but also the ordinary notion of human in the sense of *menscheln*.

of Creation has been transformed into an ecclesiastical order, or in other words, in which the cult has been institutionalized. This is the constellation that constitutes the insolent secularization for which Stifter has been introduced as representative.

In contrast to the unambiguous positioning of Stifter as an exponent an *allmenschliche* "credo of Austrian worldliness" or, alternatively, of a "patriarchal (*altväterliches*) credo" (SelWr 2.437ff.), the status that Benjamin ascribes to Kraus is more ambivalent, although the reading of Stifter leads immediately to his portrait of Kraus. The diagnosis that he operates in "the span between Creation and Last Judgment" without finding any "redemptive fulfillment" (437) remains valid, however, for Kraus as well. Landscape is for Stifter's prose what history is for Kraus, so that "for him, Kraus, the terrifying years of his life are not history but nature, a river condemned to meander through a landscape of hell." This image makes it clear that Benjamin's critical gaze is not just directed at the mythologizing process, at the perception of history as nature; what particularly interests him is the virulently theological topology (the "landscape of hell"). For Kraus, Benjamin writes, history is "merely the wilderness wasteland (*Einöde*) separating his genus (*Geschlecht*) from Creation, whose last act is world conflagration" (II.I/341; SelWr 2.438). And further: "As a deserter to the camp of the creaturely—so he measures out this wilderness (wasteland)." An apocalyptic worldview and devaluation of history are therefore not just two sides of the same coin. In Benjamin's perception, they also evoke an attitude in which the human subject allies itself with the animal creature and finds itself mirrored in it. The role of the animal creature thus becomes a symptom of an *anti-historical theological mythologization* of modernity, an attitude Benjamin describes as a legacy of the Baroque.

Benjamin elaborates the stance toward the creature from both of its sides: in terms of affection toward animals, and of their transformation into Creation's mirror of virtue, which is an act of imagination. He sees an echo of the "all-human credo" wherever "Kraus concerns himself with animals, plants, children" (340, 437). Benjamin treats the way in which Kraus "inclines toward" the animal "in the name of creature" with undisguised irony. For Kraus, writes Benjamin, the animal is "Creation's true mirror of virtue, in which fidelity, purity, gratitude smile from times lost and remote" (SelWr 2.438). His irony is directed at the projection involved when virtues that have emerged only in the course of human cultural history are mistaken for the innocence of paradise and where "purity" is discerned in, of all things, animals. The name 'creature' stands precisely for this projection of the state of Creation onto history. When the human being sees its own face in the mirror image of the animal creature, Creation and history merge into one. As emblems of Kraus's attitude, Benjamin discovers something "infinitely questionable" in the animals, above all because they are his own creations, "recruited solely from those whom Kraus himself first called intellectually to life, whom he conceived (*zeugte*) and convinced (*überzeugte*) in one and the same act" (438). Here Benjamin takes Kraus's work as an example of an autopoetic system wherein his own imaginative projections are regarded as the embodiments of Creation, and in whose mirrorings a reflection of the Creation falls back upon the author. The critique is then intensified in Benjamin's image of the "temple of creature." Benjamin poses a grave objection against such a procedure, one central to present-day debates about fictionalized works of Holocaust witness:[7] "His testimony can determine only those for whom it can never become an act of procreation (*Bestimmen kann sein Zeugnis nur die, denen es Zeugung nie werden kann*)" (II.I/341; SelWr 2.438). With this statement, Benjamin criticizes reference to animals as the representatives of a creaturely state of innocence, as if conferred upon them by divine Creation, a reference that disregards the real living animals. Instead Benjamin reserves the act of witnessing (*Zeugnis*) for a constellation free of 'intellectual' procreation (*Zeugung*), that is, the generation of 'life' through an act of imagination.

His commentary on the ambiguity of meaning that is characteristic of Karl Kraus's speeches and writings cannot be discussed in detail here. However, in the course of his discussion of the concrete themes, objects, and motifs in Kraus's texts, Benjamin comes back again and again to the basic structure of a significant historico-philosophical topography: the "span between Creation and Last Judgment." For Benjamin, Kraus embodies a stance that—in the midst of modernity and its technological features—takes up a relation to the theological inheritance through such

---

7. In respect of the aftermath of the Holocaust, I have analyzed the concept of *Zeugnis* by differentiating between the gesture of witness and the historical and legal notion of testimony; see my article "Zeugnis und Zeugenschaft. Klage und Anklage. Zur Geste des Bezeugens in der Differenz von identity politics, juristischem und historiographischem Diskurs," in *Zeugnis und Zeugenschaft. Einstein Forum Jahrbuch 1999* (Berlin: Akademie 2000), 111–135.

concepts as that of creature, although without leading into a redemptive history. He presents Kraus to us as a *persona* operating in a complex and complicated intermediate space between the world of Genesis and the present. By neglecting history, which would fill this intermediate space in the form of a time-span, Kraus finds himself in a position on "the threshold of the Last Judgment" (SelWr 2.443). Benjamin compares this perspective to the foreshortening found in Baroque altar painting. Where Creation and Last Judgment abut one another in a relation of immediacy (that is, with no intervening historical time), their orders come into conflict, a conflict of principles: "If he ever turns his back on *Creation*, if he breaks off *lamenting* (*Klagen*), it is only for *accusing* (*anzuklagen*) at the *Last Judgment*" (II.I/349; SelWr 2.443, emphases S.W.). *Anklage*, the language of the law, and *Klage*, the language of creatures, are directed at different authorities; they are not only incompatible but in direct conflict with one another. This conflict finds expression in a multiplicity and polyphony of linguistic and bodily gestures. Polemicism, headstrong stubbornness, biblical pathos, theological tact, lamentation, and demonic voice are all the effects of a stance in which the speaker, maintaining his position on the threshold, turns first in one direction, then in the other, addressing himself as he does so to different authorities. At issue in the Kraus essay (first published in four parts in the *Frankfurter Zeitung* in 1931) is not so much the historical figure of Karl Kraus as the illumination of this intermediate space and the clarification of the aftereffects of the theological inheritance in specific present concepts. Benjamin's commitment is directed at a precise analysis of the various overlays, substitutions, transformations, and references that connect contemporary concepts to ideas derived from a divine order.

In two of the central motifs—that of the creature as the mirror of virtue or morality and that of the perception of history as nature—Benjamin's Kraus essay comes back to his book on German Baroque theatre, developing ideas first set out there concerning secularization. There he explored the Baroque attitude toward the world in *The Origin of the German Mourning Play* in the view of which history itself appears as a mourning play. In such drama, history and Creation have become indistinguishable. And this is precisely the theological legacy of speculations from the seventeenth century which for Benjamin belong to the prehistory of that insolent secularization through which the 'wonders of nature' are seen in the literature of the nineteenth century as the effects of higher laws.

## The Secularization of the Historical
## in the State of Creation in the Baroque

In Benjamin's book the Baroque serves as the site and stage of the sovereign prince who, on account of his Janus-like stance between "the unlimited hierarchical dignity, with which he is divinely invested" and his state as a poor human being, can develop in both directions: to become a tyrant as well as a "victim to the disproportion" between the two states (Origins 70). Yet also in this book, the creature takes on a similar significance to that in the Kraus essay:

> The creature is the mirror within whose frame alone the moral world was revealed to the baroque. A *concave mirror*; for this was not possible without distortion. Since it was the view of the age that all historical life was lacking in virtue, virtue became of no significance also for the inner constitution of the *dramatis personae* themselves. It has never taken a more uninteresting form than in the heroes of these *Trauerspiele*, in which the only response to the call of history is the physical pain of martyrdom. And just as the inner life of the person *in the creaturely condition* has to attain mystical fulfillment, even in mortal pain, so do authors attempt to freeze the historical events. The sequence of dramatic actions unfolds *as in the days of Creation*, when it was not history which was taking place. (I.I/270; Origins 91; emphasis S.W.)

In the conditions of history in which virtue and historical life have become separated, the person reverts to the creaturely condition—a constellation which for Benjamin is characterized by three elements: the standstill of history, physical pain, and the meaninglessness of inner virtue. This description may help to explain Benjamin's barely comprehensible interpretation of the Baroque as the complete secularization of the historical in the state of Creation (Origins 92).

*The Origin of the German Mourning Play* occupies a particular position in Benjamin's works as in it he writes explicitly of secularization, using the term itself. It is admittedly less striking when he calls the Baroque *Trauerspiel* a "secularized Christian drama" (78) or when he refers to the king in the Spanish Baroque drama as a "secularized redemptive power." The notable formulation concerning the "comprehensive secularization of the historical in the state of Creation," which he describes as the last word in the escapism of the Baroque, is, however, not so easy to understand. The unusual reference to the "secularization of the historical," which runs counter to conventional notions of secularization as a process of transformation moving from the sacred or theological to the historical, and not vice versa, already introduces a complex dialectic into secularization. With the "secularization of the historical in the state of Creation," Benjamin thematizes a form of transformation of history back into a precarious version of a natural state, a kind of "restoration of the timelessness of paradise" (92) with the effect that history merges into the setting of the scene (*Schauplatz*), thus disappearing in its capacity *as* history.

For the concept of secularization being addressed here, then, the image of the creature is central. If Benjamin understands the reduction of the human being to the creaturely state as secularization, then this process must be accompanied by the withdrawal of that significance which points beyond the creaturely and belongs to the historical. Even if this significance has accrued to the human being within history, it is an indication of his origin in another sphere. Elsewhere, in the "Critique of Violence," Benjamin wrote of the double meaning of such words as 'existence' and 'life' as being derived from their reference to "two distinct spheres" (SelWr 1.251). What is withdrawn from the human being in the "secularization of the historical in the state of Creation" is the aspect of existence that is *more* and *other* than "mere natural life" (200, 250). Originating in a biblical concept, human existence—understood as simultaneously both natural and supernatural—is a product of history. Awareness of the other sphere, the consciousness of loss that finds expression in the concept of the creature, is nevertheless informed by the knowledge of it. When persons who find themselves reverted to mere life understand themselves to be in the state of Creation, then their notion of the creature refers to the loss, and not to the original state of Creation. In this sense, an origin in Creation is inscribed into the concept of the creature just as much as the *distance* from the "innocent first day of Creation" (I.I/253; Origins 74). This implies that the concept of secularization in this context appears as a kind of counterconcept to messianism. The *messianic* aims at redemption through the fulfillment of history; *secularization* here means the withdrawal of sacred significance within history, the transformation of existence back into the creaturely state or of history back into nature.

In another passage concerned with the figure of the tyrant, Benjamin ascribes the utopia of a "restoration of order in the state of exception" to the dictatorship of the tyrant: this, too, is then a form of transformation of history back into nature, or, more precisely, into the "iron constitution of the laws of nature" (Origins 74) whereby standstill, in the sense of petrifaction, is seen as both the ideal and goal of dictatorial force. The image of a counterhistorical or antihistorical stance appears as a leitmotif in the Baroque drama, establishing the framework within which the Baroque is constituted without being able to lessen its distance from the "innocent first day of Creation." Since there can be no return to the paradisiacal state in which nature and Creation were still identical, the world image that is the product of an antihistorical attitude bears the features of an (in the final analysis impossible) imitation of Creation: "The sequence of dramatic actions unfolds as in the days of Creation, when it was not history which was taking place" (91). Benjamin speaks in this context of an antihistorical re-creation. This renewed creation is not only directed against history but also presumes, in opposition to history, to be able to orient itself in respect of the world of Creation.

One example of the embodiment of an "antihistorical new-creation" is for him the case of the "chaste princess" of the martyr-drama, who, like Gryphius's Catharina, resists the tyrant despite being subjected to torture. Her "chastity" is as far removed from "innocence" as nature is from paradise. Rather, it is the result of a stoic technique, not dissimilar to the "iron laws of nature" the tyrant attempts to substitute for history. The difference is that, unlike in the case of the tyrant, it is the result not of unlimited absolutist power but rather of a kind of empowerment to "a state of exception of the soul, the rule of affects," through "stoic technique" (I.I/253; Origins 74). Analogies to this in the Kraus essay are biblical pathos and the phrasings described by Benjamin as a "spawn of technology" (II.I/336ff.; SelWr 2.435).

In comparison to the complex constellation of secularization in *The Origin of the German Mourning Play*, the relevance of secularization to modernity in the Kraus essay is patently reduced, whereas the theological heritage of the Baroque is above all tied to the concept of creature. Perhaps this also helps to explain why in "Karl Kraus" he speaks only of an insolent secularization. In claiming that the *Allmensch* has won back for Creation the "insolently secularized thunder and lightning, storms, surf, and earthquakes" by turning them into a Last Judgment's answer to the criminal existence of men, Benjamin here emphasizes the other side of secularization. It is characterized less by the withdrawal of a supernatural significance in the state of nature than by the tacit sanctification of "natural wonders" as the "effects of far higher laws," a notion that goes hand in hand with the idea of Creation.

## The Kraus Essay:
## Nodal Point of Controversial Readings of Benjamin

When one reads the Kraus essay, a number of aspects and strands of the critical reception of Benjamin's works come into play. There is in the first place the debate about Benjamin's position vis-à-vis theology and secularization, which began with the diagnosis of the "rescuing abandonment of theology, its unrestrained secularization," as Adorno formulated it in his introduction to the first, two-volume edition of Benjamin's *Schriften* of 1955.[8] It was continued, for example, by Hans Heinz Holz, who thought to have discovered in Benjamin's work a connection between a "metaphysics grounded in a philosophy of religion" and Marxist philosophy of history,[9] and with Heinz-Dieter Kittsteiner's refusal "to interpret Benjamin theologically."[10] Gerhard Kaiser intervened in this debate, turning above all against Adorno and arguing that Benjamin does not belong in the intellectual history of secularization since his thought moves in a counterdirection that draws very clear distinctions between the profane and the messianic.[11] At the same time he observed in Benjamin a freedom "to think strictly theologically while at the same time, without there being any contradiction to this approach, surrendering the human being to his autonomy."[12]

This debate is largely founded upon the paradigm of transferal, whereby secularization is understood as the transferal of religious or theological meanings into worldly affairs. It is motivated by an opposition

8. Theodor W. Adorno, in Walter Benjamin, *Schriften*, eds. Th. W. Adorno, Gretel Adorno, F. Podszus (Frankfurt/M: Suhrkamp, 1955), xxii.

9. Hans Heinz Holz, *Philosophie der zersplitterten Welt. Reflexionen über Walter Benjamin* (Bonn: Pahl-Rugenstein Nachf, 1992).

10. Heinz-Dieter Kittsteiner, Die "Geschichtsphilosophischen Thesen," in *Materialien zu Benjamins Thesen, 'Über den Begriff der Geschicht', ed.* Peter Bulthaupt (Frankfurt/M: Suhrkamp 1975), 38.

11. Gerhard Kaiser, "Walter Benjamins 'Geschichtsphilosophische Thesen'. Zur Kontroverse der Benjamin-Interpreten," in ibid., p. 74.

12. Kaiser, 73.

between messianism and history and in large part circles around the question of which side is given priority in Benjamin's writings—though Benjamin himself, as the so-called *Theological-Political Fragment* demonstrates, has shaped the relationship between the two as an interacting counter-striving constellation. In 1992, Uwe Steiner rescued the issue of secularization from the two opposing camps (the supporters of theology on the one hand and those of Marxism on the other) by trimming it back to the question of secularization as a descriptive historical category.[13] It was a reasonable and liberating step for critical reception of Benjamin's work in view of the previous deadlock, but it circumvented the problem that there can be no contribution to the history of secularization that does not adopt a position vis-à-vis its preconditions, because theories of secularization always imply certain ways of addressing concepts derived from the spheres of cults, theology, Holy Scripture, and religion. This is certainly true in Benjamin's case.

This was already noticeable at the beginning of the controversy, for example when Adorno suggested that Benjamin's position is close to that of Karl Kraus: "Reading profane texts as if they were holy ones is not the least of the operations by which theology is secularized for the sake of its own salvation. This was the basis of Benjamin's elective affinity with Karl Kraus." However, when Adorno argues that the historical appears in Benjamin's work "as if it were nature," then he is overlooking the fact that Benjamin talks of the secularization of the historical, not of theology. The same can be said of Adorno's diagnosis of a mythical trend in the "imagistic character of Benjamin's speculations," which, he argues, comes from the fact that "beneath the contemplative gaze what was historical was transformed into nature on account of its own frailty and everything that was natural into a piece of the story of Creation."[14] Here he fails to see that Benjamin ascribes this process to the "escapism of the baroque" and does not subscribe to it himself.

At the heart of this reading is a misunderstanding of the concept of nature in Benjamin's book on the *Trauerspiel*. Adorno reads it as evidence of a "deep, somewhat antiquarian allegiance of Benjamin's to Kant, above

13. Uwe Steiner, "Säkularisierung. Überlegungen zum Ursprung und zu einigen Implikationen des Begriffs bei Benjamin," in *Walter Benjamin, 1892–1940*, ed. U. Steiner, Uwe (Bern: Peter Lang 1992), 141.

14. Adorno (note 9), p. xvi.

all to his conclusive distinction between nature and the supernatural," and he claims to discover in Benjamin an "involuntary reformulation and alienation" of Kantian categories, whereby he additionally equates Benjamin's idea of the supernatural with reconciliation.[15] Yet although the category of the supernatural in Kant's essay "The Only Possible Argument in Support of a Demonstration of the Existence of God" (1763) is relevant to the supernatural character of divine Creation, Benjamin uses this word in order to discuss the double meaning of the term "life": as mere and higher life, or as natural and supernatural, as can be seen in his essay on Goethe's *Elective Affinities* (SelWr 1.308).

An offshoot of the controversy concerning Benjamin's position vis-à-vis theology is the debate over his relation to Schmitt, which has in part picked up the confessional gesture that meanwhile has cooled down in the arguments over theology. Although this debate is still conducted in terms of pros and cons, the aspects of the two writers' references to one another as well as their major differences have nevertheless been usefully elucidated in a number of contributions dealing with the differences between Benjamin's interpretation of Baroque sovereignty and Schmitt's theory of modern sovereignty, as well as those between their specific conceptualizations of the state of exception. It must be said, however, that the consequences these differences have for the understanding of and the approach to secularization have not yet been analyzed.

A further development of the controversy about theology is to be found in the discussion of Benjamin's stance vis-à-vis Jewish tradition and doctrine. At the center of debate here is Benjamin's complicated dialogue with his friend Gershom Scholem, which will be analyzed in the sixth chapter of my book. The controversy touches upon the demarcation line between the Jewish and the Christian traditions, which in Scholem's view needs to be strictly observed,[16] but which Benjamin constantly crosses in his work, in particular when referring to biblical or Adamite language. The most important site of this argument is Benjamin's essay on Kafka and the differences in their understanding of Kafka that emerged between Scholem and Benjamin in its wake. Stéphane Mosès recently provided a lengthy account of the intellectual dialogue between the two dissimi-

---

15. Adorno, ibid., xviii–ix.

16. Gershom Scholem, "Zum Verständnis der messianischen Idee im Judentum," in *Judaica 1* (Frankfurt/M: Suhrkamp, 1986).

lar friends and of their sensitive personal relationship in an article in the Benjamin handbook.[17]

The contributions on Benjamin's approach to the Jewish tradition have produced a separate strand concerned with the significance of the creature and creaturely life in the context of the German-Jewish tradition, taking the significance of creatures and beings such as Kafka's Odradek as its starting point. This has generated a canon of literary reference points that are also paradigmatic for the deconstructivist reception of Benjamin: Büchner, Kierkegaard, Nietzsche, Rilke, Kafka, Heidegger, and Celan.[18] Eric Santner has recently broadened this strand of debate in his book *On Creaturely Life* (2006). There, he argues the case for a natural history of the present and an ethics of the neighbor, pursuing his theme into the post-Benjaminian present and adding the name W. G. Sebald to the canon.

Finally, there is the debate on the concept of "bare life" initiated by Agamben, whose book *Homo Sacer*[19] was motivated by a remark in Benjamin's "Critique of Violence" that it would be worthwhile tracking down the "origin of the dogma of the sacredness of life." The debate that ensued paid no attention to the sentence that follows, however, which sees this dogma as a kind of surrogate, "*last mistaken attempt* of the weakened Western tradition," the aim of which is "to seek the saint it has lost" instead "in cosmological impenetrability." Already in this work, written ten years before the Kraus essay, Benjamin criticized the tacit substitution of the holy with a cosmological dogma: in the Kraus essay, the problem is the substitution of the divine with higher laws; in the "Critique of Violence," with the sanctification of mere life. Even in this context, the substitution is rated as questionable or worth further reflection: "Finally, this idea of man's sacredness gives grounds for reflection that what is here pronounced sacred was, according to ancient mythic thought, the marked bearer of guilt: mere life" (II.I/202; SelWr 1.251).

· · ·

17. Stéphane Mosès, "Gershom Scholem," in *Benjamin-Handbuch. Leben-Werk-Wirkung*, ed. Burkhardt Lindner (Stuttgart, Weimar: Metzler 2006).

18. See, for example Beatrice Hanssen, *Walter Benjamin's Other History: On Stones, Animals, and Angels* (Berkeley: U of California P, 1998).

19. Giorgio Agamben, *Homo sacer. Die souveräne Macht und das nackte Leben* (Frankfurt/M: Suhrkamp, 2002); *Homo Sacer: Sovereign Power and Bare Life* (Stanford: Stanford UP, 1998).

In addition to the triad of the *law*, the *holy*, and the *creature*, the concepts discussed in the Kraus essay include *justice*, the relation between *Last Judgment and Creation*, and that between *witness and procreation*. With these concepts, the themes of the various strands of the reception of Benjamin discussed above become entangled in a single site. Various traces of Benjamin's work on a dialectic of secularization, addressed in earlier essays in relation to single themes using a number of registers, such as Eros, language, justice, history, sovereignty, also converge in this essay. If one looks back from the Kraus essay over these preceding texts, then the work on a dialectic of secularization becomes visible as a constant motif in Benjamin's writings. It pertains to the theory of language in his early texts, one derived from the caesura between Adamite language and the language of signs. This dialectic is relevant to his interpretation of translation as the measure of the distance from pure language ("The Task of the Translator"), his analysis of the relation between justice and the law ("Critique of Violence"), and the development of the figuration, instructive for the theory of history, of the counterstriving constellation of the profane and the messianic—all of which come from the early 1920s. It is relevant, too, to his critique of the attempt to appropriate a divine mandate into the theology of poetry propagated by Stefan George and his disciples, the discussion of the idea of a nexus of guilt among the living (in the essay on Goethe that followed a few years later), the examination of the Janus-like figure of the sovereign and of allegory in *The Origin of the German Mourning Play*, and the figure of profane illumination found in the essay on surrealism from the late 1920s—to mention only the most important points during this period. And of course the trail continues even after the Kraus essay, in the way Benjamin elucidates the afterlife of such theological concepts as inherited sin, guilt, and shame in the world of Kafka's *Trial*, for example. This world appears to Kafka's characters, who have lost the doctrines and knowledge of the theological origins of their concepts, as a purely creaturely world. The trail also runs through the "*Urgeschichte der Moderne*" (an ur-history or archaic history of modernity) in which the phenomena of a world saturated with technology and machines appear to those who have produced them as natural history and modernity itself becomes the time of hell, and finally through the concept of the Now or *Jetztzeit*, as the model of messianic time, in the theses "On the Concept of History."

## The Resonant Space of the Holy

In order to read these projects as Benjamin's specific contribution to secularization, a number of approaches or detours—"detour is method," as Benjamin wrote—are imaginable. One possibility would be to go through his writings tracing a line along significant concepts such as that of the *holy*. Taking this concept as the focus, one might start with the short text *Socrates* (1916) and the 'holy' question, which awaits a response that Benjamin introduces as a contrast to the Socratic question. The twenty-four-year-old Benjamin criticizes the latter as a "mere means to compel speaking," caricaturing it as the "erection of knowledge." Here, the holy forms a horizon in front of which the degradation of the question to a mere pedagogical means is subjected to a biting critique.

The Socratic inquiry is not the holy question which awaits an answer and whose echo resounds in the response: it does not, as does the purely erotic or scientific question, already contain the *methodos* of the answer. Rather, a mere means to compel conversation, it forcibly, even impudently, dissimulates, ironizes—for it already knows the answer all too precisely. (SelWr 1.53)

The question of the holy distinguishes itself from being a mere means primarily through the echo that resounds in the response—that is, through granting a space of 'life' to language. This resonant space is further illuminated by a reading of the essay written in the same year, "On Language as Such and on the Language of Man," in which speaking *about* nature with the aid of language as a medium is distinguished from the scenario in which recognizing and naming, the translation of the mute into the sonic, come together as one.

From here on, the critique of *mere means* can be traced as one of the most important leitmotifs of Benjamin's thought. When something is turned into a mere means for another purpose, when something is *enlisted into the service* of something else, as a typical phrase of Benjamin's has it, then this is an indication that the dimension of the holy within it has been eradicated. It is in this sense that the enlistment of the services of theology, which "today, as we know, is small and ugly and has to keep out of sight," by the "puppet called 'historical materialism'" (as the first thought-image of "On the Concept of History" describes it), is an indicator for the desecration of theology—a desecration that is the necessary prerequisite to its deployment as a means to an end (SelWr 4.389). This in turn recalls the

Kraus essay's diagnosis that cult and creation have been transformed into the mists of incense and church. The notion of the holy as a resonant space resists in principle a rhetoric in which "holy" is used as an attribute, be it the characteristic of the supernatural, a heavenly or theological authority, or any other kind of entity. Already on these grounds it becomes plausible that Benjamin rejects the "dogma of the sacredness of life" in his "Critique of Violence" because an entity such as mere life (at times "all animal and even vegetable life," or quite simply human life) is thus sanctified (SelWr 1.250). As an attribute, 'holy' can apply to language only to the extent that it moves within the resonant space of the holy text, as thematized in "The Task of the Translator" (1921). This essay speaks of "Holy Writ" and scripture and of the "holy growth of languages" (SelWr 1.262, 257).

In Benjamin's subsequent works, the concept of the holy disappears into the background somewhat, only to reemerge at prominent points in the Kraus essay, where it is deployed in a number of directions. Though the commentary on Stifter critiques the concealment of the holy within the concept of law, for poetic language the *sanctification of the word* takes on central importance. In a passage on Kraus's linguistic gesture, his "sanctification of the word" appears in opposition to Stefan George's use of language as a mere means to aid his ascent to Olympus. At issue is music. First, Benjamin notes that Kraus, in his lectures on Offenbach, "confines music to limits narrower than were ever dreamed of in the manifestos of the George school" (SelWr 2.450). However, this antimusical attitude does not yet make him a partisan of the school whose program, a requisitioning of a divine mandate, Benjamin had criticized in the passages on the George school in the Goethe essay (SelWr 1.323). In what follows, he immediately takes back the closeness posited between Kraus and George on account of their antipathy toward music:

This cannot, of course, obscure the antithesis between the linguistic gestures of the two men. Rather, an exact correlation exists between the factors which give Kraus access to both poles of linguistic expression—the enfeebled pole of humming and the armed pole of pathos—and those which forbid his *sanctification of the word* to take on the forms of the Georgean cult of language. To the cosmic rising and falling that for George 'deifies the body and embodies the divine,' language is simply a Jacob's ladder with ten thousand word-rungs. Kraus's language, by contrast, has done away with all hieratic moments. It is the medium neither of prophecy nor of domination. It is the theatre of a *sanctification of the name*—

with Jewish certainty, it sets itself against the theurgy of the 'word-body' (SelWr 2.451ff., italics S.W.).

In the one, language is a vehicle for the ascent of the genius. In the other, language is the site for the sanctification of the word: Benjamin sees the latter as founded in the tradition of the sanctification of the name, the *Kiddusch Haschem* (Lev. 22:32), that is the highest principle of the Jewish religion. In this respect, poetic language is seen by Benjamin as the inheritor of this religious tradition, as a kind of resonant space of the biblical linguistic scene.

When, in the continuation of the essay, he places the poetic praxis of Kraus's *The Forsaken* under the much-quoted statement that "the more closely you look at a word the more distantly it looks back" and calls it "a Platonic love of language," he is seeing it as a language that is "bound to Eros." To the features of the poetological praxis concerned with expressing this bind belong rhyme and name, dedication and quotation: "As *rhyme*, language rises up from the creaturely world; as *name*, it draws all creatures up to it" (453, emphases S.W.). With this, poetic language acquires the capacity to enable the creature to gain access to another sphere, beyond that of the creaturely world. This notion, too, becomes illuminated if one thinks back to the primal scene of naming and recognition in the early essay on language, a scene of the translation of the mute language of things into human language, the biblical primal scene of naming in which Creation receives a language through being named.

Just as in the passage quoted from the critique of Stifter, here, too, the holy and the creature are brought together, but in a context radically different from that in the Stifter commentary. If the holy is granted a surprisingly positive significance here, it is neither as a separate sphere (as for example in the opposition of the sacred and profane) nor as a quality ascribed to an authority, species, or concept. Rather, what is at issue in the sanctification of the word, described with reference to Kraus's poetic method, is a *linguistic praxis* standing in the succession of a *cultic attitude* that has disappeared from cultural history. By contrast with the *theological* inheritance of the all-human concept of creature, which resulted in an insolent form of secularization, here it is a matter of an active shaping of the afterlife of *religion* in the modern age—which now can be understood as a perspective for a noninsolent secularization.

This has nothing to do with a religious attitude toward art, nor with the worship of art in the aftermath of the "death of God"; instead

this linguistic praxis traces its origins back to biblical language. The poetic praxis that Benjamin values is that which stands in the resonant
space of the image of divine justice as language (444). It is a Jewish-
biblical notion that also underpins Benjamin's view of language as being
the mother of justice in his much-cited theory of the quotation: "In
the quotation that both saves and punishes, language proves the matrix
of justice (*Mater der Gerechtigkeit*). It summons the word by its name,
wrenches it destructively from its context, but precisely thereby calls it
back to its origin" (454). When Benjamin goes on to characterize origin
and destruction as the "two realms" (*Reiche*) that in the quotation "justify themselves before language," then he is developing his theory of quotation in accordance with a messianic model. The perfection of language
follows the pattern of the completion and end of history in salvation. He
further claims that only where origin and goal penetrate one and other—
in the quotation—is language perfected. Thus the quotation has a similar
position in relation to language as salvation has in relation to history. The
linguistic practice that is oriented toward the sanctification of the word
is based upon a messianic concept.

　　The final sentence of Benjamin's theory of quotation returns once
more to contrasting this attitude to the all-human concept of creature he
had earlier criticized. Although in the first section of the essay the creature,
in whose name Kraus 'inclines toward' animals, is caricatured as being
Creation's true mirror of virtue "in which fidelity, purity, gratitude smile
from times lost and remote" (438), it is the quotation that now becomes
the mirror of "the angelic tongue in which all words, startled from the
idyllic context of meaning, have become mottoes in the book of Creation"
(454). When in the modern age a mirror relationship to Creation is established through an approach to religious tradition, this can take place only
in language, because the idea of *Creation* stems from the book of Creation,
*Genesis*. The essay's second section deals with Kraus's efforts to develop in
his critique of the law a similar resonant space of language as the matrix
or mother of justice. Benjamin expresses this in the image of the "rules
of a linguistic court (*Sprachprozeßordnung*),"[20] an attempt he interprets as
a "Jewish *salto mortale*": "To worship the image of divine justice *as* lan-

---

20. *Sprachprozeßordnung* is a neologism created by substituting the element of penal-
ty/*Strafe* in the German word *Strafprozeßordnung* (rules for criminal proceeding) with lan-
guage/*Sprache*.

guage—even in the German language—that is the genuinely Jewish *salto mortale* by which he tries to break the spell of the demon" (444).

The concepts that preoccupy Benjamin in his essay on Karl Kraus are closely related to his work on the Kafka essay, on which he spent several years. The first sketch for this essay, the "Idea of a Mystery" (1927), presents a constellation comparable to that which Kraus embodies on the threshold between Creation and Last Judgment: "To represent history as a trial in which man, as an advocate of dumb nature, at the same time brings charges against all Creation and the failure of the promised Messiah to appear" (SelWr 2.68). And the distance is not great between the poetology that upholds the principle of a sanctification of the word and Kafka's literature that, in Benjamin's reading, takes on those questions that are orphaned in a world without religion:

Kafka's work, which is about the darkest concerns of human life (concerns which theologians have time and again attended to but seldom in the way that Kafka has done), derives its poetic greatness from the fact that it carries this *theological secret* entirely within itself, while appearing outwardly inconspicuous and plain and sober (467; emphasis S.W.).

Benjamin's concern (intensely discussed in the sixth chapter of this book) will not be to throw light on this theological secret but rather to examine how the laws and rites of tradition live on in Kafka's world of creatures without being recognizable to them as such. He adopts from Willy Haas the interpretation that the 'mysterious centre' of Kafka's *Trial*, described as 'forgetting', derives from the Jewish religion, and he quotes Haas: "The most sacred . . . act of the . . . ritual is the erasing of sins from the book of memory" (IL, 127; ellipses in the original).

At the center of Benjamin's own reflections on the *creature* and *Creation* is not the holy or the sacred but the ways in which the stance toward religious cults, consigned to the past by secularization, nevertheless still finds expression in the modern age. That the terms *secularization* and *the holy* occur relatively seldom in the course of Benjamin's pursuit of these questions must be regarded as his own theological secret. Since his reflections largely take the form of thought-images, his approach to secularization will, in what follows, be traced in relation to those figures, images, and scenes through which his work on the dialectic of secularization is articulated. The focus here is both on secularization as a descriptive historical category and on an attitude that bears the dignity of a method.

## The Site of Secularization: Remoteness from Creation

Benjamin's reflections on the theme of secularization is elaborated topographically, via historical constellations that appear in the form of thought-images and scenes (*Schauplatz*) into which history has passed. One of these images, and one which is at the very core of his theory of history, is the *remoteness from Creation*. It is a figure to be understood as literally the foundation and central thought-image of his historico-theoretical reflections.

The most important reference point for this figure is the early essay on language, in which Benjamin reads the Book of Genesis as a historico-theoretical narrative. This text presents the end of the paradisiacal state of language, or the Adamite language of naming, as a "Fall of language-mind," which arises at the moment in which language enters the state of history. This moment comes with the beginnings of a language of signs in which human beings speak about things, a language defined by characteristics such as judging, differentiation between good and evil, and the possibility of abstraction. In other words, with the entry into a language that operates within history, the access to Adamite language is cut off. Its characteristics can now find expression only through a variety of noncommunicable modes. In contrast to the mute language of nature and things, which in the Adamite state is translated into the verbal language of human beings, an "other muteness" arises after the caesura of the Fall insofar as the "overnaming" of nature by men gives rise to lament (SelWr 1.73). *Lament* is thus seen as the creature's mode of expression once it has become distanced from Creation.

Five years later, in "The Task of the Translator," the caesura marking the end of paradise and the beginning of history reappears, but now in relation to the space opened up beyond the Fall, conceived by Benjamin both as distance from Creation *and* as distance from revelation. In the messianic perspective, the gaze is directed not backwards, toward what is lost, but forwards, toward the revelation that stands at the end of history. As far as the theory of translation is concerned, the decisive epistemic step consists in the fact that he does not pursue the familiar debate about literal translation versus translation focused on meaning. Instead, Benjamin ascribes to translation a symptomatic character: it is a test of the distance from revelation. Even when he states that the interlinear version of Holy

Scripture is "the prototype or ideal of all translation" (SelWr 1.263), the issue is not how to approach this ideal but rather the reflection on the distance from the archetype. Since the task of translation catches fire upon the eternal life of the works and the perpetual renewal of language, it is up to translation to put the growth of languages to the test:

> If, however, these languages continue to grow in this way until the messianic end of their history, it is translation that catches fire from the eternal life of the works and the perpetually renewed life of language to keep putting the holy growth of languages to the test: How far are their hidden elements removed from revelation? How present can it get by *the knowledge of this remoteness*? (I.I/14; SelWr 1.257; emphasis S.W.)

It is in this sense that Benjamin understands "all translation" as a "somewhat provisional way of coming to terms with the foreignness of languages." Translation is, in this reading, a symptom of the distance from Creation and of the remoteness from revelation. Translation and lament in Benjamin form a kind of corresponding configuration. Translation presupposes a conscious knowledge of the remoteness from Creation and revelation; lament is an unreflective expression of this remoteness in the sense that it is addressed within history directly to Creation.

In the Kraus essay, published a decade later, the position "on the threshold of the Last Judgment" becomes the test to be put to the efficacy of linguistic gestures that relate back to Creation in modernity. The image of Kraus standing on the threshold between Creation and Last Judgment is a dialectical figure. The gesture of lament within it is interpreted as an attitude that addresses Creation directly, as if there were no distance from it. It turns back, rather as the lyrical 'I' does in Scholem's poem *Gruß vom Angelus* (*The Angel's Greeting*) in the line "Ich kehrte gern zurück" ("I would like to turn back"). The gesture of complaint (*Anklage*), meanwhile, arises out of a reversal or interruption of lament (*Klage*), whereby the authority to which the accusation is addressed in a world that has turned its back on Creation is modeled on an image of divine judgment, as "*Weltgericht*."[21] Although lament is completely dependent on a notion of Creation that sees history as nothing but a time of waiting before the kingdom of salvation comes, complaint is by contrast a profane form of speech, imitating a divine court. This threshold position, described in terms of

21. See note 4.

a simultaneity of incompatible linguistic gestures and thus not permitting any durable, unambiguous meaning, goes some way toward explaining the text's closing image, in which a "new angel," an a-human being (*Unmensch*), appears. On this "evanescent voice," Benjamin claims, the ephemeral work of Kraus is modeled: "Angelus—that is the messenger in the old engravings" (457).

Among the thought-images in the theses on the concept of history (written a decade later, in 1940) the a-human being reappears as the "Angelus Novus," now quite clearly and explicitly differentiated from human beings. The reversal of Creation and Last Judgment, and lament and complaint, that characterized his earlier threshold position is here transferred into a configuration of opposing forces. In it, lament and the gaze backward onto the distance from Creation are ascribed to a mute angel who fixes his stare on the catastrophe while "a chain of events appears before *us*" (SelWr 4.392). The Janus tone of lament and complaint is here distributed between two positions looking in different directions: between 'our' gaze from our standpoint as subjects within history, outside of which we cannot step except at the price of our status as human beings; and the gaze of the angel, in the direction of paradise, back to where history originated in the Fall. As the double of the historical subject, the angel embodies the knowledge of the distance from Creation that quite literally runs counter to the knowledge of the chain of events. This also means, however, that our gaze and that of the angel cannot be reconciled within a single perspective.

In the *Angelus Novus*, Benjamin presents a dialectical image of a counterstriving constellation that he had discussed almost two decades earlier as a conceptual thought-image in the "Theological-Political Fragment": the image of two arrows pointing in different directions, in which messianic intensity and the dynamic of the profane, though opposed to one another, nevertheless propel each other forward (OWS, 155). In this historico-philosophical lesson, Benjamin uses a critique of political theocracy as the basis for developing the core philosophical thought of his dialectic of secularization—a reason his theory of history should not be confused with political theology. This core thought is that the order of the profane cannot be built upon the idea of the kingdom of God. Rather, messianic intensity is inscribed within the profane as rhythm.

Benjamin describes the "rhythm of the messianic nature" as happiness and argues that the earthly *restitutio in integrum*, that is the earthly restitution to the prior condition, leads to an eternity of demise. This re-calls both the biblical notion that man is made of earth and must return to earth and the contemporary biological view of mortality as the assimila-tion of the organic to the inorganic, which Sigmund Freud adopted in the same period in his essay *Beyond the Pleasure Principle*. In Freud, the death drive is the general drive of all living things to return to an inorganic state and Eros is the life-preserving drive opposed to it.[22] Whereas Freud depicts the death drive and Eros together as a constellation of counter movements, in Benjamin the same constellation conjoins mortality and the search for happiness: "For nature is Messianic by reason of its eternal and total pass-ing away" (156). When he writes that earthly striving is directed simulta-neously toward both happiness and downfall, more precisely toward its downfall *in* happiness, then this rhythm alludes both to messianism and to the findings of modern science. Benjamin's lesson in the philosophy of his-tory, which begins with the rejection of theocracy in the order of the pro-fane, thus ends in a double reference to biblical and scientific viewpoints.

## The Language of Secularization: Ambiguity or Double Reference

What implication do these reflections have for the concepts and lan-guage on the stage of secularization? In answer to this question, Benjamin's observation that in Kraus's polemic, his rhetoric, and his gestures, progress and the archaic coincide comes to mind. Benjamin describes Kraus's po-lemic as an "intermingling of a technique of unmasking that works with *the most advanced means*, and a self-expressive art operating with *the most archaic [means]*" (SelWr 2.441). A leitmotif of the Kraus text is equivocal-ity, a specific dual semantic that must be seen as the linguistic effect of the position on the threshold between Creation and Last Judgment, and be-tween lament and complaint.

The sensations and opinions pilloried by Kraus as being the bad principles of the daily press are then countered by him, claims Benja-min, in two ways. On the one hand, they are countered with lament, as when he opposes the daily press with "the eternally fresh 'news' of the his-

22. *The Standard Edition of the Complete Psychological Works of Sigmund Freud*, eds. James Strachey et al. (London: Hogarth Press, 1953–1974), vol. XVIII, 38.

tory of Creation: the eternally renewed, uninterrupted lament" (440). On the other, he leads a linguistic battle in the name of justice, the *Sprachprozeßordnung* mentioned earlier. For in Kraus's judicial chamber, it is language that presides. Justice and language remain, for him, "founded in each other." Yet what does this mean, and what is the consequence of their foundations within one and other?

In this context, Benjamin characterizes Kraus as a zealot who places the legal system itself under accusation, attacking the law not for individual judgments (i.e., misjudgments) but "in its substance." For he accuses the *law* of its betrayal of *justice*—and Benjamin adds: "More exactly, betrayal of the word by the concept, which derives its existence from the word" (444). This abbreviation holds the key. The claim is: just as the concept derives from the word, so is the law derived from justice. Thus Kraus charges both derivations (law and concept) with high treason vis-à-vis the idea to which they owe their existence. His accusation thus relates to the betrayal of concepts such as justice and the word in whose name the complaint is simultaneously filed. In other words, complaint of this kind, conducted within history or within the order of the profane, even though appealing to notions of divine order, produces a paradox. In it the victims of the betrayal (justice and the word) and the authorities to whom the appeal is made are identical. It is only on the basis of this constellation that the full sense of the *salto mortale* that Benjamin discerns in Kraus's linguistic judicial procedure becomes clear: "To worship the image of divine justice as language—even in the German language—this is the genuinely Jewish salto mortale by which he tries to break the spell of the demon" (II.I/349; SelWr 2.444).

The passage presents Benjamin's thinking about justice in a condensed form in which justice is an idea that precedes positive law since it originates in a biblical context. Insofar as the legal order (as an historical order) takes the idea of divine justice as its point of orientation, while positive law (as human law or the law made by human beings) simultaneously marks the distance from the sphere of divine justice, then the law is characterized by a structural equivocality. Indeed, Benjamin speaks in the Kraus essay of the "constructive ambiguity of law," a formulation capturing his perception that an unavoidable dual semantic is inscribed into the constructive function of the law within history, because justice in historical terms carries within itself a reference to the idea of Justice in a pre-judicial, biblical sense. By contrast, justice in this latter sense acts destructively against the law if it is appealed to in the critique of present concrete jurisdictions. As Benjamin states in the last passage of *Karl Kraus*, "Destructive is therefore that justice, which stops the constructive ambiguities of law" (3673 456).

To conclude what has been discussed up to this point: among the dominant theories of secularization, the most prominent version assumes that secularization is to be understood as a phenomenon of transferal or translation. This places the rhetoric of secularization at the center of attention.[23] Benjamin appears distinctly within this horizon, because he rather operates in an historical scenario in which secularization is conceived of as a test of the distance from Creation or revelation—that is, always in terms of a *difference from Creation*, but in full awareness of one's own present language originating from biblical language, of its derivation from a beginning that must be thought of as always already irretrievably lost. The terms of this language cannot be simply transferred into secular concepts—justice into ethics, for example. Instead, they function as a standard that can neither be avoided nor met. Yet in this space, one defined by its remoteness from Creation, language acquires its double sense only via a detour through the clear distinction between concepts that are derived from a divine or biblical order and those of a profane order. These orders' referentiality and specific ways of alluding, each according to its kind, to biblical language, divine justice, and the idea of Creation can be discussed only on the basis of this distinction. A *reflexive secularization* that acts in the knowledge of this constellation of history does *not* express itself in transferals and translations, the results of which present themselves as the products of complete secularization while in fact being marked by the precarious ambiguity of their Janus-like form. In opposition to these, Benjamin sets forth thought-images and figures that do not seek to reconcile Creation and history or bring them onto the same level, but that reflect the double reference to both profane and religious ideas: double reference instead of equivocality.

23. Hans Blumenberg, *Legitimität der Neuzeit*, Erneuerte Ausgabe (Frankfurt/M: Suhrkamp 1996).

# 2

# The Sovereign and the Martyr

*The Dilemma of Political Theology*
*in Light of the Return of Religion*

Terrorism in Religious Disguise:
Counterfigure to *Homo Sacer*

Since September 11, 2001, the scenes of war and terror that played out in the international scene have been marked by the return of images and *topoi* one might have assumed belonged to long-since-outdated, if not historically surmounted, rhetorics and iconographies. Talk of 'holy' or 'just' war, 'rogue states,' and the phenomenon of suicide bombers who conceive of themselves as martyrs, together with the controversies over international law, sovereignty, and human rights, have motivated numerous attempts at interpretation that go beyond the discourse of political theory, if understood as more narrowly defined and with recourse to the explanatory frameworks of political theology. In these interpretations' examination of the role of religious traditions and of models drawn from artistic-political *avant-garde* movements, discussion has focused mainly on Carl Schmitt and Leo Strauss, but it has also included surrealism,[1] the situ-

A previous version of the first part of this chapter appeared in Friederike Pannewick, ed., *Martyrdom in Literature* (Wiesbaden: Reichert, 2004), 63–73; in English translation in *The New Centennial Review I,* vol. 4, no. 3 (Ann Arbor: Michigan University Press, 2005), 109–123; in Italian translation in *La responsabilità della critica. L'ospite integrato. Annuario del Centro Studi Franco Fortini I* (2004), 91–103. A previous version of the second part of this chapter appears in *After the Totalitarianism*, Part I, *Telos* No. 135 (Summer 2006), 61–76.

1. Jean Clair, 'Le Surréalisme et la démoralisation de l'Occident', in *Le Monde*, 12.12.2001.

ationism of Guy Debord,[2] and often Walter Benjamin's essay "Critique of Violence," the origin of one of the central concepts of current debate, that of 'mere' or 'bare life' (*bloßes Leben*, II.1/200; OWS 151).

The issue of the relation of 'mere' or 'bare' life to politics and the law, which Giorgio Agamben addressed in his book *Homo Sacer: Sovereign Power and Bare Life* (1998), has been propelled forcefully into the forefront of the debate by events on the world political stage in the years since the book's appearance. Above all, it is the figure of the *homo sacer*, in whom the issue appears in condensed form, which has taken on an uncanny actuality. The images of Guantanamo that have been broadcast around the world appear as visualizations of the *homo sacer*, who is defined by the fact that he "may be killed and yet not sacrificed."[3] This applies all the more to the photographs from Abu Ghraib, in which the bodies of the prisoners seem like the resurrections of those living statues with which Agamben compares the *homo sacer*.[4] Moreover, the Iraq policy of George W. Bush has provided what could be described as a textbook example of Agamben's theory of the state of exception, developed out of his reading of Carl Schmitt, and in which sovereign power and bare life are intimately related.[5] "The State of Exception as World Order" (*Ausnahmezustand als Weltordnung*) duly appears as the subtitle of a newspaper article in which Agamben interpreted Guantanamo as the *signum* of the new world order—with reference to his thesis that the prison camp should be seen as 'the "Nomos" of the Modern,'[6] of which the extermination camps of the Nazis were the historical prototype. In the same article, however, the limits of his theoretical model are revealed as he undertakes a biopolitical extension of Schmitt's theory of sovereignty and in this way seeks to bring together geopolitics and biopolitics. For here Agamben describes "the new American world order" as a strategic "fusion of the two paradigms of the state of exception and the civil war" and concludes, "in this perspective, terrorism and the state ultimately form a single system with two faces, in which each of the elements

2. See, for example, Samuel Weber, *Theatricality as Medium* (New York: Fordham UP, 2004).

3. Giorgio Agamben, *Homo sacer: Sovereign Power and Bare Life*, trans. Daniel Heller-Roazen (Stanford: Stanford UP, 1998), 8.

4. Ibid., 99.

5. Ibid., 67.

6. Ibid., 166ff.

not only serves to justify the actions of the other, but each even becomes indistinguishable from the other."[7] In this context, the "symmetry [ . . . ] between the body of the sovereign and that of the *homo sacer*,"[8] as posited in the theory of the *Homo sacer*, is transposed (post-September 11 and Iraq war) onto the relation between the state and terrorism, with the effect that in the present scenario terrorism has moved into the place occupied by the *homo sacer* along with the prisoner.

In the quotation above, the thesis that the state and terrorism have become indistinguishable is certainly problematic, but so is the fact that this equation remains underilluminated as far as terrorism is concerned. If this argumentative move serves to identify the U.S.-American state as terrorist, the equation that would in turn define terrorism as a state system is nevertheless not further explained or clarified. This lack of explanation focuses our attention on a blind spot symptomatic of the discourse on September 11 and the Iraq war in general. Preoccupied with the Bush administration's policies, the theoretical efforts toward generating a critique of violence or extension of political theology adequate to contemporary events are for the most part blind to the new forms that terrorist violence is taking. Apparently, these phenomena present a far more difficult challenge to those attempting to analyze the new world order.

Yet it is precisely this issue that could be better illuminated by the question posed in *Homo sacer* concerning the relation between bare life and politics. It is a question that has taken on concrete form not only in the images of prisoners but also in the figure of the suicide bomber, who has come more and more to occupy the scenes of international debate and military conflict. The suicide bomber who sacrifices his own life in the battle against the 'enemy' or occupying forces and who defines himself as a martyr or the terrorist who uses his own armed body as a bomb: this figure appears as the precise counterimage of the *homo sacer*. For even though the latter represents bare life that may be killed but not sacrificed, the suicide bomber embodies a life that sacrifices itself *in order to kill*. Through this act, the attacker defines his or her life as more and other than bare life, since this life presents itself as consecrated or sanctified in images that draw on the traditional iconography of passion and martyrdom and are circulated in the

7. Giorgio Agamben, 'Der Gewahrsam. Ausnahmezustand der Weltordnung,' *FAZ*, 19.4.2003. 33.

8. Agamben, *Homo Sacer*, 102.

media via videos, brochures, and placards. In this sense, the figure of the suicide bomber is a counterimage of the *homo sacer*, and it also contradicts the close association of bare life and 'sovereign power' that characterizes Agamben's "*nomos* of the modern." The central role of the suicide bomber and the new terrorism with a religious face therefore require an investigation that can move beyond the horizon of sovereignty theory.

The Suicide Bomber:
The Embodied Question of Political Theology

That the current European debate is focused so strongly on Schmitt and the concept of the state of exception coincides with the fact that the present critique of violence is concentrated primarily on U.S. policy. Schmitt is being deployed for a critique of American politics, and it is also presumed that President Bush's closest advisors have been shaped by the intellectual legacy of Leo Strauss and Carl Schmitt.[9] Moreover, Schmitt has been invoked as well in the construction of a new opposition between the United States and Europe, for example where his *Grossraumtheorie* (theory of a unified great area) has been used as a model for the projection of a European Empire: "Europe should be an empire. Carl Schmitt's *Grossraumtheorie* could help it escape from the United States' imperial universalism in an intelligent way."[10]

Bush's interpretation of the airplane attack on the Twin Towers as being an existential threat to the American state (in other words, as creating a state of exception) and America's immediate declaration of war, together with all subsequent proclamations and undertakings, might indeed very well be placed under the heading of Schmitt's motto, "Sovereign is he who decides on the exception."[11] According to Schmitt, this definition of sovereignty marked off the borderline concept and borderline case of the

9. See, for example, Horst Bredekamp's reference, in conversation with Ulrich Raulff on the 'image strategies of the war,' to an 'emphatically used and banalised Strauss': 'For the third generation of Straussians, the issue is evidently to meet the metaphysically justified attacks of enemies on a level which in turn lies beyond the banality of, for example, the economic.' In *FAZ*, 7.4.2003.

10. Carlo Masala, *FAZ*, 10.10.2004, 15; trans. Chadwick Smith.

11. Carl Schmitt, *Political Theology: Four Chapters on the Concept of Sovereignty*, trans. George Schwab (Cambridge, MA, 1985), 5.

theory of the state, since the suspension of fundamental rights *within* the state's legal framework is regulated by it. The politics recently pursued by the United States represents a borderline case to the extent that the politics of intervention combine measures to counter terrorist activity with forms of waging a war that in the course of the twentieth century were integrated into the conceptual norm of international politics through international treaties (such as the Geneva Conventions). In the run-up to the Iraq war, it was primarily the attempt to transfer the exercise of sovereignty under the conditions of the state of exception from the national, state level into the international plane that triggered the conflicts between the United Nations and the United States. Already in his books *The Nomos of the Earth in the International Law of the Jus Publicum Europaeum* (1950) and *Theory of the Partisan* (1963), Schmitt had diagnosed a trend toward overstepping the limits of normality within the wars and conflicts of the twentieth century. He analyzed this trend as one toward the dissolution of the rules for the conduct of war within the Jus Publicum Europaeum (JPE), which, as long as it remained valid, ensured an era of the successful "containment of wars" (*gehegte Kriege*). On the basis of the phenomena of "worldwide civil war," the technologically equipped "industry-partisan," and the replacement of the concrete and declared enemy with an absolute enemy, the figure of the partisan in this era had its place as the illegal complement to the army. Against the backdrop of the new terrorism, Schmitt's *Theory of the Partisan* has also enjoyed a renaissance. In 2004 it was translated into English for the first time.[12] However, since this text failed to take any explicit account of religio-cultural issues, it is of little assistance in the examination of the current phenomena of terrorism in which religious motives intermingle considerably with political issues.

In this context, the question then arises as to whether the political theology of the state of exception is necessarily blind to violence legitimated on religious grounds to the extent that this has no basis as a manifestation of sovereignty. This question highlights the significance and place of religion(s) and the relation between religious violence and state force in political theology. Since the martyr is a resurrection from the pre-secular age, this is also a question of secularization. One might, vis-à-vis political theology in the Schmittian tradition, take the much-quoted formula

12. See the special number *Theory of the Partisan* of the journal *The New Centennial Review*, vol. 4, no. 3 (winter 2004).

from his *Concept of the Political* that "The enemy is our own question in material form," and paraphrase it as "the figure of the suicide bomber is its own question in material form." In other words, the figure of the martyr embodies that which political theology must pose to itself as a question. Whether it will also prove to be the enemy of political theology, i.e., to be epistemologically inimical to it, thus necessitating a completely different theoretical horizon, will be discussed in what follows.

## Scenes from a Modern Tragic Drama

Unlike partisans and resistance fighters, who operate in secret and without official recognition within military orders, in targeted action, to strike the militarily superior enemy at a strategically sensitive spot, the underground fighters of today prefer their actions to be played out in the full glare of the spotlights. When Chechen terrorists chose a theater auditorium as the setting for a hostage taking in Moscow, the significance of spectacular dramatization for the current politics of suicide attacks was symbolically condensed: here the politics of violence became bloody theater. In the combination of theatricality and violence, the television images of suicide attacks in Israel and Chechnya, and of the wars in the former Yugoslavia, Afghanistan, and Iraq, have long since outstripped the Theater of Cruelty. What radically separates terrorist politics from theater, however, is that the actions of the former take place in front of a large audience, and the audience itself becomes a target. This is the reason for the controversy that flared up concerning the possible proximity between the avant-garde and terrorism after September 11, sparked by Jean Clair's statement that surrealism (for example, André Breton's fantasy of shooting into the crowd of passers-by) was to be seen as a precursor of terrorism.[13]

Other associations that go far back in historical terms come to mind for me when viewing the images of the attacks. The bloody acts of public violence, staged by preference in densely populated areas; the presentation of the victims and their dismembered bodies; the dramatization of the suicide attackers as martyrs; and the ritual display of the wounded and dead of military revenge attacks borne through the streets by the combat-

---

13. Jean Clair, 'Le surréalisme et la démoralisation de l'Occident' (note 1). Cf. Luca di Basi, 'Die besten Videos drehte al-Qaida,' *Die Zeit*, 14.8.2003, 34.

ants all contribute to the impression that on the present political stage, the theater of the Baroque has taken over the director's chair. Reversing Benjamin's observation of the "radical adaptation of the theatrical to the historical scene" in the seventeenth century, at a time when the name *Trauerspiel* came to apply equally to historical events and to a dramatic form (I.I/244; Origins, 64), it seems that today politics is adapting to the media-fed desire for theatrical images.

Yet the topicality of Benjamin's book *The Origin of the German Mourning Play* (1927) goes beyond such associations of today's scenes of violence with the display of dismembered bodies in the dramaturgy of the Baroque. In his book, Benjamin investigates Baroque theater as the drama of tyrant and martyr. It is already on account of its central figures (the sovereign, the tyrant, and the martyr) and the scenes in which they play (frequently in locations in the Orient, in the form of dramas of Eastern rulers) that a reading of this book so urgently recommends itself in the present situation. More significant still, though, is Benjamin's discussion of tragic drama in terms of a dialectic of secularization. In view of the political power of religion, which has in recent times so forcefully reasserted itself, it is not very helpful to distinguish, as Jürgen Habermas did in his 2001 *Paulskirche* speech, between a "secularization which is elsewhere running off the rails" and a supposedly "post-secular" Western culture of common sense—to differentiate, in other words, between a bad and a good form of secularization.[14] For Europeans, a far more useful endeavor toward the goal of understanding the influential force of religion is to look at the long-neglected traces left by the history of religion in their own culture. A number of Benjamin's writings offer interpretative models that have as yet been relatively underexplored in this context, notably his reading of the Baroque mourning play.

Although the reception of the book on the German mourning play is above all focused on Benjamin's view of melancholy and allegory, Baroque sovereignty, and his epistemo-critical prologue, the present-day topicality consists first of all in the fact that he interprets the mourning play as the search for a *secular* answer to the *religious* concerns of its time, for which, despite the unabated influence of Christianity, there were no longer any solutions or promise of redemption at hand: "For all that the worldliness

---

14. Jürgen Habermas, speech on occasion of receiving the Friedenspreis des deutschen Buchhandels, in *Glauben und Wissen* (Frankfurt/M: Suhrkamp, 2001), 12.

of the Counter-Reformation asserted itself in both confessions, religious aspirations did not lose their importance: it was just that this century denied them a religious solution, demanding of them, or imposing upon them, a secular solution instead" (Origins 79). Conversely, it may be observed that in many of the present-day conflicts religious interpretive frameworks and patterns of action become more attractive where political solutions appear hopeless.

The most significant result of the framework of the dialectic of history, religion, and theater developed in the book on the German mourning play is that it distinguishes Benjamin's conceptualization of sovereignty from Schmitt's sovereignty theory. Schmitt's concept of the political is founded in a *sublation* (*Aufhebung*) of theological concepts in national-legal terms; Benjamin analyzes the interrelationship between both. These differences can be seen more clearly if the comparison between Benjamin's and Schmitt's concept of political theology is not just discussed in terms of their conceptualization of the *state of exception*, *sovereignty*, and *decision*, as is usual in the Benjamin-Schmitt debate, but undertaken with the aim of shedding new light on the issue of sovereignty via its respective counterpart in the two theories: in Schmitt, the *partisan*, and in Benjamin, the *martyr*.

## The Scope of Schmitt's Political Theology

To the extent that the recent reception of Schmitt's works has reached beyond the strictly scholarly discussion of national and international law to touch upon his political theology, it is striking that interest has been directed mainly toward two texts, both from the period before 1933: on the concepts of sovereignty and the state of exception from the small volume *Political Theology: Four Chapters on the Concept of Sovereignty* (1922), and on Schmitt's friend-enemy theory from the volume *The Concept of the Political* (first published 1927, extended edition 1932). Remarkably little continuity, however, can be identified in terms of an echo of these central concepts of political theology in Schmitt's own writings *after* 1945. Some degree of continuity is to be perceived in his characteristic reservations vis-à-vis the law, legality, Jews, liberalism, economics, and technology. Yet after the Second World War he does not return to the specific issue of the relation between the state of exception and the theory of sovereignty with which his name has become most closely associated.

It is notable that his weightiest work, *The Nomos of the Earth*, transposes the concepts of politics and sovereignty from the plane of national law to that of international law (in German, *Völkerrecht*, an expression that literally means "the law of the peoples"). With this move, the conceptualization of sovereignty, which still today counts as the pathos formula of Schmitt reception ("Sovereign is he who decides on the exception"),[15] recedes into the background. The focus of the 1950 work is rather a European law of nations, the history of which is analyzed as an era of the successful "bracketing (*Hegung*) of wars"[16] characterized by a number of elements: the overcoming of civil wars fueled by "confessional dogmatism" and the transformation of the crusades, feuds, and 'Holy wars' of the Middle Ages into wars between "equal sovereign states."[17] On the basis of the distinction, introduced in Roman law, between the *hostis* and the robber or criminal, the enemy appears in the JPE as the opponent in war. This conceptualization is no longer concerned with the evaluation of the enemy as *justus hostis* or *hostis injustus*; nor does it have recourse to any form of legitimization outside of politics. With the ideal of the sovereign state being for Schmitt embodied in the *Ancien Régime* and with France as the first sovereign state with a judicial consciousness of itself, the JPE thus essentially refers to the historical inter-state wars within the European area in the eighteenth and nineteenth centuries, which are as it were complemented and completed through the colonization of non-European territories.

The concept of the *state of exception* reappears at a significant point in this work when Schmitt invokes it as an analogy to the legal institution of the *occupatio bellica*, that "complicated legal construction which steers a path through the two state sovereignties" in order to regulate the "military occupation of enemy territory" without challenging the latter's continuing existence as a sovereign state.[18] (Following on from his discussion of

15. Schmitt, *Political Theology*, 5.

16. Carl Schmitt, published in English as *The Nomos of the Earth in the International Law of the* Jus Publicum Europaeum (New York: Telos Press, 2006), 184. German edition: *Der Nomos der Erde im Völkerrecht des Jus Publicum Europaeum* (Berlin: Dunker & Humblot, 1997). Further references to these editions are indicated parenthetically by publication date. As with the citations of Benjamin, in cases where both versions are indicated by date (the German source preceding the English publication), this formatting indicates *translation modified*.

17. Schmitt, *Nomos*, (1997), 113, 128.

18. Ibid. (1997), 180; (2006), 206.

the principles whereby the *occupatio bellica* is legitimized, Schmitt speaks of a "curious affinity of character (*Wesensverwandtschaft*)" between "the institution within international law of the militarily occupied territory and the state of siege or exception within the constitutional state."[19] In terms of the relationship between Schmitt's state of exception (as a concept from his 1922 theory of the state) and the *occupation* of enemy territory as defined in international law in *The Nomos of the Earth* of 1950, this affinity includes a decisive shift in the meaning of sovereignty. The sovereign is no longer the one who decides on the exception. Instead it is the occupier or the one who is victorious who is sovereign!

The question here presents itself as to what this *Wesensverwandtschaft* might mean for the role of secularization in Schmitt's political theology. If all the concepts of the modern theory of the state are secularized theological concepts, as the second emblematic formula of his political theology has it, then how is secularization represented in the JPE? Schmitt's *Nomos* study, in which the history of secularization appears in the figures of overcoming and *Aufhebung*, provides an emphatic answer: "At the inception of the new European law of nations we find a call from Albertus Gentilis, exhorting the theologians to be silent on the matter of just war: *Silete Theologi in munere alieno!*"[20] (And indeed, the more absolute version, the abbreviated "*Silete Theologi!*" runs throughout Schmitt's late work like a leitmotiv.) The silencing of theology thus marks the beginning and the foundation of the projection of his political theology of modernity into space and historical time.

Schmitt imposed this exhortation upon his own thinking with complete consistency. Thus his *Theory of the Partisan* (1963), to which he gave the subtitle *An Intermediate Commentary on the Concept of the Political*, also adheres to the command. What is striking about this text when read from today's perspective is above all the contemporary relevance of the category of the "absolute enemy." For the trend toward overstepping the limits of "normal warfare" is here linked primarily to the transformation of the actual enemy into an absolute enemy, whereby war becomes absolute war. This is the situation with which we are in fact confronted today. From the perspective of the United States, this is manifest in the image of the "axis of evil" and the declaration that "whoever is not for us is against us." On the

---

19. Ibid. (1997), 182; (2006), 206.
20. Ibid. (2006), 121.

other side, too, a war is being fought against an absolute enemy, whether under the name of the West, of Israel, or of globalization. Under these circumstances, two complementary political concepts have become completely invalidated. On the one hand, the concept of war as understood in the European tradition of international law loses its validity. This was the form of law whose emergence is described in *The Nomos of the Earth* as being bound to the "overcoming" of older, pre-modern wars fought on religious grounds;[21] to the limitation of the enemy to a concrete opponent, an "actual enemy"; and the adherence to certain rules, such as the declaration of war, for example. In the *Theory of the Partisan*, Schmitt notes, "A declaration of war is always a declaration of an enemy."[22] On the other hand, the partisan, as the figure who fights an illegal battle against a militarily superior power, and usually an army of occupation, also disappears. For Schmitt, four criteria define the partisan: irregularity, heightened mobility, intensity of political commitment, and telluric (i.e., earth-bound) character.[23]

Historically speaking, the classical concept of the partisan already begins to fracture where the interests of a third party come into play, where partisans are supported, for example, by the supply of arms from outside, which is the case for almost all "freedom fighters" in the Middle and Far East. The concept of the partisan comes up against its limit, according to Schmitt, in ideologically motivated struggle, and even more so in the "professional revolutionary of global civil war,"[24] embodied for him in the person of Lenin: "The partisan, then, has an actual, but not an absolute enemy. A further boundary of enmity follows from the telluric character of the partisan. He defends a patch of earth to which he has an autochthonic relation. His basic position remains defensive, despite the heightened mobility of his tactics."[25] Schmitt finally saw a further infringement of the concept of the partisan in the latter's potential adapta-

21. Ibid. (2006), 141.

22. Carl Schmitt, *Theory of the Partisan: Intermediate Commentary on the Concept of the Political* (New York: Telos Press, 2007), 85. German edition: *Theorie des Partisanen. Zwischenbemerkung zum Begriff des Politischen* (Berlin: Dunker & Humblot, 2002). Further references to these editions are indicated parenthetically by publication date. As with the citations of Benjamin, in cases where both versions are indicated by date (the German source preceding the English publication), this formatting indicates *translation modified*.

23. Schmitt, *Partisan* (2007), 16.

24. Ibid., 93.

25. Ibid. (2002), 93; (2007), 93.

tion to technology, in the emergence of a new type, "let us call him the industry-partisan."[26] With the aircraft attacks of September 11, this has also become a reality, so that the present battles are indeed taking place beyond the conventional conceptual limits of war and partisanship.

It is also the case, however, that with the rise of the suicide attackers who dramatize themselves as martyrs and refer to themselves as God's warriors, a figure has emerged to take the place of the classic partisan. This figure did not and could not have appeared within the framework of Schmitt's argumentation because the scenes of today's warfare are dominated not just by the technologically better-equipped successors of armies and partisans but also by the sovereign and the martyr. That Schmitt could not envisage such a development can be explained by the fact that all references to the history of religion in his political theology have disappeared from the *Theory of the Partisan*—and with them, the possibility of considering the *topos* of 'Holy War.' This is all the more remarkable when considering the fact that his *Political Theology* is above all identified with the much-quoted dictum that all significant concepts of the modern theory of the state are indeed secularized theological concepts.[27]

## The Dilemma of Political Theology vis-à-vis Secularization

Schmitt concretized his thesis of secularized theological concepts in the figure of sovereignty, a concept he maintained had not fundamentally changed since the seventeenth century. The basis for this claim was that in the seventeenth-century theory of the state the monarch is identified with God, and although the state occupies a position exactly analogous to that attributed to God vis-à-vis the world in the Cartesian system:

All significant concepts of the modern theory of the state are secularized theological concepts not only because of their historical development—in which they were *transferred* from theology to the theory of the state, whereby, for example, the omnipotent God became the omnipotent lawgiver—but also because of their systematic structure, the recognition of which is necessary for a sociological consideration of these concepts. The state of exception in jurisprudence has an *analogous*

26. Ibid. (2002), 81; (2007), 79.
27. Schmitt, *Political Theology*, 36.

meaning to the miracle in theology[. . . . ] I have for a long time referred to the significance of such fundamentally systematic and methodological analogies.[28]

Out of this argument, a double limitation arises as far as the phenomena of secularization are concerned. Methodologically, Schmitt's thinking becomes tied to the figures of analogy and transfer between theology and the law, while thematically it becomes tied to the scholarly field of state theory. If the thesis of a conceptual transfer adheres to a relatively mechanistic notion of secularization, the consequence is that *after* a transfer of theological concepts into other registers has taken place, religious aspects within the latter no longer have to enter the consideration. If the legitimacy of sovereignty has in the modern age been entirely subsumed into the law of the state, then paradoxically religion is excluded from this kind of political theology. It also shuts out the possibility of conceiving of relationships between politics and theology in a different way, other than in the figure of transference.

Because Schmitt's concept of the political (notably also in his commentary or remark on the concept of the political in the *Theory of the Partisan*) remains de facto subjected to the commandment *Silete Theologi!* the question of whether and how the traces of religious violence continue to operate within those "secularized theological concepts" is obscured. This means that Schmitt is to be regarded as a representative, rather than as an analyst, of secularization. Indeed, he is a representative of the type of secularization that traces the genealogy of modernity from an earlier Christian tradition until it ends in the *Aufhebung* of Christian concepts in secular terms. The result, however, is in effect a (more or less) unacknowledged theological charging of these terms. In this respect, political theology in Schmitt's sense amounts in the end to a theologization of the political.[29]

This explains why Schmitt reacted so polemically, if not with downright irritation, to Hans Blumenberg's *Legitimacy of the Modern Age* (1966), which criticizes the concept of secularization as the last *theologoumenum*. It also explains why his counterargument appears only in the afterword to his *Political Theology II*, published in 1970. The subtitle of this work, "The Legend of the Expendability of any Political Theology," clearly sig-

28. Ibid., 46 (emphasis S.W.).

29. Raphael Gross comes to a similar conclusion: see his *Carl Schmitt und die Juden* (Frankfurt/M: Suhrkamp, 2000), 167. Gross speaks of the fact that "Schmitt takes an *atheistic* political-theological tradition to its extreme" (ibid., 170).

nals Schmitt's intention to disprove this legend and rescue or reinstate the claims of political theology. This intention is then enacted in the main part of the work in the form of a polemical philosophical treatise in which Schmitt engages Erik Peterson's *Monotheism as a Political Problem*, a work published in 1935, three and a half decades before, as if it had just appeared. Having concluded his critique of Peterson's arguments with a reference to the clarification of the "great Hobbes" in his own work, the "*Political Theology* of 1922,"[30] he turns in the afterword to confront another form of making political theology dispensable, which he evidently felt Blumenberg's book to have been.

He concludes his argument with seven theses that present a picture of an utterly "de-theologized, modern-scientific superfluousness of all political theology" and declares this to be the counterimage of his own position, something that had become clearer to him through his reading of Blumenberg. His theses are like a caricature of a world purified of every connection to secularization, i.e., of a modernity utterly without genealogy. For example: "The Process-Progress produces not only itself and the New Man, but also the conditions of possibility for its own renewal of the New," or "The New Man is aggressive in the sense of the continual progress and continual new positing."[31] What this shows is that, when every reference to theological origins becomes discredited, the historical phenomena of the New can be explained only as generating themselves. In this sense, Schmitt's polemic reveals a grave historico-theoretical problem in Blumenberg's critique: the fact that in the end, after any critique of both the concept and the rhetoric of secularization, however carefully and differentially done, one cannot do without reference to the paradigm of secularization.

This afterword, in which Schmitt reiterates in 1970 the central theses of his earlier theory, this time "within the horizon of the problem in its current situation,"[32] makes his own dilemma legible: it is the dilemma of a political theology under the sign of a self-imposed silence vis-à-vis theology. It seems that, in those places where Schmitt finds himself explicitly confronted with the epistemological role of secularization, he can formulate

---

30. Carl Schmitt, *Politische Theologie II. Die Legende von der Erledigung der Politischen Theologie* (Berlin: Dunker & Humblot, 1996), 84. Subsequent references given in the text are to this edition.

31. Ibid., 97.

32. Ibid., 85.

his own position only as a counterimage to the discredited caricature (of a totally secularized history), not, however, in positive form. One of the central theses of *The Nomos of the Earth*, which he reiterates in this afterword, proposes that the state within the JPE had attained the "hitherto greatest rational 'advance' of human history in the doctrine of war according to the law of nations, namely the differentiation between the enemy and the criminal."[33] In situating this advance on the threshold to the modern era characterized by the clarion call of *Silete Theologi!* Schmitt finds himself faced with a problem: "A consideration of the fate of the concept of the enemy in a consistently de-theologized and now only human new world becomes for us unavoidable."[34] As the legal concepts of the era were "completely characterized by the state" as Schmitt claims, he considers postwar Europe to be anew on the threshold of a new era: "the epoch of statism now draws to a close," as he writes in the foreword to the 1963 edition of *The Concept of the Political*. The question of which meaning theology takes at the turn of the twentieth century remains implicit in Schmitt's polemic against Blumenberg, without being explicitly elaborated.

Schmitt's attempt to actualize and therefore rescue political theology—or more generally, an understanding of secularization that proceeds from the overcoming and *Aufhebung* of religious meanings in secular concepts—is put to the test by the reappearance or return within modernity of figures from pre-modern, pre-secular contexts. In terms of Schmitt's own writings, this applies to the *topos* of the 'just war.' It should have become clear that this constellation is of particular relevance for today's situation, since the terminology of 'rogue states' just as much as the images of the enemy in the propaganda of the other side negate the distinction between criminal and *hostis*.

### Beyond the *Jus Publicum Europaeum*: On the Return of 'Just War' in the "new *nomos* of the earth"

The reappearance of the figure of 'just war' plays a significant role in the final chapter of *The Nomos of the Earth*. Here Schmitt discusses the dissolution of the JPE and the question of a "new *nomos* of the earth." If

---

33. Schmitt, *Nomos* (1997), 86; (2006), 147.
34. Ibid. (1997), 92.

the rhetoric of 'just war' in the twentieth century is not simply to be re-garded as a regression to a state prior to the JPE, then another interpre-tative model must be developed for it. On the manifest level of the text, this is derived from America's role, when the new spatial order laid claim to by the Monroe doctrine ("America for the Americans!"—1823) marked an end of the spatial order of the JPE. However, in this text published in 1950, impressions from the most recent past patently impinge on Schmitt's considerations. These are expressed above all in his metaphorical language, for example in the images with which America is described. The place of the United States and its role in the end of the JPE is, for instance, intro-duced at the beginning of this chapter in a poetic image: "The first long shadow that fell upon *jus publicum Europaeum* came from the West."[35] It is not until sixty-five pages later that the assessment of this image follows: "What, then, is the status in international law, according to this new *line*, of the Western hemisphere vis-à-vis a European order of international law? It is something quite extraordinary, something *chosen (Auserwähltes)*."[36]

If the breach of the JPE through the decision of another sovereign power external to it, a kind of state of exception on the level of interna-tional law, evokes in Schmitt the image of chosen-ness, then it seems the self-imposed silence of theology is put to the test. His rhetoric here over-steps his consistently secular interpretative frame. Yet this occurs without any reflection upon the theoretical consequences. And further:

It would be, at any rate for an extremely logical position, an understatement to say that America was an asylum of justice and proficiency. The true sense of this line of chosen-ness is to be found, rather, in the fact that the conditions did not exist until they were given on American soil which allow reasonable attitudes and 'habits,' justice and peace, to attain the status of normality.[37]

Formulated shortly after the end of the Third Reich and the Second World War, the anti-Semitic connotations of this passage cannot be overlooked. It is not my intention to raise once more the issue of Schmitt's anti-Semitism with this observation. The debate around this question has been sufficient-

35. Ibid. (2006), 227.

36. Ibid. (1997), 265; (2006), 289 (emphasis S.W.). The point is that, in describing America as 'auserwählt,' Schmitt's image invokes the German term for the Chosen People, *das Auserwählte Volk* (—trans.).

37. Ibid. (1997), 265; (2006), 289.

ly addressed in Raphael Gross's substantial study. Rather, what is at issue is the rhetorical role taken on here by the *topos* of 'chosen-ness.' When this term from Jewish theology, which designates the position of the Jewish people in relation to God, is here used as a metaphor describing the place of that political power (the United States), which in Schmitt's eyes exists beyond the jurisdiction of European international law and literally puts the latter in its own shadow, then the *topos* seals off Schmitt's own theory from an interrogation of religious interpretative frameworks in modernity. When Schmitt describes, at the end of the age of the nation-state in which theological concepts were sublated into "secularized theological concepts" of the modern theory of the state, the advent of a *chosen* political power, then it is striking that this does not lead him to an analysis of the return of religious *topoi* within the concept of the political. As such, his rhetoric is a symptom for the lack of reflection on religious traces within the European, and within *Nomos of the Earth* exclusively Christian, secularization.

The dissolution of the European order of war—and with it the theoretical analogy between the friend-enemy constellation in Schmitt's concept of the political and the JPE—is discussed in the final chapter of *The Nomos of the Earth*, primarily in relation to the debates on war crimes in the aftermath of the First and Second World Wars. The signal for the dissolution of the old order is above all the adoption of categories of crime into the discourse of international law. The end of the amnesty rule after declarations of peace, the "discrimination against the vanquished," and the criminalization of aggressive war[38] led to "the deep dilemma between juridical and political ways of thinking," according to Schmitt.[39] He draws a trajectory from the Treaty of Versailles in 1919, through the Hague and Geneva Conventions, and ending in the London Agreement in 1945 that ends in the "downfall of Europe": "For a moment, in the London Statute of August 8, 1945, East and West finally came together and agreed. Criminalization now took its course."[40]

The study concludes with a consideration of the "problem of just war." Here, too, the relationship between America and Europe, and more so between America and Germany, plays an important role. Already in the book's second chapter on the age of discoveries, which deals with the

38. Ibid. (2006), 262.
39. Ibid. (1997), 253; (2006), 279.
40. Ibid. (2006), 280.

historical development of "contained war," a short passage describing this concept is interrupted, not as one might expect by an account of its opposite located in a prehistory that has been overcome but rather by a sudden intrusion of the present: "The present-day theory of just war, by contrast, is striving for the discrimination of the opponent who conducts war unjustly."[41] Admittedly neither Hitler nor the Allies are mentioned explicitly here. However, in terms of the discussions about a new world order, it is indeed relevant that the *topos* of 'just war' arose in the twentieth century in the fight against Hitler and that the position of the United States as an imperial, sovereign power (beyond the conventions of the United Nations) is historically derived from the war against the Third Reich. In this sense, Germany is allocated an involuntary role in the present scenario, as the occasion for the legitimization of a state of exception in international law.

As Germany is not named at this juncture in Schmitt's argument, it does not get a mention when, in the section at the end of his study called "The war of the modern means of destruction," Schmitt considers two phenomena marking for him the culmination of the dissolution of the JPE. The first is the technological phenomenon of modern air war. This brings to an end the old spatial order of territorial land war and maritime sea war, ushering in a "deterritorialization" that demonstrates "the purely destructive character of modern air war."[42] The second is the problem of just war, in which the stronger party declares the enemy to be a criminal, in this way justifying the deployment of such means of destruction. At this point, too, the rhetoric displays what the argumentation conceals:

The bomber or hedgehopper uses his weapons against the population of the enemy country vertically, *as St. George used his lance against the dragon.* In that war today is being transformed into a police action against disturbers of the peace, criminals and pests, the justification of the methods of this 'police bombing' must also be intensified. So one is forced to drive the discrimination of the opponent to abysmal depths. Only in one respect can the medieval theses of just war possess immediate actuality even today.[43]

This rhetoric could be explained in terms of a specific prejudice on the part of the functionaries of the National Socialist state after 1945. It would

41. Ibid. (1997), 292.
42. Ibid. (1997), 298; (2006), 318.
43. Ibid. (1997), 299; (2006), 321 (emphasis S.W.).

mean that, in the thematization of a modern state of exception in international law, the Allies are seen as operating within a medieval interpretative framework, consisting of the Christian iconography of the dragon slayer and the actualization of the *topos* of just war. At the same time, the slip of the tongue within the metaphor of the "pests" points toward that concealed, other war that was conducted with modern means of destruction by Hitler's Germany against the Jews.

And thus we can see that Giorgio Agamben's *Homo sacer* touches upon a significant lacuna in political theology. If this book claims, however, to be an account of a new world order, the camp as the materialization of the state of exception and "as the *nomos* of the Modern,"[44] then crucial constellations relevant to this claim have been left out here as well. In Agamben, who unlike Schmitt again highlights theology, these are above all the framework of international law. In arguing within the horizon of a theory of sovereignty, *Homo sacer* also inherits the latter's theoretical limitations. And in respect of the analysis of the current constellations of conflict, the theoretical limitations of political theology are more far-reaching than the prejudices of the founding father of its discourse, Carl Schmitt.

The failure of political theology vis-à-vis present-day phenomena applies in particular to the appearance of new actors upon the scenes of conflict and war where international law, civil war, and religious war coincide. This failure applies to terrorism with a religious face, to the figure of the suicide bomber or martyr, and to the *topos* of just or even Holy War, to which both sides are laying claim. And it applies, too, to the overlaying of the discourses of religion and criminalization in the images both sides are making of the enemy, as well as the legitimization of action through recourse to universal concepts such as freedom, justice, human dignity, or human rights.

The fact that Schmitt's concept of the political fails to recognize the continued operation of religious traditions—because he interprets the *topos* of 'just war' only in terms of criminalization—makes clear how secularized concepts that appear to be the result of a complete transferal of theological terms into those of constitutional law are able to immunize themselves against religio-cultural connections. This even applies to the figure of the martyr. The figure makes a brief appearance at the end of *Political Theol-*

---

44. Agamben, *Homo Sacer*, 166.

*ogy II*, but only as a transitional figure between the church and the state in which the secularization of charisma appears as a form of transformation. The prototype for this is Tertullian, of whom it is said that he held fast to the *charisma of the martyr* while resisting the total transformation of charisma into the charisma of office.[45]

Here, at the end of *Political Theology II*, the unsolved problems of secularization become legible, particularly because the text remains caught in indecision, oscillating between images and counterimages, quotations and counterquotations. This indecision is clear, for example, when Schmitt on the one hand refutes the theological notion of the double nature of mankind[46] but on the other reintroduces it with a question about "what is spiritual and what is worldly and what is at stake with the *res mixtae*, of which after all the entire earthly existence of this spiritual-worldly, spiritual-temporal double-being *Man* consists, in the interval between the coming and the second coming of the Lord."[47] This, says Schmitt, is the "great Hobbes-question" of his 1922 *Political Theology*, a question that has, however, disappeared and been sublated into the "secularized theological concepts" of that book.

## The Reappearance of the Martyr

The appearance of the suicide bomber as a person acclaimed as martyr from his community can be seen as one of the phenomena most acutely relevant to the present moment in terms of the aforementioned problem of the *res mixtae*, because it confronts the present critique of violence with a figure through which scenes of battle become defined as the switching points between a human and a divine dramaturgy. At the same time, these new martyrs present a challenge to not only European but the whole of Western culture, because in these martyrs this culture encounters patterns and images from its own Christian prehistory that long since seemed to belong to the past. The figure of the martyr belongs to those motifs that Islam took over from Christianity at its foundation in the seventh century. It remains a legacy of considerable cultural-historical signif-

45. Schmitt, *Politische Theologie II*, 81.
46. Ibid., 83.
47. Ibid., 84.

icance, even if a complete adoption is disputed.[48] Though the meaning of *shahid* as martyr cannot be traced back directly to the Koran (unlike the commandment to fight *djihad*, or Holy War), the formation of the cult of the martyr is a part of the early history of Islam, since this cult is derived from both the primal scenes of the Sunni battlefield martyrs during the fights of Bar and Uhud in 624/625 and the death of Husain, a grandson of the Prophet Mohammed, in the battle of Kerbala in the year 680. These events function to this day as the object of ritual veneration, in particular among Shiites who, on Ashura, one of their most important holy days, mark the anniversary of Husain's death with flagellation processions and passion plays.

The martyr in Islam is markedly different from his Christian predecessor, however, in that he appears from the outset as a warrior, whether as one who fights for the 'true faith' and against the falsifications of the idea of the one God, of which Mohammed accused the Christians and the Jews, or as one who fights for the establishment and dissemination of the teachings of the Prophet. The Christian martyr, by contrast, appears, at least in his origins, as a figure of suffering. Derived from the Greek *martyr* = witness, the Christian martyr traces his roots back to his role as a witness of Christ's Passion and sacrifice.[49] The martyr is the witness of Christ's life, death, and resurrection who holds to his faith even at the cost of persecution, torture, and death. In this, his martyrdom appears as a form of *imitatio Christi*. Because the blood of the martyr bears witness to the confession of his faith, Gotthold Ephraim Lessing called it (in his text *The Saving of*

---

48. The question of the legacies of Christianity in Islam is a matter of controversy and cannot be discussed here. On the significance of the martyr in the Jewish-Christian history of religion, see Daniel Boyarin, *Dying for God: Martyrdom and the Making of Christianity and Judaism* (Stanford: Stanford UP, 1999). On the ubiquity of the martyr and the multiple references between the different religions, see Friederike Pannewick, ed., *Martyrdom in Literature: Visions of Death and Meaningful Suffering in Europe and the Middle East from Antiquity to Modernity* (Wiesbaden: Reichert, 2004); and Sigrid Weigel, ed., *Märtyrerporträts. Von Opfertod, Blutzeugen und Heiligen Kriegern* (München: Wilhelm Fink, 2007).

49. On the formation of the figure and concept of martyr in the course of the transition from antique Roman to Christian culture, see Sigrid Weigel, "Exemplum and Sacrifice, Blood Testimony and Written Testimony: Lucretia and Perpetua as Transitional Figures in the Cultural History of Martyrdom," in J. N. Bremmer and M. Formisano (eds.), *Perpetua's Passions* (Oxford: Oxford UP, 2011), 180–200.

*Cardanus*) "a highly ambivalent thing."[50] It is ambivalent because it has, apart from its physiological status, a second, transcendental meaning. As a symbol of blood witness, it raises the body of the martyr into another, sacred sphere. And if blood distinguishes the martyr as a blood witness, it is also in blood that there is condensed an as-it-were sacred evidence: as the sign of witness of the Passion. In this respect blood distinguishes the martyr in a double sense: it both marks him out and ennobles him.

And so it is that the Christian iconography of martyrdom appears as a both gruesome *and* sublime tableau of multifarious forms of torture. In the representative paintings from the fifteenth to the seventeenth centuries, from Cranach and Dürer via Altdorfer, van Dyck and de Ribera to Tiepolo, martyrs who remain steadfast under torture dominate the scene. Venerated in these images as saints, they have necessarily undergone every imaginable form of physical torment—and the repertoire of atrocities is not worlds apart from the reports of the massacres that took place during the Balkan wars of the 1990s. Benjamin's dictum that "blood is the symbol of mere life" (SW 1.151) is targeted precisely at this symbolism. This means he denies blood has any significance that is not physical, just as he more generally derives his critique of the violence of martyr and tyrant from their double referentiality both to a creaturely and to a sacred order, as will be demonstrated below. The veneration of the suicide bomber as a martyr assumes the reduction of his or her life to mere, naked life, because only as such can it transform into a deadly weapon in order to become an instrument in a holy war—and subsequently be sacralized postmortem.

In Christianity, the ambivalence of blood in martyrdom culture has given rise to the dynamic of an affective economy in accordance with which passive suffering could be transformed into excitation. Since the rhetoric of persistence (Lat. *constantia*) and joyful-impassioned devotion to torture and death was already common in the early Christian acts of the martyrs, the subsequent poetic, musical, and iconographic martyr worship became a culture of the transformation of suffering into passion, a prerequisite for a cultural history in which the *passio* could become passion in the sense of a state of affective excitement.[51] The dramaturgy of the Baroque mourning play de-

50. Gotthold Ephraim Lessing, 'Rettung des Cardanus,' in *Werke*, ed. Helmut Göbel, vol. 7: *Theologiekritische Schriften I* (München: Carl Hanser, 1976), 20.

51. See Erich Auerbach, 'Passio als Leidenschaft' in Auerbach, *Gesammelte Aufsätze zur romanischen Philologie* (Bern and Munich: Franke, 1967), 161–175.

velops its dynamic from this transformation, an example being when Gryphius's *Catharina von Georgien* resists not only the courtship of the Persian king who is keeping her prisoner but also the ordeal of torture so that she "completes her lamentable life full of joy-full patience at the stake."[52]

The arming of the Christian martyr to make of him a 'warrior of God' or 'Christ's soldier' did not take place until the context of the Crusades. It was only in the battles for Jerusalem that the Christian martyr was transformed into an aggressor.[53] It is quite different in the Islamic tradition, where the figure of the martyr originates in the scene of (mainly inner-Arabic or inner-Islamic) battles. His sacrificial death represents a privilege in that he receives a place in paradise without having to undergo judgment. Although the blood of the Muslim martyr does not function as witness (of his confession),[54] he is nevertheless distinguished by his blood. It is said, for instance, that the wounds the *shahid* receives in the course of *djihad* will shine like blood and give off a scent as of musk on the Last Day.[55] Also, there is a hierarchy among the martyrs that has always placed those who have lost their lives in battle (*shuhada al-ma'raka*) above those who have not died a bloody death (*shuhada al'akhira*) by giving to the former the entitlement to a particular burial rite. In order that their blood can bear witness to their heroic deaths at the Last Judgment, their corpses are not subject to the usual ritual washing.[56] Their deaths are often interpreted as a *rite de passage* stylized in poetic images as a wedding (*'urs al shahid*). Following in this tradition, the bomb attacks by Palestinian agents today are metaphorically represented as a marriage with their native soil.[57]

Unlike the retrospective transformation of victims (those fallen in war, in the resistance, or through persecution for their faith) into martyrs,

52. Andreas Gryphius, *Catherina von Georgien. Trauerspiel* (Stuttgart: Reclam, 1975), 7.

53. See Steven Runciman, *A History of the Crusades*, 3 vols. (Cambridge: Cambridge UP, 1951–1954).

54. "The fallen Muslims had nothing to testify": Fritz Meier, 'Almoraviden und marabute,' in *Bausteine II. Ausgewählte Aufsätze zur Islamwissenschaft*, ed. Erika Glassen and Gudrun Schubert (Stuttgart: Steiner, 1992), 713.

55. See *Enzyklopaedie des Islam*, ed. M. Th. Houtsma et al. (Leiden and Leipzig: Brill 1934), vol. IV, 279. See also Adel Theodor Khoury, "Enführung in die Grundlagen des Islam," in *Religionswissen-schaft-liche Studien* 27 (Würzburg: Oros, 1993).

56. E. Kohlberg, 'Shahid,' in *Encyclopaedia of Islam*.

57. Angelika Neuwirth, "From Sacrilege to Sacrifice: Observations on Violent Death in Classical and Modern Arabic Poetry," in *Martyrdom in Literature* (note 24), 259–281.

through which an unbearable death is given meaning after the event by those who commemorate it, the current recourse to the concept of the martyr by suicide attackers transforms a religious concept into a programmatic political instrument. Here, the martyr becomes a deadly weapon. This enactment creates a knot of political and religious aspects that it is far from easy to untie. Understood within the framework of Benjamin's book on mourning play, these phenomena may be described as a radical adaptation of the political into theological scenarios, or as the recourse to religious interpretations to political problems in a situation in which politics does not appear to offer any answers—in short, as a modern *Trauerspiel*. The seventeenth century's transition from Christian eschatology to the secularization of the historical, which in view of general hopelessness and despair redirected the Baroque's flight from the world into an absolute immanence, is countered today by a reversed constellation of transition. Here, the promises of modernity that are not kept are answered by the flight into religious fundamentalism, which holds out the promise of transcending struggles for which there is no prospect of an outcome.

## The Sovereign as Tyrant: The Tyrant as Martyr

Walter Benjamin's book on mourning play provides useful interpretative models for the analysis of the present-day return of religious iconography and rhetorics into politics for the precise reason that he considers the figures of the martyr, the sovereign, and the tyrant in the context of a theory of sovereignty that, unlike Carl Schmitt's political theology, does not work with secularized theological concepts but rather focuses on the question of the *res mixtae* that in Schmitt's work remained unresolved. Thus Benjamin describes the Baroque *Trauerspiel* as a drama of tyrant *and* martyr, emphasizing how the two meanings coincide or are converted one into the other. For in the Baroque *Trauerspiel*, the monarch, who stands for history, also embodies the sovereign's transformation into the tyrant who brings destruction upon himself and his court or state:

In the Baroque the tyrant and the martyr are the janiceps of the coroneted. They are the necessarily extreme manifestations of the princely essence. As far as the tyrant is concerned, this is clear enough. The theory of sovereignty, which takes as its example the special case in which dictatorial powers are unfolded, demands the completion of the image of the sovereign, as tyrant. (I.I/249; Origins, 69)

In the "completion" of the sovereign *in* the tyrant, Benjamin reflects the double positioning of the Baroque sovereign between theology and the theory of the state in its fatal consequences. For it is in the tyrannical figure that the exceptional status (*Ausnahmezustand*) is made manifest that is latently inscribed into the sovereign's godlike position in the sphere of worldly power, bringing to the surface its violent aspects. Benjamin here, in his *Trauerspiel* book (1927), takes up a lesson from his "Critique of Violence" (1921), though it is applied now to the state rather than to revolutionary violence. It is concerned with the transformation of *embodied power* into bodily, physical violence.

If all concepts of a modern theory of the state are secularized theological concepts, then it is only through examining their theological prehistory, which continues to operate within them, that the legacy can be recognized. In the Baroque period, it was precisely *not* the case that he who decides on the state of exception is the sovereign, but rather vice versa: the one who is the sovereign has the power to command the state of exception! This decisive reversal between the historical and the modern concept of sovereignty is concealed in Benjamin's text in a barely noticeable turn in the argument: "Whereas the *modern* concept of sovereignty *amounts to* a supreme executive, to princely power, the *baroque* concept *emerges from* a discussion of the state of exception, and makes it the most important function of the prince to avert this" (245, 65; emphasis S.W.).[58] This means that, whereas protection from the state of exception is the lynchpin of Baroque sovereignty, the state of exception is, in a precise reversal, the effect of sovereignty in its modern form. At this point in Benjamin's text comes a much-debated reference to Schmitt in a footnote, after which Benjamin, reversing Schmitt's dictum "Sovereign is he who decides on the exception," continues: "The ruler is *designated from the outset as the holder of dictatorial power* if war, revolt, or other catastrophes should lead to a state of exception" (245ff., 65). Benjamin describes the goal of this power within the state of exception as a type of standstill of history and its retransformation into nature, a movement he identifies as the utopia of a dictator: "The concern of the tyrant is the restoration of order in the state of exception: a dictatorship whose utopian goal will always be to replace

58. On this distinction, see also Samuel Weber, 'Von der Ausnahme zur Entscheidung. Walter Benjamin und Carl Schmitt,' in Elisabeth Weber and Georg C. Tholen (eds.), *Das Vergessen(e). Anamnesen des Undarstellbaren* (Vienna: Turia + Kany, 1992), 152.

the unpredictability of historical accident with the iron constitution of the laws of nature" (253, 74).

In Benjamin's presentation, the Baroque and the modern concepts of sovereignty thus differ fundamentally. The theological foundation of absolute authority in the person of the Baroque sovereign forms the condition of possibility for his tyrannical transformation, and more than this, for his consummation *as* tyrant: "the seventeenth century ruler, the summit of the creaturely, erupting into fury like a volcano and destroying himself and his entire court" (250, 70). Benjamin thus interprets the *Trauerspiel* as the scene in which this consummation is performed. Its dynamic is founded in the contradiction that necessarily follows upon the idea of a "mortal God," to the extent that the latter is caught between omnipotence and a life under creaturely conditions—between being "the prince of the world" and a "heavenly animal." And it is precisely in this doubled form that he becomes a martyr, as "he falls victim to the disproportion between the unlimited hierarchical dignity, with which he is divinely invested and the humble estate of his humanity" (250, 70). The tyrant as martyr is, then, not the victim of his faith, but the victim of a theologically founded politics, which allows of no distinction between the person and his authority and therefore knows no limit.

It is suggestive to think of Saddam Hussein in connection with such descriptions and to consider the tyranny and the fall of Saddam in terms of *Trauerspiel*. But then the question poses itself in his case as to what role religion played in legitimizing his sovereignty—the case of the dictator in the midst of a religiously defined culture. Unlike in the traditional conceptualization of the 'Islamic state,' Saddam's dictatorship was not founded in the imperative of the unity of religion and politics. (Incidentally, some Muslim scholars evaluated the absence of such a unity as a danger that could lead the state to transform itself into a tyrannical organization.) And yet Saddam could, despite the different interpretations applied to the question of political rule and its legitimacy within Islam, rely on one of the principles within Islamic cultures, namely that whoever rules, rules by God's will. And insofar as the Iraq War was in part represented as a war against the person of the ruler, or rather against his image—as the U.S. soldiers destroyed the monumental statues, the larger-than-life-sized images of him and the insignia of his power in front of the running cameras—the tyrant seemed, in the eyes of his supporters, to be raised to the status of martyr in whose name the resistance against the occupying forces was ignited. But the image of the lone individual hunted by the world's greatest army, who, just because he is the target of a superior military force, is transformed for his supporters into a hero, imploded in the end at the sight of Saddam's wretched appearance when he was found in a foxhole. In the way the captured dictator was presented to the world's media, his weakness made him unsuited to appearing either as a heroic figure for his supporters or the figure of the dangerous enemy for the occupying forces. This implosion of the tyrant—in his double capacity as martyr and enemy—added a new act to the dramaturgy of the modern mourning play: tragic drama.

Already in the early modern age, as Benjamin shows, the transformation of sovereign into tyrant and the discussion about tyrannicide formed a difficult complex:[59] "The old textbook case of tyrannicide" asserts itself in the seventeenth century, Benjamin claims, in the focal point on the formation of a new concept of sovereignty and the controversy on the legal doctrines of the Middle Ages. It was a debate that had not least been ignited by the murder of Henry IV of France: "Among the various kinds of tyrant defined in earlier constitutional doctrine, the usurper had always been the subject of particular controversy. The Church had abandoned him, but beyond that it was a question of whether the people, the anti-king, or the Curia alone could give the signal to depose him" (Origins 65). Benjamin interprets the fact that the position of an *absolute inviolability of sovereignty* ultimately prevailed before the Curia as the dismissal of a theocratic claim, which he attributes mainly to Protestantism: "Despite the alignment of the respective parties, this extreme doctrine of princely power had its origins in the counter-reformation, and was more intelligent and more profound than its modern version" (65). It follows the previously cited reference to the role of the Baroque princes in excluding the state of exception. This means that a murder of these princes cannot easily be legitimized on the basis of the same exclusion that is guaranteed by his sovereignty. It is striking that Benjamin, in this context, considers the doctrine of absolute princely power to be an "extreme doctrine" with which he judges the unlimited exercise of sovereign power itself to be an extreme case of power.

In the historical dispute over tyrannicide, there were no easy answers. It is no different today, and perhaps even more difficult, since the

---

59. On the cultural and religious history of the tyrant since classical antiquity, see Wolfgang Pircher and Martin Treml (eds.), *Tyrannis und Verführung* (Vienna: Turia + Kant, 2000).

"inviolability of the sovereign" is no longer opposed by any authority whose norms may limit and contain absolute sovereignty—that is, unless one would ascribe to bi- and multilateral agreements and international treaties a comparable counterposition to the sovereign, much like the Curia in the early modern era. Every argument in support of tyrannicide requires legitimization by another superior order, which has the side effect of touching and relativizing the concept of sovereignty as such. It is for this reason that the U.S. government could not define the removal of Saddam as the goal of the war, for that would possibly have meant weakening or calling into question the political concept of sovereignty altogether. For in George W. Bush and Saddam Hussein, there stood opposed, from the U.S. perspective, as it were, an *imperial* and a *tyrannical* sovereign. For this reason, the United States took refuge in the argument that Iraq had failed to meet the terms of the international accord on the nonproliferation of nuclear weapons. With this argument, however, the United States fell back on the significance of international agreements that bind the decision on the state of exception to specific rules and so set a limit upon the American president's claim to unilateral sovereignty in the international arena. In this way, the politics of the Bush administration move between imperial acts of sovereign power (which places sovereignty as such in question) and the submission to the conventions of international law (which limits the decision-making power of absolute sovereignty through agreements).

Benjamin's reading of the *Trauerspiel* as existing on the threshold between theology and politics integrates aspects of the thinking from his earlier "Critique of Violence," the text from which the category of 'bare life' is derived. This text moves beyond the limitations, described above, of a form of political theology whose concept of secularization is founded on historico-philosophical figures such as overcoming and *Aufhebung*. Benjamin's reflections, in contrast, take as their starting point the problem of the derivation of political, legal, and philosophical concepts from theological or biblical traditions, focusing on the issue of the double referentiality of human existence, between natural and supernatural life, in order to develop a critique of the dialectic of secularization. Thus, his critique of violence (both in the essay of that title, which is discussed below, and in other writings by him) is targeted above all at the precarious intermingling of concepts of divine power with the concepts of the political. As such, it is directed against the requisitioning of theology as a *means* of achieving political or legal ends, as much as against a pure transferal of sacred concepts into profane ones in which aspects of religious violence continue to operate in concealed form. He proceeds from the assumption of a radical incompatibility of human and divine order. It is only against this background that the specific forms of transferal and the figurations through which traces of an earlier religious history live on—in transformed and displaced fashion—within secular concepts can be properly examined. I do not claim that Benjamin's "Critique of Violence" can explain the current situation in its entirety. But it is capable of penetrating a sphere against which political theology, with the assistance of secularized theological concepts, has sealed itself off.

# 3

## Disregard of the First Commandment in Monstrous Cases

*The "Critique of Violence" Beyond Legal Theory and 'States of Exception'*

The analytic potential of the 1921 essay "Critique of Violence" ("*Kritik der Gewalt*") has by no means been exhausted as regards the current debate on contemporary forms of violence. This is because Benjamin subjects not only the borderline cases of the modern legal order—such as martial law and the death penalty—to a historico-theoretical analysis of the forms of violence used. He also extends his critique to those expressions of violence that appeal to a higher legitimation. In other words, he also examines those instances of violence that justify their actions as legal beyond all applicable law and thus, as it were, suggest a divine mandate for them. The essay also undertakes to reflect on secularized theological concepts, with Benjamin once again exploring the origin of core elements of legal theory in notions that have preceded law. Here, the emphasis is on the persistence of *mythic violence* or *divine violence* in modern forms of state *and* revolutionary violence. The occasion and his starting point was the contemporary debate on revolutionary violence, in particular those arguments that relied on absolute principles, whereby Benjamin analyzed their heritage in the sphere of fate and the saintly.

As has often been indicated, the concept of *Gewalt* is to be understood here in a comprehensive sense that goes beyond physical violence. This is the case in the sense that the word '*Gewalt*' can mean both violence and power, and also because the range of Benjamin's investigation goes back well before the historical differentiation between *potestas* and *violentia*, between legitimate and illegitimate violence. Yet many commentators have overlooked the fact that Benjamin's essay introduces the concept of "violence in the concise (*prägnant*) sense of the word" with quite a different meaning in mind, namely as neither physical *violence* nor institutional *power* but rather *as a reason* (*Ursache*) that "intervenes in ethical relations." He adds that the sphere of these relations is defined by the concepts of law and justice (SelWr 1.236). In other words, Benjamin is interested less in the exertion of physical or political violence and more in the way *a reason* intervenes in law and justice, which is to say in the procedure of justification or legitimation. To be more precise: the focus is on the transformation of a reason into *violence* by way of its *intervention* in the concepts of law and justice.

In order to develop standards for a discussion of the legal justifiability of violence, Benjamin opts for a "philosophico-historical view of law" (238). Yet the complexity of his essay can be explained first and foremost by the fact that he presents these historico-theoretical preconditions of the legal order in a dual light. First he discusses them with a view to the origin of law in the mythic sphere of fate, and second as regards the derivation of the idea of justified violence from the concept of divine *justice*. The first and more extensive section of the essay (236ff.) focuses on the former, while the shorter and far denser second section (248ff.) addresses the latter.

## Boundary Cases:
## On the Myth of the Schmitt-Benjamin Correspondence

The scholarly response to the "Critique of Violence" was for a long time dominated by a discussion of Benjamin's reference to Georges Sorel's *Réflexions sur la violence* of 1908.[1] Since Jacques Derrida's *Force of Law* (1991), however, it has been focused on the constellation formed by Carl Schmitt and Walter Benjamin and, most recently, above all on the renaissance of political theology and the concept of the 'state of exception.' The one letter Benjamin sent to Schmitt gained considerable weight in the critical discourse through Derrida's assertions of there having been a *correspon-*

---

1. On Sorel, see Hans Barth, *Masse und Mythos. Die Theorie der Gewalt: Georges Sorel* (Hamburg: Rowohlt, 1959).

*dence* between Schmitt and Benjamin, thus suggesting a linkage between the two thinkers that, in reality, never existed *in that form*. Benjamin's letter to Schmitt of December 9, 1930, written when he sent him a copy of his book on the *Origin of the German Mourning Play*, does provide evidence of his having studied Schmitt, at least his *Political Theology* (1922) and *Dictatorship* (in the second edition of 1928; 3/558). The only other proof of Benjamin mentioning Schmitt in his correspondence is the letter to Richard Weissbach of March 23, 1923, in which Benjamin mentions that he had left his copy of Schmitt's *Political Theology* at Weissbach's house (2/327).

Benjamin's letters prove that he did concern himself with Schmitt's writings, and he quotes Schmitt's theory of sovereignty in his book on the Baroque mourning play just as he uses the concept of the 'state of exception' both there and in his text "Theses on the Concept of History" (1940). This has all served to connect Benjamin so closely to Schmitt that one is obliged to talk of a Schmitt-Benjamin paradigm in the discourse on political theology. This has continued to be the case even after Samuel Weber first drew attention in 1992 to the fact that Benjamin's definition of sovereignty in the Baroque "diverges ever so slightly, but significantly" from Schmitt's famous maxim "Sovereign is he who decides on the state of exception."[2] This has by no means led to the two names being less linked in scholarship. On the contrary, it has recently once again been reinforced by Giorgio Agamben's argument, in his book *The State of Exception* (2005), that Carl Schmitt's *Political Theology*, which appeared one year after Benjamin's essay, was written in response to Benjamin, and that Schmitt's introduction of the concept of decision is to be seen as a "countermove to Benjamin's critique."[3] Benjamin's quotation from Schmitt in the book on Baroque tragic drama is there interpreted in turn as a response to Schmitt's reception of Benjamin, providing the basis for what Agamben refers to as a Benjamin-Schmitt "secret dossier." It is only through the assumption of this kind of dialogic continuum that the essay on the "Critique of Violence" has been included in the discussion of the state of exception.

The fact that Benjamin does not yet use the expression 'state of exception' in this context but instead, as quoted above, speaks of "an extreme case" and of *monstrous* or *tremendous cases* (*ungeheure Fälle*) indicates a far

2. Samuel Weber, "Taking Exception to Decision: Theatrical-Theological Politics. Walter Benjamin and Carl Schmitt," in *Walter Benjamin 1892–1992* (Frankfurt/M: Suhrkamp, 1992).

3. Giorgio Agamben, *State of Exception* (Chicago: U of Chicago P, 2005), 66.

more significant difference. As regards the *extreme* case, his discussion does
not bear on matters of constitutional law, but rather on the legitimacy of
revolutionary force, specifically the justification of tyrannicide or the question of whether "revolutionary killing of the oppressor" (SelWr 1.250ff.) is
forbidden by a universal injunction on killing. While contemplating this
extreme case, the "Critique of Violence" leaves the terrain of constitutional
law and legal order, which was discussed in the preceding passages in terms
of the right to strike and martial law. The essay moves from legal theory, and
thus from "all the forms of violence permitted by both natural law and positive law" (247ff.) in which there is no single one "free from the gravely problematic nature of all legal power," to the philosophy of history. It is precisely
at this point that the concept of *salvation* (*Erlösung*) comes into play. The
assumption that the conception of *solutions* (*Lösungen*) to human tasks, or
even a *redemption* (*Erlösung*) from "all the hitherto existing world-historical
conditions," cannot be conceived of without the exclusion of all violence
raises the question of form of violence free of the "gravely problematic nature" (247). In other words, the question of a concept of violence or power
beyond all legal theory is at stake. What is striking here is the fact that the
word *Erlösung* marks the limit for concepts drawn from legal theory. In the
English version, Benjamin's emphasis on the relationship between *Lösung*
and *Erlösung* is lost in translation (*Erlösung* is rendered as deliverance).

It is true that Benjamin discusses phenomena that—like Schmitt's
*Political Theology*—must be considered borderline cases of the legal order.
However, although Schmitt personifies this borderline case of constitutional law by referring to the figure of the sovereign who decides on the
state of emergency, the borderline case for Benjamin serves as an example
of the fundamental problem of all legal force, namely its dependency on
terms that are prior to or outside the law, such as fate and justice. When
Schmitt, in his *Political Theology*, defines the concepts of constitutional
law as secularized theological concepts, theology is sublated in constitutional law. By contrast, Benjamin works at a dialectics of secularization by
discussing in detail the precarious relationship between law and justice in
different cases and historical constellations. This brings him up against the
limits of legal-theoretical concepts, from which he moves into historico-
philosophical considerations. Here, what is involved is the origin of divine
power and justice, terms that refuse to be transformed into profane concepts. The very basis of his "Critique of Violence" lies in the distinction

between the law-preserving power of human legal orders and their mythic predecessors as well as the preconditions for this in the history of religion. He draws a line between these and both mythic law-making violence—whose primordial image Benjamin discerns in the mere manifestation of the (ancient) gods—and law-destroying divine violence (that of monotheism), which is to be located beyond all bloody violence and bare, naked, or natural life: "Justice is the principle of all divine endmaking, power the principle of all mythic lawmaking" (248).

## "Critique of Violence": Diptych of Law and Justice

There are two thematically distinct parts to the "Critique of Violence," which, since it is hardly an accessible text, are only discernable after countless readings. The first part pertains to *Law*, and the second to *Justice* beyond the sphere of legal theory. The first analyzes the reciprocal relationship of *law-making* and *law-preserving* violence; the second, that of *law-making* and *law-destroying* violence with reference to mythic and divine power.

Benjamin had already reflected on the divine origin of justice in his *Notes for a Work on the Category of Justice* (*Notizen zu einer Arbeit über die Kategorie der Gerechtigkeit*), which have come down to us in Gershom Scholem's transcription. They appear after Scholem recounts an evening spent reading together in his diary for the year 1916:

Justice does not seem to relate to the good will of the subject, but constitutes a state of affairs in the world; justice refers to the ethical category of the existent, virtue to the ethical category of what is required of him. Virtue can be required, justice can, in the final analysis, only exist as a state of the world or as a state of God. In God all virtues have the form of justice, the prefix all in *all-binding* (*all-gültig*), *all-knowing* (*all-wissend*) etc. is an indication of this.[4]

Having established the divine, as it were, *a-human* character of justice, Benjamin is already attempting to grasp its position vis-à-vis the law, speaking of "a vast gulf which yawns between the very nature of law and justice." He evidently presumes that this gulf is less visible in German owing to the close etymological relation between both terms (*Recht* and *Gerechtigkeit*),

---

4. Gershom Scholem, *Tagebücher 1913–1917 nebst Aufsätzen und Entwürfen bis 1923*, vol. I, half-volume 1913–1917, ed. K. Karlfried Gründer and Friedrich Niewöhner, with the collaboration of Herbert Kopp-Oberstebrink (Frankfurt/M: Jüdischer Verlag, 1995), 401.

because he notes that other languages indicate this difference. As evidence, he cites the opposition between the Latin *ius* and *fas*, followed by their Greek and Hebrew equivalents:

"ius θεμις [themis] מִשְׁפָּט [mischpat, law] / fas δικε [dike] עֶדֶק [zedek, justice]."

With the juxtaposition of *ius* and *fas*, Benjamin apparently refers to an older interpretation of the classics, one that unequivocally interprets *fas* as divine Law, juxtaposing it to human law, that is, *ius*. But such distinctions cannot be considered static. In Roman law, *fas* was the formula for an action that was not forbidden by any form of taboo and thus not regarded as *sacer*—i.e., not as "something imbued with a supernatural power and therefore taboo."[5] As far as these etymological considerations are concerned, it is debatable whether the Latin *fas* would not be better translated into Greek as *hosie*, meaning sacred custom or divine right, rather than as *dike*, which is the version Benjamin offers, because in Greek *hosie* apparently gives more emphasis to the sacred character of the Law than *dike*. That said, the shift in meaning of *dike* from myth (*dike* as a personification within the realm of the divine) to legal concepts (*dike* as a concept for litigation before a court) underscores just how religious connotations have entered into legal history and then become unrecognizable there. What is remarkable about Benjamin's note of 1916 is that by referencing the language he indirectly also points to these varying cultural contexts. Thus his question as to the relationship of law and justice covertly moves from the Biblical, monotheist context (the justice of divine power) and into the ancient world. Five years later, he was to tread this path again in the final passages of the essay the "Critique of Violence," yet this time quite overtly. Among other things, he points to the fact that the consequence of unwritten laws is that their transgression is not sanctioned by punishment, but by atonement, because the concept of guilt for such transgressions originates in an ancient notion of fate.

Benjamin initially perceives the violence that exists at the root of law itself in the first section of the "Critique of Violence": it is the dialectic of *law-making* and *law-preserving* violence. The former relates to the making of new law (overthrowing existing law), be it asserted through criminal or revolutionary force, or through external or internal warfare, while the latter relates to violence as a means to achieve legal ends or violence

---

5. Kurt Latte, Religiöse Begriffe im frührömischen Recht, in: *Zeitschrift der Savigny-Stiftung für Rechtsgeschichte, Romanische Abteilung*, vol. 67, 47–61, 50–51.

as a means used to the state's ends, a use Benjamin also terms "threatening" (242). In his critique, violence *as a means* thus becomes the key criterion for the fundamental "problematic nature of law" (243). On the basis of the distinction between law-making and law-preserving violence Benjamin, however, focuses specifically on their structural admixture and the interaction of the two forms of violence. In the *death penalty* the prehistorical origins of the legal order, namely law's roots in the sphere of *fate*, "jut manifestly and fearsomely" into existing law. Here, Benjamin emphasizes that the significance of the death penalty is not that it penalizes an infraction of the law, but rather that it is the moment in which "the law reaffirms itself" and thereby calls attention to the enduring element of law-making violence in the death penalty. To this extent, he uncovers "something rotten in the law" that is heralded in the highest instance of violence, i.e., the "exercise of violence over life and death" (242). By contrast, the *Polizeirecht* (police law) is described as a "spectral mixture" of the two types of violence. And Benjamin discovers in it an "ignominy" that results when it abrogates "the separation of lawmaking and law-preserving violence" (243). On the other hand, he recalls the (necessary) latent presence of violence in the legal system that owes its dominance to violence:

When the consciousness of the latent presence of violence in a legal institution disappears, the institution falls into decay. In our time, parliaments provide an example of this. They offer the familiar, woeful spectacle because they have not remained conscious of the revolutionary forces to which they owe their existence. . . . They lack the sense that they represent a lawmaking violence. (244)

All these phenomena are symptoms of the interaction of law-making and law-preserving violence, the historical interaction of which Benjamin captures in the term "law of oscillation" (*Schwankungsgesetz*): "The law governing their oscillation rests on the circumstance that all law-preserving violence, in its duration, indirectly weakens the law-making violence represented by it, through the suppression of hostile counter-violence" (251). In other words, the "law governing their oscillation" refers to a historical law owing to which, in every violent act that successfully overthrows an existing power, the elements which signified upheaval and the reassertion of power tend to disappear at the very moment of their establishment.[6]

---

6. There is a regular constitutional-law counterpart to this law governing their oscillation that stems from a voluntarist act of desired forgetting, in the principle of *damnatio*

Although most of the essay is devoted to the analysis of legal power and the mythic violence intrinsic to it, the concept of *justice* nonetheless becomes the impetus for the critique of violence that goes beyond the borders of legal theory. This 'beyond legal theory' is discussed specifically in the essay's final section, in which Benjamin addresses "what kinds of violence exist other than all those envisaged by legal theory" (247). This question has to address the problem that the sphere of political violence/power, although it still refers to that idea as its model, is structurally separated from the sphere in which the concept of justice originates—namely the Biblical idea of justice. Since Benjamin identifies this divine violence as being the primordial image of justice, it can never function as a "means of sacred dispatch," a point he urges in the last sentence of his essay.

Both parts of the essay are linked by the concept of *law-making violence* to the extent that it is examined in each, if from respectively different directions. In the first section, the focus is on the manner in which law-making violence extends into existing legal institutions, while the second concentrates on its mythic precedents. Law-making violence as that which overthrows an existing order and establishes new law thus constitutes the primary terrain in which Benjamin explores the intricate connection between justice and law. The link forged by violence between legal theory and the debates on the legitimacy of revolutionary violence is expressed in the discussion—encountered on both sides of the argument—about *just ends* (*gerechte Zwecke*) and *justified means* (*berechtigte Mittel*). In the first section, Benjamin outlines a basic dogma of legal theory shared by both natural law and positive law and in which they meet: "Just ends can be achieved by justified means, justified means used for just ends, Natural law attempts, by the justness of the ends, to 'justify' the means, positive law to 'guarantee' the justness of the ends through the justification of the means" (237). Benjamin reasons that this circular argumentation may be abandoned only if one takes over another vantage point in order to gain "mutually independent criteria both of just ends and of justified means" (237). Yet this, Benjamin suggests, is not possible at least as regards the ends, so long as one remains within the framework of legal theory. Thus, he returns to the question of just ends and justified means in the second section of

---

*memoriae*. This prohibits the destruction of the records of negotiations by assemblies enacting constitutions and other founding debates in order to save established legal titles from being potentially weakened by subsequent hermeneutic controversies as to their intentions.

the essay, whose argumentation goes beyond the borders of legal theory, thereby shedding new light on the concept of justice.

## Beyond Legal Theory

In the essay, the decision to move beyond the boundaries of the terms of legal theory is triggered, as stated, by the concept of salvation (*Erlösung*), the religious palimpsest of *solution* (*Lösung*). Once Benjamin has established the fact that within natural and positive law there is no domain of power that could be free of the severe problem of any legal violence, he returns to the debate with the gesture of a "however":

Since, however, every notion of a conceivable *solution* to human problems, not to speak of a *salvation* (*Erlösung*) from the confines (*Bannkreis*) of all hitherto existing world-historical conditions, remains impossible to perform (*unvollziehbar bleibt*) if violence is totally excluded in principle, this imposes the necessary question for different kinds of violence other than all those envisaged by legal theory. (II.I/196; SelWr 1.247; emphasis S.W.)

The question of "other kinds of violence" that is associated here with a Messianic perspective through the use of the concept of salvation not only takes us beyond the realm of legal theory. It is also immediately transposed into a fundamental investigation of that basic dogma that poses the question of violence by weighing up *just ends* and *justified means*, and thus opens them up to consideration by reason. Here, Benjamin identifies within the dogma an "irreconcilable conflict" that stems from the fact that the two concepts under investigation originate in quite different spheres. 'Justified means' arises from the realm of *fate*, and 'just ends' from a divine agency: "For it is never reason that decides on the justification of means and the justness of ends, instead fate-imposed violence decides on the former, and God on the latter" (247).

In this context, a key role is played by the concept of justice. It occupies the significant threshold between legal theory and the sphere that Benjamin, in a side piece to the essay, namely the so-called *Theological-political fragment*, terms "the essential teachings (*Lehrstück*) of the philosophy of history" (SelWr 3.155). Although justice, with talk of 'just ends,' is fashioned as an attribute of ends in order to be able to integrate it into legal-theoretical concepts, Benjamin insists that the concepts in the above-mentioned legal-theoretical dogma differ in their origin. In this context, the semantics of the concept of violence come to bear. Unfortunately, however, they are lost in the English translations of "Critique of Violence." This is because Benjamin ties the concept of *enacted* violence (*ausgeübte Gewalt*), which first makes possible the notion of violence as a means, to *enacting* power (*ausübende Gewalt*), that is to say, *Gewalt* in the sense of an agency or power. Its primordial image is mythic violence: "Power (is) the principle of all mythic lawmaking" (SelWr 1.248).

All legal concepts rely on a mythic concept of violence that precedes all legal theory to the extent that law-making violence is shaped in the primordial image of mythic violence, Benjamin argues: "Lawmaking is making of power (*Machtsetzung*), and to that extent an immediate manifestation of violence" (II.I/198; SelWr 1.248). And it is this violence, as always inscribed in lawmaking, which turns a legal-theoretical discussion of violence's character as a means into discussion of the "gravely problematic nature of all legal violence." If the category of *justice* is then introduced into existing law in order to gauge violence (this happens in the figure of "just ends"), then this again refers to a sphere before or beyond law. In this case, however, it stems from another set of ideas, namely religion instead of myth. In other words, the legal-theoretical dogma that enables us to measure violence relies on nonlegal concepts in two ways: on the mythic violence of the gods, on one hand, and on divine justice on the other. Put differently, it refers to both Athens/Rome *and* Jerusalem. These reflections form the conditions of possibility for a discussion of the issue of *pure violence*. Thus the realm beyond the legal-theoretical dogma into which the question of other types of violence leads is placed in a dual referential frame, i.e., to myth and to the Bible. At the very least, this double index in the philosophy of (religious) history highlights the complexity of the essay's concluding passage. If revolutionary violence cites justice, it legitimizes itself in line with the model of divinely ordained ends, while also emulating the principle of all mythic lawmaking in its intention to justify new law. This follows from the sentence with which Benjamin closes the passage in question: "*Justice* is the principle of all divine *endmaking* (*Zwecksetzung*), power the principle of all mythical lawmaking (*Rechtsetzung*)" (SelWr 1.248; emphasis S.W.).

In the second part of the essay, Benjamin initially describes the other form of violence that leads to thinking beyond this dogma as one that functions "not as means at all" to just ends, and as neither a justified nor an unjustified means, but, as he puts it, "irgendwie anders." This "some different way" concerns a nonmediate (*nicht mittelbare*) function of violence.[7] Benjamin initially discerns this other form of violence in *manifestation*. The only example he is able to cite, however, stems from experience in everyday life: "As regards man, he is impelled by anger, for example, to the most visible outbursts of a violence that is not related as a means to a preconceived end" (248). The evident difficulties in giving more concrete shape to the discussion of violence in "some different way" and giving it a more vivid presentation show that Benjamin is endeavoring here to enter new epistemological terrain, for the discussion of which there were apparently no examples at hand in history hitherto. The existence of a realm beyond legal theory is a primordial theme and entails recourse to a literal *u-topos*, a not-yet-existing site. The fact that at this point a shift in perspective is necessary, as Benjamin now addresses mythic violence by highlighting the "mere manifestation of the gods" (248) as the archetypal image of mythic violence, makes clear that only beyond legal theory can the horizon of law's prehistory within the history of religion become apparent and be negotiated. Otherwise it remains something that functions covertly in the genesis of the legal order. Benjamin's discussion, via the detour through mythic violence, of *manifestation* as a different form of violence, leads him to reject the idea. The mythic manifestation of immediate violence does not open up some "purer sphere"; instead it transpires that mythic violence shares the problems of all legal violence. This permits Benjamin to claim with certainty that its historical function can perish, and from this he goes on to inquire as to what possible other forms of violence can exist, with a view to "pure immediate violence that might be able to call a halt to mythic violence" (249).

With the introduction of the concept of "pure immediate violence," Benjamin introduces a second criterion to determine this different type of violence: first, it may not be defined in any way as a means, and second, it is pure. Although its 'immediacy' derives from his critique of the legal-theoretic dogma of justified means and just ends, the criterion 'pure' is introduced as the opposite of mythic violence. The basis for the opposition of mythic-pure stems from the relationship of mythic and divine violence, because Benjamin uncovers the primordial image of pure violence in divine violence. To summarize the underlying opposition: on the one

7. The English translation mistakes this as "non-immediate" (SelWr 1.247–8).

hand there is *mythic violence*, which he defines as lawmaking, demarcating, giving rise to guilt (*verschuldend*), expiatory (*sühnend*), threatening, and bloody. On the other hand, there is the *divine pure violence*, which he states destroys law, is boundlessly destructive, de-expiatory (*entsühnend*), strikes, and is lethal without spilling blood.

## In Monstrous Cases: *in ungeheuren Fällen*

In the following passage, which is among the most difficult of the essay, he then proceeds to introduce the concept of *mere life*. The focus here is on the question of whether mere life can be an argument for or against revolutionary violence. Benjamin's line of argumentation then moves along a dual track, persistently switching between mythic and divine Law, or to put it differently, between Athens/Rome *and* Jerusalem. Giorgio Agamben has taken from this passage the notion of the "dogma of the sacredness of mere life" (SelWr 1.251) to make it the starting point of his book on *Homo sacer*. In contrary, it is precisely the other, the trace of the Biblical, that Benjamin himself takes up. This leads him completely out of the sphere of the state of exception, since from that perspective the argument does not concern a "decision on a state of exception" centered on the ruler's sovereignty. Instead, Benjamin's focus is on the responsibility of the acting subject if he or she, in the event of "ungeheuren Fällen" (monstrous cases), disregards the commandment "Thou shalt not kill." This disregard of the commandment is expressed as 'vom Gebot *absehen*'—which should not be understood as the act of simply 'ignoring it.' This case by no means places the actor in a sovereign position and certainly does not impair the otherwise ongoing validity of the commandment. For the commandment is construed as an "irreducible answer to the question" of "may I kill?" (250).

Though the state of exception intervenes as a *cause* in the legal order, and thus in terms of the "Critique of Violence" should be considered "violence in the most precise meaning of the word," in contrast disregarding the commandment "Thou shalt not kill" cannot effectively render the commandment invalid because:

This commandment precedes the deed (*steht vor der Tat*), just as God was 'preventing' the deed (*'davor sei', daß sie geschehe*). But as well as it must not be fear of punishment that enforces obedience, the commandment remains inapplicable, incommensurable towards the accomplished deed. No judgment of the deed can be derived from this commandment. (II.I/200f.; SelWr 1.250)

In profiting from the linguistic relationship between the phrase '*davor sein*' (a phrase evoking an authority who is able to hinder something to happen) and to precede (*davor stehen*), Benjamin emphasizes the correlation of two aspects of 'vor'—namely, the mere temporal dimension of time in respect to the succession of actions and the dimension of authority. The superior always comes prior to the subject. It is the sovereign who, within the state of exception, aims to abrogate this whole structure and who, in order to do so, adopts a position similar to that of God: by deciding over the new order he gains the position of the superior. In contrast, the actor who does not obey the commandment remains directly, and thus *immediately*, subordinated to divine Law.

It [the commandment—S.W.] exists not as a criterion of judgment, but as a guideline for the actions of persons or communities who must come to terms with it in solitude and, *in monstrous cases*, to take on themselves the responsibility to disregard it (*von ihm abzusehen*). (200 f.; 250; emphasis S.W.)

Since this mode of action must be valued as a monstrous deed, it tends to mirror the "monstrous cases" to which it responds. The fact that the English version translates "*ungeheure Fälle*" as exceptional cases may be understood as one of the main reasons for the assimilation of "The Critique of Violence" into the Schmitt-Benjamin paradigm, which has strongly influenced the international theoretical discussion. The interpretation of the essay within the framework of political theory is for the readers of the English Benjamin, in addition, supported by the fact that the cited passage is superimposed by an attitude of voluntary decision when the phrase *in ihrer Einsamkeit sich auseinanderzusetzen* gets translated as "to *wrestle* with it in solitude."

What is particularly striking here is that Benjamin uses *ungeheuer* to characterize a unique, tremendous case that goes beyond any criterion. Taking into consideration that he was a brilliant reader of Hölderlin, one invariably thinks here of Hölderlin's idiosyncratic translation of the chorus in the second act of Sophocles' *Antigone*, namely the translation of the verse "*Ungeheuer ist viel. Doch nichts ist ungeheuerer als der Mensch.*" Hölderlin translates δεινός (deinos) not as frightful, frightening, or violent but as *ungeheuer*.[8] This brings with it associations of the *Ungeheuer*, the monstrous and thus the in-human or a-human being. It instills Benjamin's remark—that the commandment is not a yardstick for judgment but a guideline for action—with an additional meaning. If adherence to the commandment not least occurs for the actor's own sake, then it is because he therefore proves himself to be human and by doing so places himself in the position of a human being, worthy of precisely that Biblical "likeness of God" that ensures he is no longer a creature. This is the reason behind Benjamin's statement that the commandment is not applicable. As an irreducible answer it cannot become the cause for intervening in ethical considerations, i.e., not become "violence in the precise sense of the word."

The commandment "Thou shalt not kill" therefore relates to precisely the dimension of human life that goes beyond mere natural life. In the context of the discussion on the legitimacy of a "revolutionary killing of an oppressor," on that "extreme case" that is treated in the final section of the essay, Benjamin juxtaposes his reflections on the commandment directly to the "more distant theorem" that postulates the holy inviolability of mere life: "This is the doctrine of the sanctity of life" (SelWr 1.250).

## Dogma of the Sanctity of Mere Life

Yet, let us first follow the systematics of Benjamin's arguments. As regards the issue of revolutionary violence, he focuses on two types of the *absolute* negation of violent killing: first on the negation justified by the commandment "Thou shalt not kill" (the Judaeo-Christian justification), and second on the justification by that "more distant theorem," the doctrine of the sanctity of life (a mythic justification). When he discusses them in terms of the diametrically opposed notions of sacrifice that are innate to them, these two theorems become linked to the previously discussed juxtaposition of the two archetypes of violence that lie beyond and before law, namely mythic and divine violence: "Mythic violence is bloody power over mere life for its own sake; divine violence is pure power over all life for the sake of the living. *The first demands sacrifice, the second accepts it*" (250; emphasis S.W.).

---

8. Friedrich Hölderlin, *Antigone*, in *Sämtliche Werke. Frankfurter Ausgabe*, Bd. 16: *Sophokles*, Michael Franz, Michael Knaupp, D. E. Sattler, eds. (Frankfurt/M: Strömfeld Verlag, 1988), 299.

Equally significant are the differing notions of time that adhere to the historical natures of the two extralegal reference points. Mythic violence constitutes a justification system from prehistory, which persists in myths, for example, in the notion of a fateful guilt (*Verschuldung*) of mere natural life.[9] In the essay on *Schicksal und Charakter,* written two years earlier, he claimed that "fate is the guilt nexus of the living" (204). This guilt has nothing to do with a religious context and does not appear as the reason for a legal judgment, but conversely here the judgment precedes the guilt; to be more precise, it should read that the judgments of the ancient *gods* precede the actual guilt *of mankind.* Here, the focus on law and justice is already at stake.

Mistakenly, through confusing it with the realm of justice, the order of law—which is merely a residue of the demonic stage of human existence, when legal statutes determined not only men's relationships but also their relation to the gods—has preserved itself long past the time which inaugurated the victory over the demons. (203)

In other words, Benjamin here identifies an afterlife of the archaic relation between men and the gods within Law. The idea of the guilty person emerging from that realm is condensed in the concept of *fate.*

"Divine violence," by contrast, entails a different concept of time and history, one Benjamin terms real presence: "This divine power is not only attested by religious tradition but is also found in *present-day life* in at least one sanctioned manifestation" (250; emphasis S.W.). This notion brings to mind the "immediacy to God of each single day," as Gershom Scholem later formulates it in his essay "The Messianic Idea in Judaism" (Scholem, 1986). Benjamin thus emphasizes the asynchrony between the language of the commandment on the one hand, and the criteria of legal judgments or judgments by men on men on the other.

As regards the other aforementioned theorem on the "dogma of the sacredness of life," Benjamin rejects the idea that mere life stands higher than "the happiness and justice of existence," a notion that leads to creaturely, natural life being considered sacred or its bodily state declared sacred. Instead he argues: "Man cannot, at any price, be said to coincide with mere life of man, neither with mere life in him nor with any other of his conditions and qualities, including even the uniqueness of his bodily

9. The English translation renders *Verschuldung* as 'expiation' (ibid., 250).

person." In this statement, he understands mere life as a human state but not as "existence in itself," as was the case in Kurt Hiller's *Anti-Kain*, against which Benjamin argues here. A paragraph from the *Anti-Kain* is taken as representative of those thinkers who rely on the sentence of the sanctity of mere life:

> Their argument, exemplified in an extreme case by the revolutionary killing of the oppressor, runs as follows: "If I do not kill, I shall never establish the world dominion of justice . . . that is the argument of the mental terrorist . . ." We, however, profess that higher even than the happiness and justice of existence stands existence itself. (250ff.)

It is precisely this postulate that Benjamin rejects with the certainty that it is "false, indeed ignoble," and returns to the commandment, which for him implies the need "of seeking the reason for the commandment no longer in what the deed does to the murdered, but in what it does to God and the doer (*Täter*)" (II.I/201; SelWr 1.251). The inviolability of human life is, according to Benjamin, justified not by mere natural life but precisely by human beings' participation in a life that is more than mere, natural life. The idea for this different concept of life arises from, among other things, the biblical notion of Creation, according to which God created man in his likeness.

Less than a year later, Benjamin pursues this double reference of the concept of life to both a natural *and* a supernatural (*übernatürlich*) life (that is to say, more than mere life) at greater length in his essay on Goethe's *Wahlverwandtschaften* (*Elective Affinities*). In the "Critique of Violence," he counts the concept of 'life' among those words whose dual meaning is illuminated by their relationship to two distinct spheres, doing so within the context of his critique of the dogma of the sanctity of mere life. The assertion that existence in itself is of a higher order would first be accurate if "'existence' or, better, 'life'—words such as 'freedom' whose ambiguity [*Doppelsinn*] is readily dissolved through their *reference to two distinct spheres* means the aggregate state of 'man'" (II.I/201; SelWr 1.251; emphasis S.W.). The special treatment of the word 'man' indicates that, here, Benjamin is referring to the *concept* of man that exceeds the definition of natural life, which describes only one of its states or conditions. Sacrality can be attributed to man only in this comprehensive sense: "However sacred man is (or however sacred that life in him which is identically present in earthly life, death, and afterlife), there is neither sacredness in his conditions nor in his bodily life vulnerable to injury by his fellow men" (SelWr 1.251). The double referentiality in the concepts of life and of the human being raised in this context means something quite different from the double nature of the human being in the body-soul paradigm. At issue here is the fact that the dimension pointing beyond the creaturely has in the final instance emerged from biblical ideas.

Benjamin explains that it is first the historical loss of sacredness that brought forth the dogma of the (cosmic) sanctity of natural life. He thus considers this dogma an effect of secularization and criticizes it as the re-transformation of lost sacred aspects into natural law. What originated in a world of cult is, after its loss, reformulated as nature. In this sense, Benjamin evaluates the dogma as the "*last mistaken attempt* of the weakened Western tradition to seek the saint it has lost in cosmological impenetrability." And further: "Finally, this idea of man's sacredness gives grounds for reflection that what is here pronounced sacred was, according to ancient mythic thought, the marked bearer of guilt: *life itself*" (251; emphasis S.W.). It is, then, no coincidence that Benjamin's text, which rejects precisely the theorem of the "sanctity of mere life" Agamben took as the point of departure for his study of the *Homo sacer*, also develops a "Critique of Violence" in which the figure of disregard of the commandment (*Absehung vom Gebot*) furnishes an answer to the dialectic of secularization. It is an answer, moreover, that goes beyond the political theology of the state of exception/emergency in which the theological origin of the secularized constitutional concepts has been subsumed.

### The *Salto Mortale* of 'Pure Violence'

Following Benjamin's discussion of commandment and dogma, the essay's concluding passage returns to the question of violence, namely as a question of a pure violence, the horizon of which first emerges beyond the law of oscillation that governs lawmaking and law-preserving violence and beyond any violence as a means. Benjamin identifies this horizon "beyond" with nothing less than the beginning of a new historical age, grounded in a "suspension of law with all the forces on which it depends, as they depend on it, finally therefore on the abolition of state power" (251ff.). Only after such a suspension of law (and this does not indicate an attack on a particular existing legal order, but on law itself) would the existence of violence beyond law also be ensured. Under such conditions, the danger of pure violence's manifestation reverting to mythic violence would seem to have been averted, because it is here, "outside the law," that Benjamin posits revolutionary violence to exist. This is the name for the "highest manifestation of pure violence by man."

This violence can be *immediate* only if it is not deployed as a means to just ends, and pure only if taking a cue from divine violence for its measure. To this extent, Benjamin comments on this perspective specifically as regards the difficulty in identifying such pure violence *per se* in history or reality, and he links this to the impossibility of deciding "when pure violence has been realized in particular cases" (II.I/203; SelWr 1.252). Since a genuine feature of divine violence is its covert nature, it will "not be recognizable as such," as Benjamin writes. Therefore, the epistemological dilemma of a theory of pure violence beyond the law, which aligns the possibility of pure violence with the measuring stick of divine violence and the concept of justice, consists in its essential covertness and thus in the uncertainty as to whether we will recognize it. If the essay's parting gesture cites "pure divine law" again, then the concept of pure violence is, as it were, *returned to God*. What remains, at least as regards the question of pure violence, is the certainty: "Divine violence, which is the sign and seal but never the means of sacred dispatch, may be called ruling (*waltende*) violence" (II.I/203; SelWr 1.252). The fact that the English translation renders the phrase *waltende Gewalt* here as "sovereign violence" makes this one more passage that may trigger a connection between Benjamin's essay and Carl Schmitt's *Political Theology*.

With an act of immense acceleration and concentration, the arguments and concepts in the essay's final passage culminate in reflections on pure violence beyond law. The text moves in such a way that one feels the concepts are trying to outdo one another, similar to the *salto mortale* Benjamin was to observe a decade later in Karl Kraus's attempt to revere the image of divine justice as language. By returning pure violence to God in the concluding sentence of the "Critique of Violence," Benjamin leaves the question he raised unanswered. A passage from his essay on Goethe's *Wahlverwandtschaften* penned a little later can definitely also be construed as a critical reflection on the possibility of pure violence seen against the horizon of human action. The focus here is on presuming a divine mandate in the vocabulary of a mission or task (*Aufgabe*). In the section on the George School, Benjamin criticizes the notion of literary work as mission:

This school assigns to the poet, like the hero, his work as a task; hence, his mandate is considered divine. From God, however, man receives not tasks, but only exactions (*Forderungen*)[. . . . ] Moreover, the notion of the task is also inappropriate from the standpoint of the poet. The poetic work in the true sense arises only where the word liberates itself from the spell of even the greatest task. (SelWr 1.323)

What he describes here as regards the literary work also sheds light back on Benjamin's attempt to derive the concept of pure violence from a mission in the "Critique of Violence," namely the task to destroy the "perniciousness" of the "historical function" of mythic violence, just as it is also still expressed in legal violence: "This very task of destruction poses again, ultimately, the question of a pure immediate violence that might be able to call a halt to mythic violence" (249). In 1921, Benjamin may have been prompted to return it to a divine authority by the fact that he sensed the difficulties inherent in such a task. What is striking is how he uses the term *decision* in this context, namely as the diametrical opposite of the concept of 'state of emergency/exception.' For Schmitt the definition of that *state of exception/emergency* was based on the notion that "he is sovereign who decides on the state of exception." By contrast, for Benjamin here the focus is on the fact that humans *cannot decide* on pure violence, namely that humans do not have the possibility to "decide when pure violence has actually happened in a particular case." Humans' inability to recognize and gain knowledge about the mere existence of pure violence situates the latter outside any human sphere.

When later in his life Benjamin used the concept of the state of emergency quite explicitly, this occurred in a quite different historical situation and manner than in Schmitt's *Political Theology*. Once the Nazi regime had lent permanence to a constitutional state of exception, thus turning the sovereign into a dictator, when a case that Benjamin had already theoretically reflected in the context of his Baroque book actually took place, he was to write in his historico-philosophical theses that the "state of exception in which we live is the rule." Against this, the idea of a "real state of exception" thus comes into play and becomes the task (Schmitt 697). The word "real" signifies the difference between this state of exception and one defined by the terms of constitutional law. The fact that, in 1940, he again programmatically formulated a task (*Aufgabe*) can be explained by a historical constellation that caused the "extreme case" that Benjamin had discussed in 1921 to become acute in theoretical terms. The question of an assassination attempt on Hitler provides the most factual form of the monstrous case imaginable, in the context of which Benjamin had discussed disregarding the commandment—two decades before writing the theses on the concept of history. In contrast to the conception of a politically exceptional case in the sense of constitutional law, this could actually count as an "*ungeheurer Fall*" and a *real* exceptional case (from obeying the commandment).

Although the "Critique of Violence" leaves undecided the question as to pure, immediate violence, Benjamin's essay formulates a series of fundamental insights and terms by critically engaging the contemporary debate on the nature of violence. Alongside a critique of "violence in the concise sense of the word" (namely, any kind of legitimizing an intervention into law and justice), the essay offers a fundamental historico-theoretical analysis of the relationship of law and justice with the intent to secure such central concepts as 'life' and 'man.' In the process, Benjamin concealed his own answer to the fierce debate over the extreme case of killing a tyrant within his considerations on the responsibility of, in tremendous cases, disregarding the commandment to not kill.

SOMETHING FROM BEYOND THE POET
THAT BREAKS INTO POETIC LANGUAGE

# 4

# The Artwork as a Breach of the Beyond

*On the Dialectic of Divine and Human Order
in "Goethe's* Elective Affinities*"*

[Not] this *Nazarene character* but rather the symbol of the *star* falling down over
the lovers is the form of expression appropriate to whatever of *mystery* in the exact
sense of the term indwells the work.

(I.I/200; SelWr 1.355; emphasis S.W.)

By setting the Nazarene character against the falling star in the last
passage of his essay, "Goethe's *Elective Affinities*" (which appeared in two
parts in 1924 and 1925 in the *Neuen Deutschen Beiträgen*), Benjamin formulates a significant objection to Goethe's novel, a work that he otherwise
deploys as the virtually ideal model for a discussion of a series of themes
and motifs that lay close to his heart and that he had already examined in
some of his previous essays—such as the concept of *critique*, or of myth,
fate (*Schicksal*), and character; of hope, redemption, and revelation; and
the connection between natural and supernatural life. Although his text
otherwise refrains from passing judgment on the novel and instead develops fundamental art-philosophical reflections on poetic works (*Dichtung*)
from his reading, Benjamin, with this one objection, immediately dis-
misses the entire ending of the novel. As he writes, "[T]hose Christian-
mystical moments [ . . . ] at the end" arise "from the striving to ennoble
everything mythic at ground level" (SelWr 1.355). These elements are, according to Benjamin's description, "out of place" (*fehl am Ort*).

## Reconciliation vs. Hope

When he interprets precisely these aspects of *Elective Affinities* as the "Nazarene character" of the novel, he, in principle, works against a literary narrative style that transfigures and idealizes the image of Christian reconciliation. This critique refers in particular to the last sentence of *Elective Affinities*, in which the *topos* of a 'union of lovers in death' (well-known from classical mythology) ends in the (Christian) image of a future resurrection: "So the lovers are side by side, at rest. Peace hovers over their dwelling-place, other cheerful images of angels look down at them from the vaulted ceiling, and what a sweet moment it will be for their eyes when on some future day they wake together."[1] However, Benjamin's assessment of the narrator's lapse as being Nazarene also pertains to the previous passage in the novel, in which Eduard praises Ottilie's death as martyrdom, thinks of her as a *saint*, and then dies with these thoughts in mind. Perhaps more precisely, he could be said to be blessedly asleep, since Goethe writes: "and since he had passed away thinking of his saint, he might rightfully be called blessed" (262). Benjamin's critique, however, pertains less to a secularization of Christian martyrs in the form of a human *Imitatio Christi* than it does to the opposite: the Christian ennobling of mythical motifs. The blend of myth and Christian reconciliation produces a heightened pathos that awakens the impression of kitsch among today's readers. Benjamin sees this as Christian mysticism at work.

His real concern, however, is for another moment. As he illustrates, his critique of the Nazarene comes about because of hope. In Goethe's novel, it is the kind of hope that the narrator had cherished in the lovers six chapters earlier, before the ending that Benjamin criticized (i.e., in the thirteenth chapter of the second part), and it is represented in the symbol of the falling star above them: "Hope shot across the sky above their heads like a falling star" (SelWr 1.355). Benjamin takes this sentence as an occasion to reflect on a concept of hope clearly distinguished from the colloquial, secular meaning of the word. For him it is *not* about hope

---

1. Johann Wolfgang Goethe, *Die Wahlverwandtschaften*, m.e., Nachwort von Peter von Matt (Zürich: Manesse, 1996), 386ff.; the cited English translation is *The Sorrows of Young Werther, Elective Affinities, Novella* (*Goethe: The Collected Works*, vol. 11) (Princeton: Princeton UP, 1995), 240. Further references to this work will be given parenthetically within the text. Modified translations will be indicated by citing both editions.

as a subjective expression of self-referential sentiment; it rather concerns the hope that comes from the culture of a funerary cult and care for the dead, the "hope for redemption that we nourish for all the dead" (355). Benjamin then ascribes a unique meaning to this kind of hope when he observes: "This hope is the sole justification of the faith in immortality that can never be inflamed by one's own existence" (I.3/839; SelWr 1.355). As the essay is concerned with the living's emotions for the dead and *their* salvation, it places hope into a religious-historical perspective. Not only does the belief in immortality—as a human response to the experience of mortality—stand at the origin of religious concepts,[2] but hope for salvation in the beyond also originates in this context. Thus Benjamin's concept of hope is not simply a secular counterpart to the concept of redemption, which would be the concept of a secularized messianism. This can be confirmed with reference to the "Theological-Political Fragment." There, the rhythm of messianic intensity in the order of the profane is described not as hope but as happiness. Hence, Benjamin gave expression to his stance toward the history of the Christian and Jewish religions in an unambiguous, unequivocal manner at the end of "Goethe's *Elective Affinities*," while also clearly commenting on differing concepts of 'the beyond.' For Benjamin, the beyond alone is the space for redemption—not, however, for resurrection. Thus, he explicitly emphasizes the fact that hope does not correlate to *one's own* personal salvation; he does not treat messianism as a matter of faith—faith as defined by a subject's bearing toward a religion, originally a commitment to it, *confessio*. In contrast, the messianic is for him a phenomenon of cultural history that originates in the attitude of the community toward the dead.

This does not mean that, for Benjamin, there is no earthly hope. Hope is indeed the vanishing point of the essay, to which also the disposition in Benjamin's working notes attests. In the essay's triptych (as thesis:

2. In this context, Benjamin's notes on his reading of François-Poncet are germane: "The Nazarene elements are in need of the severest critique. Poncet rightly stressed the inability to face bare, naked death in Goethe. Either he remains almost imperceptibly gentle or one meets it with beautified, serene pageantry[. . . . ] The Nazarene is deep serenity and catholic tendency within it is related to the otherwise deeper pagan tendency—but not subject to it[. . . . ] Poncet also observed that Goethe avoided the burial, and later the grave, of his mother." Walter Benjamin, *Gesammelte Schriften Vol. I.3* (Frankfurt/M: Suhrkamp, 1974), 839.

the mythic; antithesis: redemption; and hope: their synthesis)[3] hope constitutes the endpoint of a dialectic composition. Its place is literature: "For in the symbol of the star, the hope that Goethe had to conceive for the lovers had once appeared to him" (SelWr 1.354). The narrator relates to his or her characters just as we foster hope for the dead—as Benjamin illustrates at the beginning of the passage about the symbol of the falling star in *Elective Affinities*:

"Hope shot across the sky above their heads like a falling star." They are unaware of it, of course, and it could not be said any more clearly that the last hope is never such to him who cherishes it but is the last only to those for whom it is cherished. With this comes to light the innermost basis for the "narrator's stance." It is he alone who, in the feeling of hope, can fulfill the meaning of what happens. (354)

When regarded as the narrator's bearing, this hope refers not to the event itself but rather to the manner in which hope can "fulfill the meaning of what happens." In this respect, this hope is not part of what is presented (*des Dargestellten*), but rather concerns an aspect of representation (*Darstellung*) itself, that is to say an aspect of the work of art. Such 'last hope,' whose emergence comes simultaneously with 'sealed fate,' cannot be contained or secured in a single image—of the future resurrection from the dead, for example. As "that most paradoxical, most fleeting hope," it closes itself off from translation into a positive notion, or into the language of rhetorical convention.

Benjamin thus places the narrator's stance in the vicinity of messianic hope without, however, equating them. The narrator's hope seeks not redemption but rather the fulfillment of the novel's events. Furthermore, this literary version of hope is not described as one that permeates the events of the novel, nor as one that supports the plot. It instead surfaces, as Benjamin writes, only fleetingly in the same moment in which the "semblance of reconciliation" expires (343). Thus when he then describes the "semblance of reconciliation" as "house of the most extreme hope" (355), he conceives of both in an interrelationship similar to the relationship of the noncommunicable and communicable (in the 1916 essay on language), that is, of the mimetic and semiotic in language ("Doctrine of the Similar" 1933): "That most paradoxical, most fleeting hope finally arises from the semblance of reconciliation" (355). In "Goethe's *Elective*

3. See GS 1.3, 835–837.

*Affinities,*" such a constellation is rewritten in multiple places and with different imagery. Benjamin, in the concluding passage, ponders these moments in terms of the concept of mystery, or more precisely, in terms of "something *of mystery* in the exact sense of the term that indwells in the work" (355; emphasis S.W.). If the work is described as the abode not for mystery but for the something of mystery, then precisely this 'something' condenses into the image of the star falling over the lovers. Benjamin understands the image as a symbol, as an expression of mystery in the work, and simultaneously as the work's caesura: "That sentence, which to speak with Hölderlin contains the caesura of the work and in which, while the embracing lovers seal their fate, everything pauses" (354). In another place, this complex constellation is expressed in the succinct but ambiguous phrase: "something beyond the poet interrupts the language of poetry" (341). This lowercase *beyond*[4] is thereby not to be confused with the Christian notion of the beyond, in which what lies beyond the authority of the writer is translated into concrete theological concepts. In this respect, Benjamin's philosophies of literature and art have nothing to do with a 'religion of art' (*Kunstreligion*) in which art avails itself of theological concepts.

## *Dichtung* as a Breach

Outside of Christian iconography, this lowercase and worldly 'beyond' can only be expressed in the form of a symbol. Where the author of the novel introduces the falling star as a simile ("Hope shot across [ . . . ] *like* a [falling] star"), Benjamin regards the star as a symbol that marks the element of mystery in the work or art. He understands the "falling star" as "an analogous moment of representation" from analogy to mystery in drama: "that moment, in which it juts out (*hineinragt*) of the domain of language proper to it into a higher one, unattainable for it," and thus "can never be expressed in words but is expressible solely in representation" (355). This means that the star alludes to a domain situated beyond the work of art, or

4. Translator's note: In German, all nouns begin with capital letters. In this case, "beyond" (jenseits) begins with a lowercase letter, indicating that this 'beyond' is adjectival and therefore a different "beyond" from the more common nominative, which is usually used in a religious context—"the beyond" (*das Jenseits*).

to another mode of language altogether. Benjamin thus redefines the status of the mystery in the work, or the relation of the beyond-to-poetry to poetic language, via the figures of 'jutting into' (*Hereinragen*), 'indwelling' (*Einwohnen*), and 'falling into' (*Einfallen*). As a "form of expression appropriate to the something of mystery in the exact sense of the term that indwells the work," the symbol of the star signifies an acknowledgement both of a domain of meaning that extends beyond poetry and that is not expressed in the presented event but rather in the stance (*Haltung*) of the narrator in the manner of representation.

The theory of the artwork formulated here implies that, on the one hand, the poet must limit himself to his (human) faculty; yet on the other hand, he is to mark and rupture the limit of his own language in representation and the narrative stance by using it as a symbol of a different realm that lies beyond, thus allowing a "mystery in the exact sense" (355) to 'indwell' in his work. The exact sense of mystery originates from ancient Greek, where *mysterion* denotes secret knowledge. Such a configuration is only possible, however, if based on a clear distinction of domains and languages—on one side, the language proper to poetry or drama, and on the other, a language that points to a higher and unreachable sphere. Such a mode of representation is thus possible only on the condition that the difference between human terms (or concepts) and those that belong to a divine order be recognized and reflected upon. Just as history in Benjamin is conceptualized structurally, as the distance from Creation, human language is defined by its difference from those terms that belong to a divine order. In contrast, the Nazarene end of Goethe's novel presents the human imitation of a divine power—the resurrection of dead—through which the human characters of the novel assume a divine position, because resurrection is a faculty that, in theological tradition, belongs only to the Christian God's son. In Benjamin's philosophy of art, the divine is admitted a site within the language of the artwork, or, better stated, a breach (*Einbruchstelle*) through which what lies beyond the work juts into its language. At the end of Benjamin's essay, these remarks on hope and mystery solidify a motif that permeates the whole text as a compositional or structuring element—not in the thematic sense but rather as a moment of representation: the line of demarcation between human faculty and that which lies *beyond the poet* and also bears the name of the divine.

## On the Forgetting of the Divine
## in the Reception of Benjamin's Essay

Remarkably, this moment of representation, and indeed the interpretation of sacred terms in "Goethe's *Elective Affinities*," constitutes something of a forgotten and silenced motif[5] in the reception of Benjamin's essay. The literature on this essay usually focuses on those passages in which Benjamin casts the figure of Ottilie as an allegory of the artwork, out of which he develops his theory of the impossibility of unveiling (*Unenthüllbarkeit*) as the essence of beauty, which Benjamin also discusses in respect to the distinction between a human and a divine sphere, since the impossibility of unveiling is reserved for those who are immortal: "Nothing that is mortal is therefore unrevealable (*unenthüllbar*)." In addition, the differentiation between commentary and criticism and, in particular, between the material content (*Sachgehalt*) and the truth content (*Wahrheitsgehalt*), have received due attention, and no less so than Benjamin's discussion of the novel's mythical content and of the "expressionless." Understood in contradistinction to semblance (*Schein*) in the artwork, the expressionless functions as the point of junction between "Goethe's *Elective Affinities*" and the history of aesthetic theory, especially the aesthetics of the sublime.[6]

The trace of the *beyond* and the interpretation of terms that originate in a divine order and traverse the essay has, in contrast, been scarcely considered, glossed over, or ignored in its reception. This is all the more surprising considering the central importance that the "divine imprint" has for Benjamin's theory. It is established early in the first part of the essay concerning *critique* and *commentary*.[7] Benjamin here casts the relationship between the artwork's *content* (*Gehalt*) and *matter* (*Sache*) in the famous

5. An exception is the chapter on "Goethe's *'Elective Affinities'*" in Astrid Deuber-Mankowsky's book on the early Benjamin and Hermann Cohen: *Der frühe Walter Benjamin und Hermann Cohen. Jüdische Werte, Kritische Philosophie, vergängliche Erfahrung* (Berlin: Vorwerk 8, 2000).

6. See, for example, Winfried Menninghaus, "Das Ausdruckslose: Walter Benjamins Kritik des Schönen durch das Erhabene," in Uwe Steiner, ed., *Walter Benjamin, 1892–1940* (Bern: Lang, 1992), 33–76.

7. The headings of each section function hermetically given the absence of the text, but as its composition is actually systematic, it can be reconstructed from the detailed outline that is preserved in the notes (1.3/835–837).

image of the signet:[8] the content must be conceived of as the seal that presents the matter. The idea of imprint remains implicit in this image. One line later, he writes that the matter is "graspable only in the philosophical experience of its divine imprint, which is evident only to the blissful vision of the divine name" (300). This proposition stands in relation to his reflections on marriage, in which Benjamin critically reflects on Kant's definition of marriage as well as its mythical grounds in order to establish that married love (*Gattenliebe*), rather than marriage, is thematized in Goethe's novel.[9] For even when Benjamin speaks of the perception of beauty as a secret, he brings the "divine" into play by calling this secret the "divine ground of the being of beauty" (351). In this respect, the theory of poetic works posed at the end of the essay (which is drawn from the dialectic between *Dichtung* and a higher sphere) does not contradict the theory of art Benjamin formulated in the context of the allegory of Ottilie. This theory presents Ottilie as the embodiment of beauty and of beauty as semblance (*Schein*).[10] With talk of the "divine ground of the being of beauty," also the appearance of the beautiful as art finds the ground of its 'being' in the divine, and thus in the secret, "since only the beautiful and nothing else can be essentially veiling or veiled" (I.I 195; SelWr 1.351). It is true, according to Benjamin, that "the task of art criticism is not to lift (*heben*) the veil but rather, only through the most precise knowledge of it as a veil, to raise (*erheben*) itself to the true view of the beautiful" (SelWr 1.351). Veiling, semblance, and the secret are therefore for him genuine properties of a "true work of art": "Never yet has a true work of art been grasped other than where it ineluctably represented itself as a secret" (351). This is why Benjamin conceives the secret as the "divine ground of being of beauty," a conception that gives rise to a concept of *semblance*, which has

8. On the topic of the signet, see Fritz Gutbrodt, "Wahl: Verwandtschaft. Benjamins Siegel," in *Modern Language Notes*, vol. 106, no. 5 (1991); 555–588.

9. For a closer reading of this aspect of Benjamin's essay see my article "Fidelity, Love, Eros: Benjamin's Life Science," in Eckart Goebel and Vivian Liska (eds.), *True to Benjamin*, forthcoming from Northwestern University Press.

10. The German word *Schein* opens up a variety of meanings; it is related to both 'appearance' (*Erscheinung*) and 'shine' since the verb *scheinen* can mean 'to shine,' 'to seem,' and 'to appear as if.' In ordinary language one often talks of mere *Schein* with a negative connotation. Benjamin, however, refers to the figurative character and the beauty surface of art that can't be unveiled and transformed into something lying behind mere or surface appearance.

nothing to do with a discourse of critiques of ideology and the attendant categories of 'false semblance' (*falscher Schein*) and 'pseudo correlation' (*Scheinzusammenhang*).[11] *Schein* is rather understood as art's genuine form of expression, which distinguishes itself from philosophical formulations or discursive discussions in the medium of conceptual language. Benjamin defines the appearance of beauty as follows:

> not the superfluous veiling of things in themselves but rather the necessary veiling of things for us. Such veiling is divinely necessary at times, just as it is also divinely determined that, unveiled at the wrong time, what is inconspicuous evaporates into nothing, whereupon revelation takes over from secrets[. . . . ] Like revelation, all beauty holds in itself the orders of the history of philosophy. For beauty makes visible not the idea but rather the latter's secret. (351)

This theory of the artwork is explained by Benjamin's remarks on the relationship between art and philosophy, which he defines as a sibling relation. He derives this kinship from work on the "ideal of the problem" (334) common to both. By this phrase, he designates the ideal, yet indeed impossible, formulation of a problem that comes into appearance only in its multiplicity. From the assertion that the "truth is not in itself visible," it follows that its emergence can only touch on "traits *not* its own" (351; emphasis S.W.), namely on a sort of "virtual possibility of formulating the truth content of the work of art." What critique therefore reveals in the artwork is "the virtual possibility of formulating the work's truth content as the highest philosophical problem" (I.I; 173; SelWr 1.334). The description of art as the site of a virtual formulatibility (*Formulierbarkeit*)[12] of truth content provides for the proper process of Benjaminian *critique*: the mining of the problem that in its multiplicity is buried in the work. Indeed, he adds that awe of the work and respect for the truth demands to stay away from this "formulation itself" (334). This means nothing other than that the artwork's formulations cannot be translated into the formulation of the problem without losing their essence. The artwork's truth content is legible, but not translatable into concepts. The restraint that

11. The diagnosis of *Scheinzusammenhang* is part of a somehow trivialized discourse in the reception of the Frankfurt School.

12. This term belongs to a whole register of terms (*Erkennbarkeit, Lesbarkeit, Übersetzbarkeit* etc.), all with the suffix *-barkeit*. To this typical Benjaminian linguistic figure see Samuel Weber, *Benjamin's -abilities* (Cambridge: Harvard University Press, 2008).

critique shows before the phrasing itself corresponds to the recognition of the secret as a "divine ground of the being of beauty," so that the latter represents a type of matrix for Benjamin's theory of art that can be ignored only at the price of great distortion of his philosophy of art.

By this point, it should have become clear how this theory of art (developed in the essay already finished in 1922) corresponds exactly to the essay on language Benjamin wrote six years earlier. There, the history of (human) language originates in a caesura: "the spirit of language to be sought in the Fall of Language-mind" (II.I/153; SelWr 1.72)—in which paradisiac language loses its magical elements and turns instead into a system of signs. This language is then "not only communication of the communicable but also, at the same time, a symbol of the noncommunicable" (SelWr 1.74). This function of language as a symbol of something ungraspable in words is described quite vividly in "Goethe's *Elective Affinities*" as an event that concerns words themselves. If it is expressed here as "something beyond the poet that interrupts the language of poetry," then this interruption (*ins Wort fallen*) must be read as an event that appears as a caesura or counterrhythm close to an eruption. Benjamin uses the same phrase, "ins-Wort-fallen," with regard to the expressionless shortly before the formulation of something beyond the poet that interrupts the language of poetry—harmony interrupts and calls a halt to semblance. According to Benjamin, "the expressionless compels the trembling harmony to stop, and through its objection immortalizes its quivering" (340). If this 'beyond' in "Goethe's *Elective Affinities*" mainly points to a higher or divine sphere, then this constellation of the breaching through of another knowledge may be considered also as a presupposition to bring Benjamin's later work into conjunction with the language of the unconscious as conceived of by Freud for psychoanalysis. And this is not least due to its figurative character, namely that the *Einbruchstelle* is also a key Freudian term.[13] This connection, however, presupposes an understanding of psychoanalysis and an engagement with the language of the unconscious, understood as a language that is concerned not with the unveiling of a 'truth' but rather with the specific nature of another type of appearance.

13. The increasing pervasiveness of concepts from Freudian psychoanalysis in Benjamin's writings is the subject of my previous book on Benjamin and does not need to be recounted again here. See Weigel, *Entstellte Ähnlichkeit. Walter Benjamins theoretische Schreibweise* (Frankfurt/M: Fischer, 1997).

The language of the unconscious also exhibits a type of virtual formulation of a 'truth' that cannot be resolved in or translated into an ideal formulation of a problem.

### The Line of Separation Between Art and Redemption

In "Goethe's *Elective Affinities*," the theory of art derived from the dialectic between human and divine orders offers an alternative model to that of the George School and Gundolf. By elevating Goethe in particular, and the writer in general, Gundolf ascribes divine attributes to poetic works themselves, and thereby turns art into a pseudo- or quasi-religion. Although, as Benjamin establishes, the separation of art and philosophy in antiquity coincides with the decline of myth (and its indifference to the category of truth), he observes a tendency toward remythologization in the program of poetry as a quasi-religion. Benjamin counteracts this tendency by drawing a strict line of demarcation between the discourse of art and "speech vis-à-vis God." Precisely because of this, his essay touches upon a current phenomenon, namely the reestablishing of art *as* cult or *as* mystery, which takes place not least in the aesthetic of the sublime: art as a substitution for religion in a postsecularized age.[14]

At the beginning of the second part of the essay, Benjamin develops his critique of the hubris of a *divine mandate*, in which he grapples with problems of biography, namely in the context of his commentary on Gundolf's book on Goethe (322–324). His critique concerns the commingling of art and religion—above all in Gundolf's understanding of the author as a mythic hero, "demigod," "hybrid of hero and creator," and as "superhuman type of savior" through whose work humanity steps in for the starry sky. From here, a strict line of separation runs through Benjamin's essay with which the terms of discourse on art are distinguished from such concepts as belong to another, divine system of meaning. Although his critical reflections on myth (which represent a kind of leitmotif, espe-

14. As a prototype for this, one would mention Barnett Newman, who began a renaissance of the sublime with his programmatic text *The Sublime Is Now* (1948), and rather indiscriminately integrated motifs from the Christian, Jewish, and Native American religions into his own imagery. See Barnett Newman, *Schriften und Interviews 1925–1970* (Bern and Berlin: Schiedegger & Spiess, 1990); and Jörg Herrmann et al. (eds.), *Die Gegenwart der Kunst. Ästhetische und religiöse Erfahrung Heute* (Munich: Fink, 1998).

cially in the first section) have found much attention in scholarship on Benjamin, this work on language, whose reflections on the terms play a fundamental and structuring role for Benjamin's thought in the essay, have to date been largely ignored.

### Task (Aufgabe) vs. Exaction (Forderung)

For Benjamin, "the poetic work in the true sense" can emerge only where the word frees itself from the spells of the task (323). His critique of the confusion of literary works of art and divine mission or mandate targets the image of the poet in the George circle:

> This school assigns to the poet, like the hero, his work as a *task*; hence, his *mandate is considered divine*. From God, however, man receives not *tasks* but only *exactions* (*Forderungen*), and therefore before God no privileged value can be ascribed to the poetic life. Moreover, the notion of the *task* is also inappropriate from the standpoint of the poet. (323; emphasis S.W.)

This radical rejection of any "task" seeks to prevent the legitimization of the poetic work on the basis of an authority alien to it, whatever its nature and description. Only with language's liberation from a determination of tasks can the "true work of art" spring forth. With the suggestion that only exactions and not tasks would come from God, secularization is also criticized, as it makes divine authority into a type of employer and thereby levels the inevitable difference between God and humans without which the divine terms forfeit their meaning.

### Creation (Geschöpf) vs. Formed Structure (Gebilde)

The fact that Benjamin sees in the contemporary "heroizing attitude of the poet" a perpetuation of the hubris already connected to the old concept of the genius is evident in his reflections on the discourse of the production of art that retains the metaphor of art as Creation: "And indeed the artist is less the primal ground or *creator* than the origin or form *giver* (*Bildner*), and certainly his work is not at any price his creation but rather his *form* (*Gebilde*)" (I.I/159; SelWr 1.323, emphasis S.W.). This difference between composition and creation does not, however, resolve itself in the simple differentiation between culture and nature. This is apparent in the following passage, in which Benjamin brings the concept of redemption into play: "To be sure, the form, too, and not only the creation, has life. But the crucial difference between the two is this: only the life of the creation, never that of a shaped form (*des Gebildeten*), partakes, unreservedly, of the intention of redemption" (I.I/159; SelWr 1.324).

Although Benjamin alludes here to the "afterlife" (*Nachleben*) of works by means of the life of works (about which he has more to say elsewhere, especially in "The Task of Translator"), the exclusiveness with which he ascribes redemption to the life of the creation implies the exclusion of the artwork from the sphere of the messianic. As stated: the narrator's hope seeks not redemption but rather the fulfillment of the sense of the novel's events. Thus, Benjamin's theory of art does not attribute a messianic quality to the literary work of art itself, because hope can be expressed only in the author or artist's bearing. Such hope, however, does not apply to the author but to his characters. Thus Benjamin claims that Goethe, in Ottilie's name, truly tried to "rescue someone perishing, to redeem a loved one in her" (199; 354).

### Choice (Wahl) vs. Decision (Entscheidung)

The line of demarcation also plays a significant role in the discussion of the concepts of love and marriage. Whereas Benjamin qualifies Gundolf's description of marriage as mystery and sacrament as mysticism, he discusses 'marriage' himself in terms analogous to those in the "Critique of Violence," where he considers concepts such as 'life' and 'man' as notions whose double meanings are determined by their relationship to two different spheres. The meaning of marriage is thus derived from the interplay between its "natural moment" (sexuality) and "divine component" (fidelity; 326). He thus ascribes a transcendent moment to marriage. Whereas "the dark conclusion of love, whose daemon is Eros," implies a natural incompleteness of love, insofar as Eros is "the true ransoming of the deepest imperfection which belongs to the nature of man himself" (345), marriage is an expression of continuance in love (i.e., for its supranatural endurance) and for seeking fulfillment and perfection. Benjamin sees this moment in the moment of *decision,* a concept that he would like to understand as strictly distinguished from choice (*Wahl*): the decision "annihilates choice in order to establish fidelity: only the decision, not the choice, is inscribed in the book of life. For choice is natural and can even belong to the elements: decision is transcendent" (346).

If this decision is bound to a legal act, then theology juts into civilian life in the "divine moment" of matrimony, "For what is proper to the truly divine is logos: the divine does not ground life without truth, nor does it ground the rite without theology" (326). Thus it is important to him to stress that marriage does not draw its justification from legislation, because then it would be regarded merely as an institution. For Benjamin, marriage is legitimated only by being an expression of continuance in love. When he writes that, furthermore, love seeks this expression (that is, the expression of constant love) "by nature [ . . . ] rather in death than in life," then the supernatural (not: unnatural) element of marriage is once again grounded. Thus Benjamin's readings do not see the presentation of competing laws in Goethe's novel—roughly understood as the struggle between natural and marital laws. For him, those forces that emerge from the deterioration of marriage become recognizable: "These are surely the mythic powers of law" (I.I/130; SelWr 1.301).

In this case, the characters of Goethe's novel exemplify how misjudgment of the "divine moment" in marriage leads to a return of the mythic. The inability to decide, relapse into a sacrificial myth, and evocation of 'fate,' which characterizes the actions of the two couples—all of this Benjamin explains on the basis of their "chimerical striving for freedom" (332). As educated, enlightened people, superior to the order of nature, they believe they have outgrown the need for the ritual, as is most evident in the scene in which the gravestones are rearranged:

One cannot imagine a more conclusive detachment from tradition than that from the graves of the ancestors, which, in the sense not only of myth but of religion, provide the ground under the feet of the living. Where does their freedom lead those who act thus? Far from opening up new insights for them, it blinds them to the reality that inhabits what they fear. (I.I/132; SelWr 1.302)

Likewise, Benjamin's rejection of any description of Ottilie as a 'saint' (both in the novel and by Gundolf) is linked to the moment of her indecisiveness: "Ottilie's existence, which Gundolf calls sacred, is an unhallowed one, not so much because she trespassed against a marriage in dissolution as because in her seeming and her becoming, subjected until her death to a fateful power, she exists without decision" (336).

## Dialectic of Sacrifice in the Context of Secularization

Among other things, "Goethe's *Elective Affinities*" (1809) recounts how a martyr is produced without the enlightened protagonist being aware of the process. Within the framework of Benjamin's distinction between profane and sacred meanings, the novel becomes legible as a representation of a precarious secularization that, among other things, functions through a leveling of the various dimensions of sacrifice. On one hand, *sacrifice* is understood in the sense of a *sacrificium* that has religious-historical origins and demands a sacrifice of life, while on the other hand, the profanation of the semantics of sacrifice in everyday speech indicates that some*thing* can be sacrificed. In *Elective Affinities*, the latter occurs above all in the negotiation between the enlightened partners that again and again concerns who or what one is willing to sacrifice. Thus the discussion of whether one should or could "sacrifice" something (*aufopfern*) in the sense of 'to give up' is a leitmotif in the conversations Eduard and Charlotte conduct about their way of life. That this profaned use of language represents the accompanying and much-further-reaching forgetting of the cultic in enlightened, secular society (which believes to have overcome or suppressed the origins of their culture in the cultic) is visible in the already mentioned graveyard scene of the novel. While engaged in planning their landscaped garden, the couple takes the path through the old churchyard together. Without recognizing the sacrilege present in his words, Eduard admires how Charlotte "with the greatest care for the old monuments," created a pleasant space: "She had done honor to even the oldest gravestone. She had stood the stones up along the wall, inserting and arranging them according to their dates; in this way, the church's high foundation acquired charm and variety" (Goethe 1996, 23ff.; 1995, 101).

In this concise description, a radical break with tradition intensifies. The rearrangement of the old gravestones that Charlotte resolved to undertake transforms a site of a funerary cult into a piece of landscaping whose shape reflects the contemporary order of things: a harmony of knowledge and beauty that is shown in the chronological arrangement of stones according to their age and in accordance with their function as ornament. Goethe's remark that Eduard used to take care to avoid the path through the churchyard is an indication of the taboo surrounding the place. Because the origin of the taboo in the proscription against disturbing the rest of the dead was forgotten, it remained to him only as a vague fear. It is thus no wonder that the suppressed religious violence, which is inherent in the things and words[15] they use in such a profane manner, catches up with the protagonists, who are themselves so unenlightened about the basis of their own enlightened culture.

They employ the natural sciences, applying the chemical law of elective affinities to experiment on themselves. These experiments trigger a deadly dynamic inherent in the equalization of the natural elements and human nature, reducing them to mere, natural life. It occurs initially through the death of Charlotte's drowned son, and in this way (and in distinction from the model of chemical elements) manifests itself as an uncontrollable element. The way in which his 'sacrifice' is interpreted by the protagonists remains suspended between a death (self-) imposed through the experiment—the "first victim of an ominous fatality (*ahnungsvollen Verhängnisses*)" (1996, 346; 1995, 244)—on the one hand, and, on the other, a "necessary" sacrifice "for the happiness of them all" (1995, 243), i.e., a sacrifice with which a new order could be founded. Indeed, with Ottilie's subsequent death, the unrecognized religious force of the *sacrificium* obtains validity in the enlightened rhetoric of the sacrifice—when Ottilie, unnoticed by the others, wastes away in her asceticism and dies a martyr. Ottilie, who had entered the scene of the novel as the embodiment of beauty and as a sort of *tableau vivant*, has thus finally and decisively become an image—namely, that image whose origin in the funerary cult is likewise as repressed as the secularization of sacrifice in the bourgeois ethic of renunciation.

Analogous to Eduard's unexamined fear of the graveyard, Charlotte feels an equally vague aversion to portraits, especially to the claim that they may be the "fairest memorial" of a person in "preserving the living form" (1995, 178). Thus, she just as involuntarily thematizes the relationship between the cult of images and the funerary cult. In particular, she rejects the idea that the image of a person constitutes his or her memorial (*Denkmal*), what in the parlance of the time amounted to "the actual resting place" (1995, 177). With this idea, she clarifies her concomitant "peculiar reaction toward portraits" because they always point to something departed (1996, 193ff.; 1995, 121). The fact that the likenesses of the dead were regarded as their visible substitute is one of the origins of Western visual culture. With these images, the resting place of the dead is marked as a site of a cult and

---

15. As regards the religious violence in language, see Gershom Scholem's notes on the "secularization of language" discussed in the last section of this chapter.

thereby made taboo for the purpose of utterances of life. Therefore, the *tableaux vivants*, with which the society in the novel passes the time, are a dangerous enterprise; they are but imitations of memorials in the original sense—images as proxies for the dead.

Goethe characterizes the society of *Elective Affinities* in a twofold manner as regards their dealings with images. The nearly solemn contact with vestiges of the past that are collected, ordered, and restored stands in opposition to the desecration of the gravestones. The former thus metamorphose into objects for the imagination in order to plunge into "ancient times" (199, 179). The society of *Elective Affinities* indulges a visual culture that reveres the remnants and old portraits like relics: "The most everyday doings seemed to shine with divine life, and a worshipful aspect appeared to clothe every character" (180). Thus the cult of beauty and effigies repressed the relationship between the funerary cult and the image and caused the forgetting of it. Yet at the same time it inherited the cult value of images. Ottilie's gradual assimilation into an image allows the inherent dynamic in which sacrifice and sacralization combine to manifest itself in the figure of the martyr as a saint. When Goethe's novel relates how the profanation of the gravesites and the concept of sacrifice coincide with the sacralization of images and the treatment of the remnants of the past as relics, it reflects a significant logic within the dialectic of secularization. The elements of the culture of martyrdom continue to have an (unnoticed) effect in the Enlightenment, and their misrecognition in an apparently secular culture sets in motion a return of the repressed.[16]

## Of "The Guilt Nexus of the Living:"
## A Critique of Destiny and the Death of Atonement

Wherever the Goethe cult praises the "suprahuman" (*Übermensch-lich*), Benjamin counterposes a subject position grounded in a dual reference to *natural* and *supernatural* elements of life. He analyzes the "fateful nature of existence," in which Goethe's characters remain entangled, as a world of ideas in which life appears as a "nexus of guilt and expiation"

---

16. For a deeper insight into the cultural history of martyrdom's trespasses into the realm of religion, see the sort anti-martyrologium: Sigrid Weigel, ed., *Märtyrer-Porträts. Von Opfertod, Blutzeugen und Heiligen Kriegern* (München: Wilhelm Fink, 2007).

(SelWr 1.307). Within this world Ottilie's death appears as a mythic sacrifice. The denial of natural life's bond to a higher, supernatural life consequently leads to a development of a "culpable life," to a notion of "guilt, which is bequeathed through life" (307). In this respect, it is precisely *mere life*, stripped of any "supernatural" demands, that manifests itself as guilt: "With the disappearance of supernatural life in man, his natural life turns into guilt, even without his committing and act contrary to ethics. For now it is in league with mere life, which manifests itself in man as guilt" (308). These reflections on "the guilt nexus of the living" (307) correspond to remarks in the essay "Critique of Violence" (published a year before the completion of "Goethe's *Elective Affinities*"), that concern the diffidence of the "guilt of mere natural life" (250, I.I/138) in myth that comes with the rejection of the "dogma of the sacredness of life" (SelWr 1.251).

In his Goethe essay, Benjamin explains these considerations through the episode involving Charlotte and Eduard's child: through the interpretation of his death as atonement on one hand, and the treatment of Ottilie's death as the death of a martyr on the other.

Thus not only is it as a "victim of destiny" that Ottilie falls—much less that she actually "sacrifices herself"—but rather more implacably, more precisely, it is as the sacrifice for the expiation of the guilty ones. For atonement, in the sense of the mythic world that the author conjures, has always meant the death of the innocent. That is why, despite her suicide, Ottilie dies as a martyr, leaving behind her miraculous remains. (309)

Benjamin's critique of Ottilie's death (which she herself refers to as sacred in an "ambiguous" manner) also applies to the relationship of holiness and expiation in the interpretation of her death by the characters in the novel. It concerns that mix of mythic and Christian notions that ultimately leads to the critique of the Nazarene end of the novel. Ottilie's death is at best "atonement, in the sense of fate but not *holy absolution*—which voluntary death can never be, but rather a death divinely imposed on human beings" (I.I/176; SelWr 1.336; emphasis S.W.).

### Expiation (Sühne) vs. Absolution (Entsühnung)

Whereas the "Critique of Violence" was about using the distinction between the terms solution (*Lösung*) and redemption (*Erlösung*) to derive how the idea of redemption continues to have an effect on the action of resolution, the distinction of expiation (*Sühne*) from absolution (*Entsüh-nung*) is a matter of the opposition between a mythical and biblical term. Absolution is linked to the biblical notion of a vengeful God: the death inflicted by God appears as divine absolution. Because such a biblical notion cannot be emulated by a self-determined death, the idea of a death of expiation (the idea of a possible atonement of human guilt by self-determined sacrifice) still partakes in the confusion of human and divine terms. An example of this is martyrdom.

### Reconciliation (Versöhnung) vs. Conciliation (Aussöhnung)

The divine terms that Benjamin would like to see distinguished from human terms originate in biblical tradition and require a conception of a transcendent sphere. The concept of the human that participates in both natural *and* supernatural life ultimately refers back to these biblical ideas, and this also pertains to secularized rationales for "natural human rights." Nevertheless, *supernatural life*, whose meaning is developed in light of these biblical notions, remains excluded from each *supramundane* sphere—and therefore from the occupation of biblical terms. Benjamin discusses the distinction between reconciliation and conciliation in a similar fashion to the way he does creation and constructed form: "For reconciliation, which is entirely supermundane and hardly an object for concrete depiction in a novel, has its worldly mirroring in the conciliation of one's fellow men" (343). Conciliation, however, has nothing in common with either clemency or toleration but rather coincides with *decision*.

Benjamin discovers a model of "false" reconciliation in the sentimentality (*Rührung*) he describes as a "semblance of reconciliation" (348). Once again, the haze that comes to knowledge through having been emotionally moved relates to the lack of distinction: "Neither guilt nor innocence, neither *nature* nor the *beyond*, are strictly differentiated from sentimentality" (I.I/192; SelWr 1.348, emphasis S.W.). In this sense, sentimentality lies like a veil over Ottilie's beauty: "For the tears of sentimentality, in which the gaze grows veiled, are at the same time the most proper veil of beauty itself. But sentimentality is only the semblance of reconciliation" (SelWr 1.348). Only there, where through a moment of violent commotion sentimentality reaches the threshold of the sublime, is the semblance represented as perishing: "That semblance which presents itself in Ottilie's beauty is one that perishes" (I.I/193; SelWr 1.349). And only there where the expressionless opposes semblance can one speak of a 'true work of art' in the Benjaminian sense, whereby the expressionless attains the position of a placeholder for the secret, the divine ground of existence of beauty: "Like revelation, all beauty holds in itself the orders of the philosophy of history. For beauty makes visible not the idea but rather the secret" (I.I/196; SelWr 1.351). The expressionless appears in the work of art as resistance against false mixtures. Only where the expressionless interrupts harmony, where it brings about a caesura or counterrhythmic interruption, can it become a "critical force" that guarantees the necessary distinctions: "The expressionless is the critical power which, while unable to separate semblance from truth in art, prevents them from mingling" (SelWr 1.340). The possibility of such a *critical power* that resists the mixing in art is based, as shown, on a twofold distinction of terms: on the one hand, between those of the human and those of divine orders, and on the other hand, between those of life and of the poetic work. In the relationship between human life, poetic works, and a transcendent sphere, literature is then in the space that is the name for what, coming from another place, beyond art, interrupts poetry.

## The Relationship of the Work of Art to the Tragic

In order to grasp this category of the expressionless in more concrete terms, Benjamin undertakes some digressions into the realm of the tragic. Thus, the drawing of a strict border between the discourse of art and a *speech before God* is corroborated by yet a different trace that carries the name of the tragic.

### The Tragic vs. Mourning

This track, too, takes as its point of departure its distinction from a myth typical of the Goethe cult, namely, the phrase that references the "tragic dimension in the life of the Olympian" (SelWr 1.320). Yet confusion abounds even in this phrase. This time, however, the confusion does not pertain to the separation of the human from the divine but rather to that of the human from the tragic order: "The tragic exists only in the being of the dramatic persona—that is to say, the person enacting or representing himself—never in the existence of the human being" (320). This concept of the tragic, too, dates back to Benjamin's early studies of language from a decade before. One of the preliminary studies to the essay on language, "The Role of Language in Mourning Play and Tragedy," focused, among other things, on the difference between mourning (a feeling, whose transformation into words is the phenomenon at the root of the *Trauerspiel*) and the tragic: "It is the pure word itself that is of immediate tragic" (59). In clear proximity to Hölderlin's "Annotation to Oedipus" and "Annotation to Antigone," Benjamin had defined the tragic in this text as the "ultimate reality of language and the linguistic order" (61) and as human dialogue, because "The tragic is situated in the laws governing the spoken word between human beings. There is no such thing as a tragic pantomime. Nor do we have tragic poems, tragic novels, or tragic events" (59).

When Benjamin mentions that Ottilie's "lingering, at once guilty and guiltless, in the precincts of fate . . . lends her, for the fleeting glance" (337), like that of Gundolf or André François-Poncets),[17] a tragic quality, then this observation is part of his critique of an understanding of the 'tragic' that fails to grasp the meaning of the concept derived from Greek tragedy. It instead uses the word "tragic" only as an empty catchphrase for pathos. To see Ottilie as a tragic figure is "the falsest of judgments" (337). Among other things, Ottilie's inability to decide, the way in which she simply lets things take their course, stands opposite the tragic, because in the tragic word Benjamin sees that the "crest of decision is ascended, beneath which the guilt and innocence of the myth engulf each other as an abyss" (337). On a crest, one can hardly walk, and even less drift aimlessly. Since the tragic is always linked to the word, it belongs to the tragic personae, to the tragic hero, whose place is likewise defined by means of a beyond, albeit, in this case, through the negation that constitutes a specific "here-and-now" (*Diesseits*): "Beyond Guilt and Innocence is grounded the here-and-now of Good and Evil, attainable by the hero alone." This is why Benjamin rejects the notion of Ottilie's 'tragic purification' as follows: "Nothing more untragic can be conceived than this mournful end" (337).

In "Goethe's *Elective Affinities*," the category of the expressionless constitutes the point of contact between the "true work of art" and the tragic. In order to demonstrate that the expressionless is "a category of language and art, not of the work or of the genres" (340), Benjamin takes a detour through Hölderlin's concept of caesura in his "Annotation to

17. See André François-Poncet, *Les affinités electives de Goethe* (Paris: F. Alcan, 1910).

Oedipus." He attributes to this text a relevance that trespasses in the theory of tragedy, one of absolutely fundamental importance for art. He quotes Hölderlin's description of the caesura as 'mere word,' i.e., as a "counter-rhythmic rupture" (340) in a rhythmic continuity of ideas, as which the tragic transport represents itself. It is "that caesura, in which, along with harmony, every expression simultaneously comes to a standstill, in order to give free reign to a power that is expressionless inside (in the realm of) all artistic means" (I.I/182; SelWr 1.341 ). The caesura therefore appears either as a silencing, an objection, or also as something "Ins-Wort-Fallen" or a breach: "in tragedy as the falling silent of the hero, and in the rhythm of the hymn as objection. Indeed, one could not characterize this rhythm any more aptly than by asserting that something beyond the poet interrupts the language of poetry" (341).

As the caesura in Hölderlin is thus conceived of as a counterrhythmic interruption, this phrase guides us to the "analogous moment of representation" (355) in the novel, with which Benjamin concludes the essay by merging the caesura with the image of the star. As a symbol of hope, the star thereby occupies the place of the expressionless in the novel (which is opposed to semblance *in* the work of art)—and in this way counters the mythologem of the sacrifice and martyr to which the characters cling. Beyond this, this interpretation of the expressionless now also explicitly conjoins with that which interrupts from beyond into the language of poetic works, and in such a way retains the meaning of "mystery in the exact sense of the term" (355). Thus, in terms of its representation in Goethe's novel, the star of hope becomes for Benjamin the "dramatic crowning in the mystery of hope" (355). In his theory of art Benjamin thus updates tragic figures to a linguistic order, absconded from tragedy and myth where the subject must instead face a different *beyond*. Benjamin's star of hope is thus placed in exactly that space in which acceptance of the secret (as divine imprint of beauty) and the acknowledgment of another language (that of the expressionless of not-communicable) merges with the figure of the caesura. This can enable only the break-in (*Einbruch*), the falling-in (*Hereinfallen*), or protruding-in (*Hineinragen*) of "something beyond poetic works."

"Goethe's *Elective Affinities*" presents itself as a place of reflection in which Benjamin's studies on Hölderlin and his conversations with Scholem intersect, in which Athens and Jerusalem connect. If the Christian world of ideas can be readily described as a synthesis of the classical world and Judaism, then Benjamin returns with these thoughts to the origin of this synthesis. From here, he works toward a distinction that provides for his own distinctive perspective: a theory of language and history informed by both Greek tragedy and Jewish messianism.

## The Holy Violence of Language

Benjamin's discourse on the "kritische Gewalt" of the expressionless is to be understood through the polysemy in the term *Gewalt*, as it is negotiated in the "Critique of Violence." By way of example, it becomes clear with the claim that in the caesura "along with harmony, every expression simultaneously comes to a standstill, in order to give free reign to a power that is *expressionless power* inside (in the realm of) all artistic means" (341, italics S.W.). The critical power of the expressionless thus inverts itself here into expressionless force. Furthermore: "Such power has rarely become clearer than in Greek tragedy, on the one hand, and in Hölderlin's hymnic poetry, on the other" (341). In Hölderlin's "Annotation to Oedipus," it is also a question of the relationship between the divine and the human. His discourse of monstrosity here bears on the fact that the Godly and human sphere mix or mingle in the tragic:

The representation of the tragic is mainly based on the fact that what is *monstrous* in the coupling of God and man and in the total fusion of the power of Nature with the innermost depth of man in moment of wrath, shall be made conceivable by showing how this total fusion into one is purged by there total separation [. . . .] Therefore the permanent antagonistic dialog, therefore the chorus, therefore the opposition against him[. . . .] All is speech against speech, that mutually rescind each other." (Hölderlin; emphasis S.W.; transl. mod.)

From Hölderlin's understanding of the *monstrous* as the commingling of God and human, a light once more shines back upon Benjamin's discussion of "monstrous cases," in which humans accept the responsibility to disregard the commandment "Thou shall not kill," thereby blending the two spheres by playing, as it were, God.

Through its illumination within the framework of Hölderlin's theory of tragedy, the motif of mixing and Benjamin's efforts toward the distinction of terms in "Goethe's *Elective Affinities*" can also be situated in a larger religious and cultural historical context. According to Hölderlin, the comprehension of this mingling through separation finds expression in the form of the tragic as speech against speech. In this rhythm, impelled "to the degree of utmost exhaustion" (107), his "Annotation to Oedipus" finds the language for a world in which "in idle time" (108) God and man communicate in "all-forgetting form of infidelity [ . . . ] so that the course of the world will not show any rupture and the memory of the heavenly ones will not expire," since "divine fidelity is best to retain" (108). The violence of the Gods, according to Hölderlin, therefore has the significance that the memory of the celestial does not altogether leave. In the "Annotation to Antigone," he takes these reflections further when he detects the violence within the language of the tragic itself and discusses the "deadly-factual" (*tödlichfaktischen*) character of the words in tragedy. Hölderlin thereby depicts the tragic as a scene of language in which divine violence discloses itself. The expressionless violence that is, according to Benjamin, grasped through the caesura in the space of poetry presents itself as an aftereffect of the tragic in prose. The violent moment of the break-in or *Ins-Wort-Fallens* is thereby to be seen as the afterlife of divine violence in secularized art.

Gershom Scholem also knew to account for the fact that, when the sacred breaks into human language, this force does not go away without violence. A letter from Scholem to Rosenzweig written two years after Benjamin's essay on Goethe contained a sketch with the title "On Our Language: A Confession" (first known through Stéphane Mosès' book *The Angel of History*), which concerns the danger of biblical power in the profane use of holy language, as with what lurks within Hebrew.[18] In exact opposition to the constellation of *breach* in Benjamin's theory of literature (in which something beyond the poet interrupts the language of poetry), Scholem's reflections on the secularization of language in Palestine concern the *breakout* (*Ausbruch*) of the sacred into modern, secularized everyday Hebrew:

What of the "actualization" of the Hebrew language? That abyss of a sacred language on which we nurture our children, must it not open up one day? The people certainly don't know what they are doing here. They think they have secularized the language, have done away with its apocalyptic point. But that, of course, is not

18. See also my article "Gershom Scholems Gedichte und seine Dichtungstheorie—Klage, Adressierung, Gabe und das Problem einer Sprache in unserer Zeit," in Stéphane Mosès and Sigrid Weigel, eds., *Gershom Scholem—Literatur und Rhetorik* (Köln: Böhlau, 2000), 16–47.

true: the secularization of the language is no more than a *Façon de parler*, a ready-made expression. It is impossible to empty the words so bursting with meaning, unless at the price of language itself. (Mosès 1994, 215; 2009, 168; transl. mod.)

In the sketch, Scholem describes experiences with a language from whose words "the power of the holy " emerges unbeknownst to the speaker: "Shall not the *religious power* of that language one day *explode* against its speaker?" (215; 169; emphasis S.W.) In Scholem's reflections, this dimension of speech is actually associated with the last judgment when he writes: "because those who endeavor to revive the Hebrew language did not truly believe in the Judgment to which their acts are summoning us" (169).

These notes are particularly interesting because they contain no moral judgment of the secular use of language, but rather they concern the historical experience of a dialectic of secularization in which divine violence breaks out precisely because the speaker seems to have forgotten the sacred meanings within language. Different from, yet still comparable to, the memory of the heavenly in tragedy, violence also comes into play here as memory, as divine memory as it were. This break-out or eruption of holy violence in an historical situation describes an inverse constellation complementary to Benjamin's figure of the break-in or irruption. Against this backdrop, the theory of *Dichtung* presented in "Goethe's *Elective Affinities*" gains yet another additional meaning: poetic works are perhaps the only form in which the expressionless power of the sacred can actually assume a nonviolent image.

# 5

## Biblical Pathos Formulas and Earthly Hell

*Brecht as Antipode to Benjamin's Engagement*
*with "Holy Scripture"*

What role does God play in *Mahagonny*? This question leads to a topic not unimportant for Bertolt Brecht's play, yet little observed in research on Brecht. It bears on the significance of biblical language, religious motifs, and the Christian order in Brecht's literature. Because the plot of the *Mahagonny* opera, which is canonized within literary history as a critique of a solely money-oriented capitalist society, called for biblical scenery to be projected onto a screen to a great extent throughout the piece, providing a framework for the plot in the process, the actual connection between religion and capitalism in Brecht's texts is open to debate. Does the biblical matrix of the plot of *Mahagonny* represent for Brecht the medium for a critique from whose perspective the established order presents itself as a wrong morality? Is it about a "theology altered in its function," as Hans Mayer wrote?[1] Is Brecht's critique thus tied up in a morality sanctioned by Christianity, or is the latter rather (whether blasphemous or parodistic) reduced to absurdity with help from epic theater? Or must one read the piece in a completely different manner and regard the perpetual hell and universalized system of pleasure in *Mahagonny* as a permanent state of exception whose significance is as a piece of a political theology or critique of violence? Since such questions play a central role in Walter Benjamin's thinking, they will be discussed in the following section from the perspective of his reading of Brecht. In the course of this discussion, however, not only will those *topoi* and concepts that Benjamin in fact discussed

---

1. Hans Mayer, *Bertolt Brecht und die Tradition* (Pfullingen: Neske, 1961), 49.

in his work on Brecht be considered, but it will also include relevant theorems from Benjamin's writings that he did not himself include in his commentary on Brecht—such as his reflections on "Capitalism as Religion" and studies on Karl Kraus and Franz Kafka.

## The "Play of God in Mahagonny"

When the third of the *Mahagonny Songs* from the *Songspiel* (also known as *Little Mahagonny*) of 1927 was integrated into the opera *The Rise and Fall of the City of Mahagonny* (Universal Edition 1929), the song was not only revamped as an ensemble scene (as the Frankfurt edition of Brecht notes) but also divided into three voices: first, the men who recognize God in Mahagonny on a gray morning; second, Trinity Moses in the role of a 'God no one expected'; and third, Jenny, who observes and names the men's reaction to this God. Along with this scenic transposition, a part of the verse refrain, "During the Whiskey / We recognized God in Mahagonny" (60), is raised to the level of a refrain for the entire play that will be enacted after the execution of Jim (alias Paul Ackermann) in the final scene. This takes place before the curtain and segues into the finale. In the revised *Versuche-Fassung*, Brecht thereby additionally accentuated the unique status of this scene, "God in Mahagonny," as a play within a play or rather a play within an opera (a genre that usually reflects the whole of the plot), in the way he modeled the "Play of God in Mahagonny" as a theatric scene. In this version, Paul takes over the role of the spectators. In doing so, his seat is swapped with the electric chair to which the accused is directed, while the four men, Jenny, and Trinity Moses (as God) take over the roles of the play within the opera. The fact that this play is addressed to Paul Ackermann,[2] who, because of a "Lack of money / Which is the greatest crime / That there is in the World,"[3] is sentenced to death moreover makes the play into the court of Mahagonny's

2. The character of the lumberjack from Alaska is named Paul Ackermann, Jimmy Gallagher, or Jim Mahoney in various editions of *Mahagonny*. In this study, Paul Ackermann is used.

3. Bertolt Brecht, *Werke. Große kommentierte Berliner und Frankfurter Ausgabe*, Werner Hecht et al. (eds.), vol. 2 (Frankfurt/M: Suhrkamp, 1988), 381. English edition: *The Rise and Fall of the City of Mahagonny*, trans. W. H. Auden (Boston: D. R. Godine, 1976), 56. All further citations to these texts given parenthetically in text as "1988" and "1976."

official answer to his objection: "You don't seem to know that there's a God" (1976, 60).

Begbick: A What?[4]
Paul: A God!
Begbick: Ever so, whether there exists a God for us? Yes, there is an answer at hand. Put on the play of *God in Mahagonny* once again for him? Just sit yourself in the electric chair!
*Four men and Jenny Smith appear before Paul Ackermann and act out the play of* God Comes to Mahagonny. (1988, 384; 1976, 60)

The only change that the subsequent text features when compared to the *Songspiel* is that the men's answers of *No* when asked by Moses (who plays God) if they recognize God in the city occurs earlier than in the *Songspiel*, where it comes at the end and countermands the previous four *Yeses*. With this gesture of negation in this version, the men, in accordance with the end of the role play, already react to their damnation to hell:

Moses:
Down with all into hellfire
Stuff your Henry Clays into your pack
Off with all of you to hell, you scoundrels
Wriggle in the Devil's crowded sack? (1976, 61)

This doubling of *No*'s reinforces the four men's denial. In the final stanza of the play within the opera, they threaten to strike, justified by the fact that the men were always already located in hell: "We'll go on strike. We will never / Let you drag us off to Hell forever / For we *are* in Hell and always have been" (62). The locution that paints life as perpetual hell allows the "play of God" to end with a moral in which the separation between this life and the beyond is sublated into a radical immanence. As an answer to the question posed by Paul Ackermann as to the existence of God, the play featuring God is thus to be read as a type of *last play*. It thus provides an answer to a question that in any case seems to have already become superfluous or unintelligible and is at best a weak and manifestly distant memory that can yet be brought to mind. Begbick's reaction shows this: "Ever so, whether there exists a God for us?" Also the answer is already known; it is

4. In German "Gibt es?"—a phrase that means "What's the matter?"—literally means "Does (it) exist?" Thus the scene cites the debate as to the existence of God.

an equally available and practiced gesture and need only be cited: "Put the play on once again for him" (transl. mod.). Hence the play seems necessary only for the yet unconvinced, while his objection is treated as a long-since-settled discourse. In this way, talk of the *death of God* is cited and itself treated as an already rejected formula.

When, however, in the *Versuche-Fassung* Paul is given the floor one more time—"Now I see it" (62)—then his *last words* become an insight or knowledge gleaned from the events of the play. As a result, the play within the opera also gains the character of a teaching play (*Lehrstück*). The deadly lesson that Paul (and with him the opera's audience) will learn is that his fate was already sealed when he came to the city in order to buy happiness, because happiness available for purchase was no happiness at all. Founded as an attempt to establish a "Paradise City" and "City of Happiness" whose image is a perpetual brothel, the project has instead created a place that offers no alternative to everlasting hell. Instead, the order of Mahagonny allowed the laws of an *earthly hell* to emerge with total clarity and severity. It is an exact inversion of the ideals of justice and humanity—as shown, for example, in the hierarchy of crimes according to which the court in Mahagonny pronounces its sentences: Paul receives only two days in prison for the indirect murder of a friend, but was sentenced to death for an unpaid bar tab. In the revision, however, the additional lesson of the condemned goes further than that, because Paul's last words bring into play notions of thirst and hunger that are not in accordance with the satisfaction of material pleasures on which the rules of Mahagonny are based. Paul's last words instead give form to a desire that invokes a spiritual lack. In the plot of *Mahagonny*, the allegory of the crane's flight during the love scene between Paul and Jenny alone corresponds to this lack. It arises from the radical immanence that determines both the eternal hell of the existing society and Mahagonny's order.

This scene must here be recalled in detail because in it one recognizes with how little clarity the question can be answered: Which role do the citations of biblical scenes and allusions to Christian motifs in Brecht's libretto play? Moreover, this difficulty is magnified in Brecht's revision, mainly through the integration of an aspect of pedagogic play (*Lehrstück*) into the execution scene. In the first edition of the opera (the Universal Edition), the "play of God in Mahagonny" is not addressed to the condemned, but neither is it posed as a precondition for Paul's last words to qualify as insight. Since it follows the execution (as epilogue) in this version, the play is to be read as a poetological commentary—that is, as a reflection on the biblical mode of narration, according to whose template the fall of Mahagonny was told. The play of God would thereby be assigned the role of staging the biblical voice that is persistently cited throughout the whole opera but may possibly be noticed only late by the audience. In other words, the role of the play is to make this voice visible while at the same time allowing it to leave the stage.

The rearrangement and revision in the *Versuche-Fassung*, however, also extends the biblical frame of reference to the scenes that follow the play within the play, or at least to Paul Ackermann's story, which is presented in the mold of a *passio Christi*. Paul smashes the stone tablets containing the rules of Mahagonny on the night of the hurricane (reminiscent of Sodom and Gomorrah) and declares new commandments for a happier order (a scene in which the *gestus* of biblical language intensifies itself). He escapes the flood in Noah's Ark, then invites his friends to a (Last) supper in a scene of drunken debauchery and is left by them with an unpaid bill. After this chain of events, and after he is sentenced to death by the court that had before (as Pilate had acquitted Barnabas) acquitted Higgins after having been bribed,[5] his *imitatio Christi* is completed in the execution scene. When Paul Ackermann's last words then end with a plea ("Give me a glass of water," 62), these words allude to those of the crucified Jesus: "I thirst!" (John 19:28) Inasmuch as the staging of his story follows the model of Christian martyrs and is thereby assigned the privilege of expressing knowledge of Mahagonny's history and lamenting their spiritual lack, this scene may also be read as showing that he, as messiah, steps into the place of the old, negated God, whose character's name, Trinity Moses, already sounds like the quasi-synthetic incarnation of an overcome 'Judeo-Christian tradition.'

No promise of redemption, however, attends to Brecht's modern passion play, as the concluding scene presents demonstrations of "those who had not yet been killed for their ideals" (63). In the middle of this scene, the corpse of Paul Ackermann is carried away in a burial ceremony with "[his] watch, revolver and cheque book on a linen cushion, also his shirt on a pole" (64). It is a parting image that arouses associations to the motif of triumphal parades in renaissance paintings (such as Andrea Mantegna's

5. For a decryption of the biblical allusions, see Sehm, 1976.

"Triumph of Caesar") as well as to both an investiture ceremony and a state burial. In this reading, the opera *Mahagonny* ends by restaging a passion play *after* God's resignation. Thus the piece would be read as a continuation of a Christian martyr morality *after* the death of God and after the disillusion of any hope for salvation—or: as an authorization of the disappointed promise of happiness through an allegorical rhetoric borrowed from the Bible. The final sentence of the piece, "Can't help us or you or no one" (65), is thereby testified to through the downfall of Mahagonny and the passion play of Paul Ackermann: the confirmation of a secularized life without God sealed through negative Christian laws or through a quasi-*divine injustice*.

## The Devil's Prayerbook

At this point, the esteem in which Walter Benjamin held Brecht during the time of *Mahagonny*, which had already engaged his research many times,[6] becomes particularly puzzling. Brechtian theater, with its practically Baroque settings (such as the funeral of Paul Ackermann in *Mahagonny*) and untragic heroes, must have no doubt held particular interest for the author of the book on German mourning play. Benjamin's engagement with Brecht is also due to a number of crucial impulses, such as the importance of gestures (e.g., II.2/507, 536), citation and interruption (534), and a theory of poverty (667). Yet despite all of these factors, it nevertheless remains difficult to imagine that Brecht's use of Christian iconography and biblical language would not *unavoidably* cause antagonism. Benjamin's stance toward the history of religion is determined by an exact counterposition to the model posed by *Mahagonny*, because for him it is defined by the perpetuation of a messianic attitude in the midst of secularization and by a program of "profane illumination" in a world without God. This position can be gleaned, for example, from his essay on Surrealism, which was produced in the same year as Brecht and Weill's *Mahagonny*. In "Surrealism" Benjamin formulated, from an aesthetic perspective, what is arguably his most radical version of revolutionary practice by seeking to combine several points from the program of surrealism (such as the cult of evil, intoxication, pessimism, and nihilism), in short by bind-

6. Particularly relevant to this point is Wizisla, 1993 and 2004; see also Yun 2000.

ing "revolt to revolution" (SelWr 2.215). The resulting interest in Satanism will also have been what allowed him to be attentive to the title *The Devil's Prayerbook*, which Karl Thieme used to name his 1932 essay "An Engagement with the Works of Bertolt Brecht."

The review by Thieme,[7] a historian and religious socialist who also reviewed some works by Benjamin and occasionally corresponded with him, is in this respect notable, as his criticism contains an ambivalent valuation of Brecht. Although Thieme assumes a moral and religious congeniality with Brecht, he nevertheless turns against *Mahagonny*. In this respect, Benjamin splits with his contemporary. Though he shared an interest in the diabolical features of Brecht's writings, Benjamin did not see in them the moral value assumed by Thieme. The question posed by the title of Thieme's article—whether Brecht's literature should be judged as devilish—is answered in therein as follows:

A work, however, that brings us to a most fruitful self-reflection, we cannot describe as satanic, may it be ever so anti-Christian: the devil never allows us to come to ourselves! It is indeed by no means the case that we would beat our breasts before Mr. Brecht, as earlier poets of social misery asked of us; rather we have found in him—and him most of all in the realm of poetry—the real adversary, with whom one again speaks and against whom one can really argue. Certainly, one can learn from the one who began to quarrel with the Christian church again in its own language. Regardless of the appraisal of his private persona, this gives him historical relevance. In the place of endless excuses he places real opposition and thus the questions of public importance that he brings about are again questions that concern Christians.[8]

Thieme thereby means to confirm an intellectual relationship with Brecht's concerns by incorporating the lines "The party sees seven states / the single man sees one city" as an epilogue to his article. He then suggests replacing the word *party* in Brecht's text each time with the word *church*. It is an extremely revealing experiment, inasmuch as it allows the confessional character of Brechtian political poetry to become clear. Thieme's debate with Brecht concerning, among other things, the *Mahagonny* opera attests to

---

7. In 1938, as Benjamin worked on the "Commentary on Poems by Brecht," he asked Thieme to send him the article because it was not at that time available to him.

8. Karl Thieme, "Des Teufels Gebetbuch? Eine Auseinandersetzung mit dem Werke Bertolt Brechts," in *Hochland. Monatsschrift für alle Gebiete des Wissens, der Literatur und Kunst*, Karl Munch, ed., vol. 29/1 (1931/32), 397–413; here 413).

the fact that after its premiere it was not only met with indignation and scandal but also found a positive reception—in this case, however, a positive reception Brecht himself would have regarded as approval from the wrong side.

Thieme can be seen as the beginning of a Christian reception of Brecht, whose positions range from appreciative to positive and continues to the present. As a most curious example of the theological reception of Brecht, perhaps the recent discussion of his theatrical aesthetics in the context of an innovative liturgical pastoral aesthetic may apply.[9] In any case, it is remarkable that the wide-reaching ignorance of the Christian armature of Brecht's polemic program, which persists in the Left's reception of Brecht, is an obstacle to their proper valuation by theologically interested parties. In contrast, those studies that have examined biblical motifs conducted in the field of literary criticism remain, in general, within the framework of a history of motifs or *topoi* and a paradigm of biblical parody or criticism.[10] An investigation that questions Brecht's stance toward religion, and thus probes the *theme* of religion, will not go beyond the thesis that Mahagonny is "a parody of the Bible that leads to a criticism of religion."[11] In my opinion, Hannah Arendt's essay on Brecht, which after all assessed *Mahagonny* as Brecht's "only strictly nihilistic play,"[12] contributed a rewarding interpretation of the question of Brecht's attitude toward religion. Arendt comments on the song "Don't let them tempt you! / There is no recurrence of life!" as follows:

Nowhere else in modern literature, it seems to me, is there such a clear understanding that what Nietzsche called "the death of God" does not necessarily lead into despair but, on the contrary, since it eliminates the fear of Hell, can end in sheer jubilation, in a new "yes" to life[. . . . ] In his jubilant rejection of all speculation about the beyond and his songs of praise to Baal, the god of the Earth, truly swings an enthusiastic gratitude.[13]

9. Cf. Marcus A. Friedrich, *Liturgische Körper. Der Beitrag von Schauspieltheorien und—techniken für die Pastoralästhetik* (Stuttgart: Kohlhammer, 2001).

10. See, for example, Sehm, 1976. He was, to the best of my knowledge, the first to undertake the task of deciphering in detail all of the biblical allusions in *Mahagonny*.

11. Gunter G. Sehm, "Moses, Christus und Paul Ackermann. Brechts Aufstieg und Fall der Stadt Mahagonny," in *Brecht-Jahrbuch 1976* (Frankfurt/M: Suhrkamp, 1976), 97.

12. Hannah Arendt, *Men in Dark Times* (New York: Mariner Books, 1970), 234.

13. Ibid., 233.

However, what is of greater importance for me than Brecht's attitude toward religion is the meaning of religious rhetoric and sacred *topoi* in his work that arises in the wake of the positing of the death of God. With reference to the methodologies of cultural studies developed by Aby Warburg, we may say it concerns the question as to which nature of the Bible's afterlife in the modern era is expressed in Brecht's texts.

## Gesture as the Dialectic at a Standstill

One of the leitmotifs in Benjamin's commentary on Brecht is that of the gestural, which, together with the concomitant critique of empathy (*Einfühlung*), constitutes the main point of contact for his thinking on Brecht's literature. Thus the third paragraph of Benjamin's first essay on the theme, "What Is Epic Theater?" (1931) begins with a statement that itself amounts to a gesture: "epic theater is gestural."[14] The postulate that later follows, "making gestures quotable" (SelWr 4.305), is taken directly from Brecht, who discussed gestures primarily from two perspectives: that of its portrayal of morals, and that of rhythm and caesura. Brecht's "Annotations to the *Threepenny Opera*" (1931) states, for example, that the actor shows "gestures, which are the mores and customs of the body, so to speak."[15] If Brecht, in his "Annotations to *Mahagonny*" (1930), wants his opera to be understood as a "portrayal of morals," then that goal shall thus be realized in drama mainly through the gestures of the actors.

In Benjamin's commentaries on Brecht, the figure of the gesture is connected to his own work on photography, film, and the shocklike temporal structure of modern apparatus and media culture. Evidently, he saw in Brecht's dramaturgy a kind of synthesis of Baroque theater and the newest media technology. From his assertion that epic theater is situated "on the level of technology," it is already evident that his essay on Brecht is related to his own media-theoretical reflections—as with his "communicating vessels." As a summary of his posthumously published study of Brecht, "What Is Epic Theater?" he writes, "The forms of epic theater correspond to the new technical forms, to cinema as well as to the radio" (II.2/524). Benjamin had introduced the concept *shock* in the closing passage of

---

14. Walter Benjamin, *Understanding Brecht* (New York: Verso, 2003), 3.
15. Brecht, *Gesammelte Werke in 20 Bänden* (Frankfurt/M: Suhrkamp, 1967), vol. 17, 997.

the "Little History of Photography" (1931) in order to mark the temporal structure of film that "paralyzes the associative mechanisms in the beholder" (SelWr 2.527). These ideas surface again in the texts on Brecht, for example in the review "Brecht's One-Act Plays" (*Brechts Einakter*), which appeared in 1938 in the *Weltbühne*: "Epic theater itself moves forward in bursts, which is comparable to the images of filmstrips. Its basic form is that of shock, through which individual, well-contained situations encounter each other" (II.2/515; a version appears in SelWr 3.331). With these observations Benjamin avoids, after all, the essential line of demarcation between Brecht's desire for innovation (*Neuerung*) and Weill's for renewal (*Erneuerung*), as well as the related competition between text and music for domination of the arts so vital for Brecht. Benjamin is able to do this by assigning both to the same economy of shock structure in which he includes the songs and then continues: "The songs, the captions of the sets, the gestic conventions of the actors set off one situation from another. This creates intervals which, if anything, undermine the illusion of the audience. These intervals are dedicated for the audience to contemplate and to respond critically" (II.2/515). When he incorporates this passage into his second essay, also entitled "What Is Epic Theater?" (1939) he inserts the sentence: "[the intervals] paralyze [the audience's] readiness for empathy (*Einfühlung*)" (SelWr 4.306).

The description of disruption and gesture forms a common thread extending through Benjamin's numerous texts on Brecht, with which he attributes an epistemic quality to two *dramaturgic* modes, which bring a specific temporal structure into play: as a breach in the plot that "opens up a clearer view of theory" (SelWr 2.560) in the review of *Mother* (published in 1932 in the *Literarischen Welt*), and as *dialectic at a standstill* in the first study of epic theater. There, Benjamin views the actors—and gestures— as being on the side of philosophy, because in his eyes the gesture "tests conditions on men."[16] In this respect, it represents for him a possibility to couple physiognomic theater without mediation to the body politic, with the "body of society" (12):

The dialectic which epic theatre sets out to present is not dependent on a sequence of scene in time; rather, it declares itself in those gestural elements that form the basis of each sequence in time[. . . . ] What is clarified, lightning-fast, in the *con-*

16. Benjamin, *Understanding Brecht*, 7.

dition—as an imprint of human gestures, actions and words—is an immanent-ly dialectical attitude. The condition which epic theatre reveals is the *dialectic at a standstill*. For just as, in Hegel, the sequence of time is not the mother of the dialectic, but only the medium through which the dialectic manifests itself, so in epic theatre the dialectic is not born of the contradictive succession of state-ments or behaving, but of the gesture itself. (II.2/530; *Understanding Brecht*, 12; emphasis S.W.)

### Gesture: Biblical Tonality and Pathos Formulas

Although Benjamin takes Brecht's gestures as a kind of vanishing point of dramaturgic elements, of historical-philosophical relationships (a reference to Hegel), and of his own physiognomic phenomenology of the social, Bertolt Brecht himself had learned his gestural technique not least from the rhetoric of biblical language. In the short article, "On Rhyme-less Lyric with Irregular Rhythm," which appeared in the March 1939 issue of *Das Wort*, Brecht comments on how gestures gained this central signifi-cance for his literature. The occasion is the question, To what degree can unrhymed lyric be called lyric? In his response, Brecht explains that his "latest lyrical works," those that indeed "have neither rhyme nor regular fixed rhythm," nevertheless feature a rhythm, which he then describes as a varying, syncopated, and gestural one.[17] In the essay, he derives his gestural technique and rhythmic notation from the study of meter and rhythm in poetic and dramatic texts from throughout the history of literature. In par-ticular, he highlights the "verse architecture" of the "Schlegel-Tieck trans-lations of Shakespeare," from which he came to realize: "I need sublime language, but I resisted the oily smoothness of the usual five-foot iambic. I needed rhythm, but not the usual chatter."[18] He links the conclusions he draws from this study, one conducted for the benefit of his own ballads, to the gestural techniques of his theatrical work and then brings the Bible into play—or, more precisely, Luther's translation of the Bible. For Brecht, Luther's verses are important for their "gestural richness," for example: "If your eye causes you to sin: pluck it out!" instead of "Pluck out the eye that causes you to sin." He comments on the gestic as follows: "The first sen-

17. Brecht, *Werke*, vol. 19, 395. Syncopation is a large reduction of sound achieved through the elimination of a short vowel in the middle of the word.
18. Ibid., 396.

tence contains a supposition and what is idiosyncratic and particular in it can fully be expressed in the intonation. Then comes a pause in the perplexity and only then follows the bewildering advice."[19] Along with the Bible, Brecht cites the "perception of social dissonance" as the premise for the "new gestural rhythmicization" of his verses and proceeds to invoke examples of "rhythm that comes from the folk (*Volk*)" that have been received into the formation of his new rhythmic style alongside the biblical language. In this way, the rhythm of *society* and the rhythm of *language* are projected directly onto one and other.

To what extent Brecht's self-commentary was already influenced by Benjamin's commentaries on him must remain an open question. A special proximity to his interpretation of rhythm in epic theater (as the dialectic at a standstill, in which the state of the body of society is visible in a flash) finds expression in a passage in which Brecht elucidates the verse-*caesura* as a rhythmic *boundary case*. Here, Benjaminian concepts underlie the linguistic material of the lyric. In his commentary on one stanza from the *Deutsche Satiren*, Brecht writes:

The end of a line of verse always implies a *caesura*. I have chosen the stanza because its second verse, if one makes two out of it and divides it:

*Could one always*
*Tell them fairy tales*

would be still easier to read, so that one can study the principle at a boundary case.[20]

Here, Brecht supplies what will be a poetological rationale for the conspicuous abundance of biblical citations and the prevalence of the biblical tonality in many of his texts. Along with the incorporation of religious forms and figures (in the *Hauspostille*, for example, there are prayer songs or *Bittgesänge*, liturgy, religious exercises, psalms, chorals, and hymns) it is above all the gesture of biblical rhetoric that shapes his works. One might think of the eleventh scene in *Mahagonny* in which the chorus ends in outcry: "Keep yourself upright! Fear ye not!" (1988, 31). In this scene, Paul declares his assault on Begbick's prohibitions: "Yes, then I, being hilarious, prefer to destroy your tablets and your laws, and your walls must go" (30). When Begbick reports on the destruction of Pensacola (a version of

19. Ibid., 398.
20. Ibid., 401; emphasis S.W.

Sodom), she says: "Slayed lie all the Constables / and the just alike with the unjust go down / They all must be off!" (30) Gunter G. Sehm has deciphered this verse as being a montage from the book, *Nahum, Hesekiel und dem 90. Psalm*, yet he also criticized it for being a "rude biblical eclecticism."[21]

If the diagnosis of eclecticism (from the Greek *eklegein* = to select or cull) is meant as a criticism or reproach, then it occurs under the largely unnamed norm or standard that either judges the incorporation of pieces from other texts as unoriginal and uncreative or regards the citation of individual ideas from various texts as an imprecise or dishonest reference that does not do justice to the content of the cited text. Understood literally as *eklegein* or rather regarded as a method, however, these selections from texts do not differentiate themselves from those that wrest linguistic fragments out of other texts, as is the case in Benjamin's theory of citation. One thinks of the description of *citation* as being a reflection of "the angelic tongue in which all words, startled from the idyllic context of meaning, have become mottoes in the book of creation" (SelWr 2.454), given in the Karl Kraus essay, which appeared shortly before the first article on Brecht. In light of this theory of citation, the initial question as to how Brecht deals with biblical citation and the mimicry of gestures from the biblical language can now be concretized: Is it to be understood in terms of Benjamin's allegorical technique, in which the continuum of tradition's transmission must be destroyed in order to place the broken-off fragments into a new context; or alternatively to be understood in the sense of authoritative citations that borrow from the aura and authority of biblical language? With an eye toward Benjamin's poetic reflections on rhyme, name, dedication, citation, and the "sacralization of words" developed in his Kraus essay, the question poses itself as to the manner in which modern literature acquits itself of holy scripture and the cultic tradition of religious speech. Already, with the fact that the poetology of the Kraus essay returns to the tradition of the Jewish Bible, another linguistic and religious-philosophic framework is established—in contrast to Brecht's reference to the Lutheran Bible. In the Hebrew Bible, we find the sacrality of a materially limited but infinitely interpretable text,[22] while in the Christian Bible we encounter a rhetoric of annunciation and of parables. As will be shown, this difference will also

21. Sehm, 88.

22. See Gershom Scholem's remarks on linguistic theory of Kabbalah: "Der Name Gottes und die Sprachtheorie der Kabbala," in *Judaica 3* (Frankfurt/M: Suhrkamp, 1973), 7–70.

play a role in the controversy about Kafka in the form of an opposition between literal wording and allegory.

Although Benjamin wanted to apprehend Brecht's postulate—
"making gestures quotable"—in terms of his own theory of interruption
and caesura, his skepticism about the spiritual tone in Brecht's poetry
comes out in various places, even if it is formulated very cautiously. By
way of example, in his "Commentary on Poems by Brecht," begun in 1938
during his stay with Brecht in Skovsbostrand, he detected a *"solemn tone"*
similar to the style of language employed by the clergy. About Brecht's
poem, "Against Temptation," he writes:

> The poet warns them [the people—S.W.] against temptations that are costing
> them dear in their lives here and now. He denies that there is a second life. His
> warnings are *uttered no less solemnly than those of the clergy*; his assurances are just
> as apodictic. Like the clergy, he uses the term "temptation" in the absolute sense,
> without qualification; he appropriates its edifying tone. (SelWr 4.223, italics S.W.)

Here, Benjamin maintains that the presence of the biblical language in
Brecht's poems concerns less citable gestures. Instead Brecht uses the pathos
formulas of religious discourse in order to provide his political program
with the required authority that can count on popular consent.[23] Since
Brecht's citations of biblical rhetoric and use of images and scenes from the
Christian tradition represent only a symptom of his mode of engagement
with theological tradition and secularization, one must ask how Benjamin
has reacted to it—beyond his critical objections to the uplifting timbre of
several of Brecht's verse.

## Brecht as Antipode: The Hell of Mahagonny

The difficult and ambivalent relationship Benjamin had with Brecht
need not be discussed again in detail here. Important in this context, how-

---

23. Because of the close connection between Brecht's gestic rhythm and the tone of religious genres, it is no coincidence that their interpretations have found the attention of play-
wrights and those involved with the theater more than by literary scholars. Some productions
of *Mahagonny* reinscribe the piece into this tradition; Giorgio Strehler's famous production of
the *Mahagonny Opera* in Milan's La Scala theater in 1964 comes to mind, where it was staged
as a mystery play. See Siegfried Melchinger, "Mahagonny als Mysterienspiel. Giorgio Strehler
an der Piccolo Scala in Mailand," in *Theater Heute 5*, vol. 5 (1964), 32–35.

ever, is the difference between his commentaries on Brecht and in comparison with his essays on Franz Kafka and Karl Kraus—all written in the same year. These essays are the result of extensive studies and preparatory work, in which both figures gained their form through lengthy and laborious work, and their profile is shaped by epistemological and historical-theoretical questions rather than biographical evidence. It is different with his texts on Brecht. The numerous reviews, articles, commentaries, and notes span a period of many years and to a large extent refer to conversations with Brecht, in part to his self-commentaries on his dramaturgy and political theory. They are indeed shaped by a historical index of the 1930s, and in particular an intellectual-political struggle held under difficult conditions between two exiles whose working and living conditions could not have been more different.

For many readers of Benjamin, as well as for many of his contemporaries, Benjamin's closeness to Brecht was and is puzzling. The clearest explanation—one he himself gave—can be found in a letter to Gretel Adorno. She confided to him in 1934 that she faced his relocation to Denmark (that is, to Brecht) "with some trepidation," and expressed her concern that Benjamin stood "somewhat under his influence," which "posed a great danger" (AB 154) to him. He replied to his friend in great detail about "the Danish question" and in the process outlined a principle fundamental for him, namely, an economy of being "in which only a few relations in fact play a role," to make it possible for him "to assert a pole of being that is the opposite one to my original being." He also asks for trust, "that these relations, whose dangers are obvious, will show their fruitfulness." Alluding to Adorno's intimate knowledge of his character, he illustrates this economy without commenting directly on Brecht:

Precisely you are not unfamiliar with the fact that my life, as well as my thinking, moves through extreme positions. The range that it thereby affirms, the freedom to bring things and thoughts next to each other, which are considered irreconcilable, only gains a face through danger. A danger my friends also only recognize as apparent in the form of such 'dangerous' relations. (AB 156)

This self-commentary reveals that Benjamin consciously sought in his relationship with Brecht a debate with an antipode to his own intellectual disposition. Yet he leaves open the question of what, exactly, this antipode is.

One could certainly name no small number of characteristics that predisposed Brecht to being Benjamin's antipode, but Brecht's satirical stance and his penchant for the infernal would be among them. In this context, Benjamin's 1935 review of the *Threepenny Novel*[24] is significant in that it acknowledges this prose work as "a satirical novel of great caliber" (III/440). In the review, Benjamin comes back to statements he made about Dostoevsky in his research for the surrealism essay, in which he had argued programmatically against the "disastrous coupling of idealistic morality with political practice" (II.I/304; SelWr 2.214). A few notes from the Paralipomena to this article, which revolve around the cult of evil and the demonic, are dedicated to Stavrogin's confession in Dostoevsky's *The Demons*. Benjamin describes the figure of Stavrogin as a "Surrealist *avant la lettre*," because he considered not only the good to be created by God but also villainy, revenge, and cruelty (II.3/1029). In the review of the *Threepenny Novel*, Benjamin then uses Dostoevsky as a foil for Brecht's literary use of crime: "Dostoyevsky was concerned with psychology; he made visible the piece of a criminal embedded in man. Brecht is concerned with politics; he makes visible the piece of crime included hidden in any business" (SelWr 3.8). In doing so, he highlights how Brecht uses the genre of the crime novel for his social critique in order to depict a social order in which the criminal possesses quasi-normality:

Bourgeois legality and crime—these are, by the rules of the crime novel, opposites. Brecht's procedure consists in retaining the highly developed technique of the crime *novel but neutralizing its rules. This* crime novel depicts the relation between bourgeois legality and crime in a proper way. (III/447ff.; SelWr 3.8; emphasis S.W.)

With the suppression of the rules of genre, the relationship between law and crime reverses itself. An opposition turns into a similarity expressed in the formal aspects of the genre, through which the similarity to crime proves itself to be a "special case of exploitation." Benjamin than takes the nexus of a critique of capitalism and social satire in Brecht's novel as an occasion to discuss satire, which, under the heading "Satire and Marx," is validated as materialist art.

    With historical distance, it is difficult not to read Benjamin's reflections on "[c]lumsy thinking" in this context as themselves satirical commentary on Brecht. Yet Benjamin was no satirist. In his criticism, it is in fact clear how literally he meant the term "economy," which he explained

24. He had been contracted to write for Klaus Mann's journal *Die Sammlung*. It was never published because of a disagreement over his remuneration.

in the earlier quoted letter to Gretel Adorno. Particularly in his remarks on dialectic thinking, which is supposedly in need of clumsy thoughts, Brecht's approach to writing is called into service as an extreme antipode to those positions Benjamin develops at the same time in other texts, notably those on Kafka and Kraus. Brecht is thereby deployed as an infernal adversary of epistemology: as a Mephisto for a melancholic, Jewish Faust in modernity.

The infernal is also negotiated thematically in Benjamin's commentary on the "Mahagonny Songs" (1938). There, he interprets the "men of Mahagonny" as eccentrics, which for him means "simply a washed-up average man" (SelWr 4.221) and is an alias for the petit bourgeois. A God that is "himself a reduced one" corresponds to them, and this degree of depletion, of eccentricity and godliness, marked by the failure of any messianic hope, thus corresponds to the locality, Mahagonny. It is not interpreted as a city or imaginary place but rather as a *topos*, as an image of its time or of an epoch. What is significant in Brecht's Mahagonny, states Benjamin, is that "with the image of this definition of place, the poet addresses his epoch."[25] He explicitly commits himself to a different image for this *topos*, namely Brecht's formulation "the Good Lord's cheap saloon" in the song incorporated into the opera in the form of the "Play of God in Mahagonny." Benjamin merges this verse with the final scene of everlasting hell—"Because we've always been in hell"—and states:

> The Good Lord's "cheap saloon" is hell. The phrase has the trenchancy of images devised by the mentally ill. "Cheap saloon" is a phrase that might be used by any ordinary man, once he has finally gone mad, to describe hell as the only piece of heaven accessible to him. (Abraham as Sancta Clara could speak of "the Good Lord's cheap saloon.") But, in a cheap saloon God has grown too chummy with the regulars. (II.2/546; SelWr 4.222)

The men of Mahagonny would have grasped this situation, with the result that under these circumstances the threat of being sent to hell would no longer make any impression on them. Because "the anarchy of bourgeois society" is an infernal one, "[f]or the people caught up in it, *there simply can be nothing more terrifying* than this society" (222; emphasis S.W.). One cannot make the accusation that Benjamin's commentaries are untouched by the larger horrors and persecution of the Jews in the following

25. Benjamin, *Understanding Brecht*, 49.

years, since he was still unaware and without knowledge of the terrible hell that began at the same time in the camps at Buchenwald and elsewhere.[26] Nevertheless, an irritation remains; it pertains to the question of how these readings relate to his own engagement with religious and cultic traditions in the modern world.

In his commentaries on Brecht, Benjamin interprets the *Mahagonny* scenario in pointed analogy to the structure of *Threepenny Novel* in his own analysis. If one applies the assertions made about the rules of genre in his review of the novel to his readings of *Mahagonny*, this would mean that the petit bourgeois's order of happiness and promise of salvation are opposites according to the rules of religion. Brecht's method consists in retaining the rhetoric of religion while discarding its rules. This manifests itself in the modern, decreased promise of salvation that corresponds to the reduced God of the petit bourgeois's pleasures. The difference between sacred and profane orders is leveled precisely through this procedure. Benjamin's interpretation indeed ends with the passage on God's cheap saloon, summed up as follows: "The sole difference between hell and this social order is that, in the petty bourgeois (the eccentric), the dividing line between a poor soul and the devil is blurred" (II.2/540; SelWr 4.222). As demonstrated, such a leveling fundamentally contradicts the genuine Benjaminian reflections on the relationship between religion and modernity, which pertain to messianic intensity *in* the profane order. To realize his 'economy of being' that is to say to assert the opposing pole of his own stance, very clearly demanded of him no small effort in his writing. This is manifest, for example, in the extensive methodological preliminary remarks to the commentaries on Brecht's poetry under the title "The Form of Commentary." There, Benjamin grounds his methodology and reading of Brecht's texts in the fact that the commentary approaches Brecht's Lyrik as a "classical text" (SelWr 4.215).

In each of the commentaries, he endeavors to defuse the obvious reproaches of Brecht's literature in advance by taking Brecht's texts literally

---

26. That in those same months of 1938, in which Benjamin undertook to write his "Commentary on Poems by Brecht," the "special treatment" of the interned Jews was already being practiced in Buchenwald, with which the Holocaust was initiated, is testified to by, for example, *Deadwood* (1946), by Ernst Wiechert, who was detained there in July and August and wrote down his memories in 1939. See the afterword to the new edition of the text by Klaus Briegleb, "Shoah 1938. Nachwort-Essay," in Ernst Wiechert, *Der Totenwald* (Frankfurt/M: Suhrkamp, 2008).

and attempting to expose a critical core in them. He obviously defends
Brecht from accusations of indecency, as when he writes that in Brecht's
*Hauspostille* such things as God, the people, homeland, and the bride are
spoken of "the way they should be spoken of before irresponsible, aso-
cial people: without shame, either false or genuine" (216). He furthermore
claims that the title, *Hauspostille*, is an ironic one: "The word comes neither
from Sinai nor from the Gospels. The source of its inspiration is bourgeois
society" (216). Yet when bourgeois society is conceptualized as a hell, it reveals that even though Brechtian verse owes itself to an infernal inspiration,
at the same time it exploits the entire repertoire of Christian iconography
and pathos that his chosen genres and *topoi* convey: a cult of capitalism as
hell, or a type of negative theology of bourgeois society depicted as infernal.

This poetic praxis also describes the exact opposite of the poetology
developed in the Kraus essay: there, it is centered on the *summoning-by-
the-name* (*Beim-Namen-Nehmen*) of the words; here, on a sacralization of
social critique.

## The Traces of Concealment
## in Benjamin's Commentary on Brecht

It is particularly eye-catching that at each point at which Brecht emerges
as the antipode or opponent for him, Benjamin barely establishes a connection to his own theoretical reflections. In this respect, the hidden traces of
Benjamin's thought on Brecht's programs are particularly symptomatic because of their position in Benjamin's writings: they concern all those thematic correspondences that are *not* voiced in the commentaries on Brecht.

Benjamin did not relate the relationship between the pursuit
of happiness in *Mahagonny* and the religious matrix of the piece to his
"Theological-Political Fragment," in which he depicts the relation of the
profane order to the messianic in an image, a counterstriving constellation,
of two arrows that point in different directions and yet foster each other.
He writes that "theocracy has no political, but only a religious meaning"
(SelWr 3.305), and from the perspective of this apodictic statement a radical critique of each elision of the difference between the profane pursuit
of happiness and messianic intensity must ensue. The same applies to the
figure of Moses and his court, who takes the figure of an avenging God as
the model for a quasi-divine injustice, when placed within the framework

of the "Critique of Violence," the matrix of whose philosophy of history is grounded in the opposition of mythic to divine violence.

Particularly conspicuous is the fact that Benjamin does not take the religious *topoi* in Brecht's critique of capitalism as an occasion to return to his own reflections in "Capitalism as Religion" (1921). This fragment does *not* present a religious stance in opposition to capitalism, but rather it analyzes the cultic character of capitalism itself, which Benjamin describes as purely a cult religion and interprets it as a type of secularized Christianity: "The Christianity of the Reformation period did not favor the growth of capitalism; instead it transformed itself into capitalism" (SelWr 1.290). These analyses of the Christian genesis of capitalism and continued existence of Christian elements *in* capitalism (such as the relationship of guilt (*Schuld/Schulden*) to money)[27] render impossible any critique of capitalism that is tied up in Christian narrative and avails itself of a Christian morality as an instrument of its critique—such as the Brechtian critique.

If the biblical commandments—which in fact obey more of a rhetoric of prohibition ("Thou shalt not . . .")—are inverted and become commandments of permissiveness in *Mahagonny*, then a deadly social order is established that appears as an anthropologic anarchy of human drives, as it were. Yet Benjamin wants them to be read as infernal anarchy of bourgeois society, and thus the horrors of this society appear greater than the horrors of hell. This image of everlasting hell in *Mahagonny* is not at this point brought into connection with Benjamin's own images with similar motifs—for example, the cultural-historical diagnosis that he made in the context of the Arcades project: "Modernity, the time of hell" (Benjamin, *The Arcades Project* 159). This statement does not bear on the social and moral relations of bourgeois society but is rather (as will be shown in Chapter 10) derived from Benjamin's studies on photography and film and the rhythm of modern life as it is conditioned by apparatuses and media.

27. Translator's note: The German word "Schuld" denotes both guilt and debt. The word thus always presents a particular difficulty when attempting to render it in English. This double meaning is often used to great effect in German texts, linking its moral sense to the economic. In *Mahagonny*, we see this confluence in Paul Ackermann's mortal "crime" or sin of owing money for his bar tab. See Sigrid Weigel, "Shylocks Wiederkehr. Die Verwandlung von Schuld in Schulden oder: Zum symbolischen Tausch der Wiedergutmachung," in Sigrid Weigel and Birgit R. Erdle (eds.), *50 Jahre danach. Zur Nachgeschichte des Nationalsozialismus* (Zürich: VDF, 1995), 165–192.

The review of the *Threepenny Novel* eventually raises the question as to how the concept of nudity in it is related to Benjamin's concept of the creaturely and his critique of law. About *Threepenny Novel*, he writes: "Brecht strips naked the conditions in which we live, removing the drapery of legal concepts. The human emerges from these conditions as naked as it will be when it is handed down to posterity. Unfortunately, it looks dehumanized, but that is not the satirist's fault. His task is to undress his fellow citizen" (SelWr 3.9). Indeed, neither in the "Critique of Violence" nor in his essay on Kraus is law judged to be a mere costume for bare life without which 'the human' would be dehumanized, because this would mean only law makes the creature into a human. In Benjamin's writings, the concept of the human is developed (as shown in the preceding chapters) through a complex relationship between two spheres, the 'supernatural' element reaching back to a prelegal, biblical notion.

## The Moment of Danger

Regarding the dialogue between Benjamin and Brecht, it is striking that the tension that grows from the two authors' differing ways of dealing with biblical tradition are rarely addressed explicitly—least of all those tensions between Jewish and Christian tradition, but with the exception of the controversy surrounding Benjamin's Kafka essay. Benjamin's diary entries hand down three conversations held with Brecht about Kafka from the summer of 1934: from July 6 and August 5 and 31. The first conversation concerns parables. When Brecht, who at this point still holds Kafka to be a great writer, takes the position that Kafka's starting point is the parable, then by 'parable' he means "the allegory, which is answerable to reason and hence cannot be entirely in earnest on the literal plane" (SelWr 2.784). From this, he follows that "in Kafka . . . parable is in conflict with the visionary" (785). Benjamin will take Brecht's contempt of the literal as an opportunity in his Kafka essay to diagnose the opposite: Kafka's parables are "not parables and do not want to be taken at face value" (SelWr 2.803; emphasis S.W.). In contrast to Brecht, he regards them as emblematic stories without attempting to translate them into a lesson.

The second conversation takes place after Brecht has already had Benjamin's Kafka essay in hand more than three weeks and after Benjamin took it back without comment since Brecht has said nothing about it during this time. The conversation begins with Brecht abruptly airing a reproach that Benjamin is not free from a "writing in diary form, in the style of Nietzsche" (786), that rips the work out of its contexts. In the meantime, Brecht has also become negatively disposed toward Kafka. Throughout his polemic, he allows himself to get carried away, describing Kafka as a "jewboy," an "unpleasant figure, a bubble on the iridescent surface of the swamp of Prague's cultural life, and nothing more" (VI/527ff.; SelWr 2.786). This polemic in no way tries to hide its anti-Semitic connotation. Ultimately, Brecht is even more decisive: "'I reject Kafka [...] the images are good. The rest is just mystery-mongering. It is nonsense'" (786). Benjamin, anything but a polemicist, suggests that the controversial assessment of Kafka's literature should be supported by a specific text and proposes the story "The Next Village," a short story of a grandfather's musings that the span of a life, in which memories crowd themselves, is so amazingly short that a young man's decision to ride to the next village seems incomprehensible. Brecht reacts by temporalizing the suggestion.

In the third conversation, Brecht sharpens his reproaches and charges that Benjamin's essay "promoted Jewish fascism. It increased and spread confusion about this figure, instead of dissipating it" (787). Brecht feels the need in Kafka for practical proposals "that could be distilled from his stories" (787). His subsequent interpretations make it clear that he treats Kafka's images in such a way that he does not take the text literally but rather interprets the story as allegory. Since Brecht did not like Kafka's 'teachings,' he adjusts them: however short life may be, "[t]his doesn't matter, because the man who started out on his journey is different from the man who arrives" (788). Although Brecht's interpretation is therefore guided by a possible message, Benjamin's follows the image logic of the story instead.[28] The true measure of life is memory: "[l]ooking back, it runs through life like lightning," just as one can "turn back a few pages" (788). From this reading, he distills an image of central importance for the Kafka essay, the image of life that, read backwards, transforms into text: "Reversal is the direction of study which transforms existence into script" (815).

In these conversations about Kafka, the controversies over the reading of literature's wording are sites wherein tensions become visible. They bear not only on the relationship to tradition and engagement with the sacred (concepts of divine orders, law, and writing) but also on the *danger* of

---

28. This contrast has been worked out in detail in Stéphane Mosès' reading "Brecht und Benjamin als Kafka-Interpretation," in Stéphane Mosès and Albrecht Schöne, eds., *Juden in der deutschen Literatur. Ein deutsch-israelisches Symposium (Frankfurt/M: Suhrkamp, 1986)*, 248.

anti-Semitism that lurks in the resentment toward writing—in particular where this is reinforced by a utilization of biblical rhetoric and the tone of holy scripture.

Although Benjamin was at first clearly fascinated by Brecht (particularly by Brecht as a dramatist and satirist), a growing alienation arose through the years despite his social network, because of Brecht's political position, which Benjamin had presumably hidden from himself for a long time, similar to the thoughts that eventually arose from his text "On the Concept of History." His distance to Brecht remained concealed until it was expressed quite abruptly and in full clarity in a critical note to the *Reader for Those Who Live in Cities* from 1938 (c.f. 6/435). Informed by Heinrich Blücher's suggestion, Benjamin now discovers that indeed "the procedures in which the worst elements of the Communist party resonate with the most unscrupulous ones of National Socialism" are reflected in several of Brecht's poems. He there now also discovers a transfiguration of the "dangerous and momentous errors into which GPU practices had led the workers' movement."[29] In his critique of Brecht's poems he thus must then include his own self-criticism of the transfiguration of these texts. With reference to his commentary on the third poem of the *Lesebuch*, Benjamin notes: "At any rate, the commentary, in the form I gave it, is a pious falsification, a *cover-up of the communal guilt* Brecht owes to the respective development" (VI/540; SelWr 4.159; emphasis S.W.).

The poem and its commentary concern the state of Jews living under Nazi policy. More specifically, they reference the expulsion of the Jews from Germany in the pogroms of 1938. Years before, Benjamin had interpreted Brecht's poem as showing "why National Socialism needs anti-Semitism" (SelWr 4.234), and in an approving tone added that Brecht interprets the attitude of the Nazis toward the Jews as a parody and caricature of a revolutionary stance: "The attitude toward the Jews that is artificially elicited by the rulers is precisely the one that would be natural for the oppressed to adopt toward the rulers. The Jew shall, according to Hitler, be treated, as the great exploiter ought to have been treated" (II.2/558; SelWr 4.234). Now, in his notes written only a short time later, he admits that Blücher is correct and had already recognized a sadistic element in the attitude of Brecht's poem itself and reads the verse "(This is how we speak to our fa-

29. GPU, Glawnoje Politischeskoje Uprawlenije, the political arm of the Soviet state police.

thers)" (SelWr 4.234) as evidence that in no way the voice of the worker is expressed in Brecht's poem, rather "that what is involved here is not an expropriation of the expropriators which is in favor of the proletariat but in favor of stronger expropriators—that is to say, the young ones" (159). Inspired by Blücher's critique, Benjamin reflects now, in the notes in his journals, on the problem of complicity and shared guilt.

Benjamin could not have remained unaffected when he realized that he had become so close to Brecht as to let himself get carried away with a "pious falsification" and a "cover-up of communal guilt" and that this happened to him, of all things, in respect of anti-Semitism. It can be assumed that this experience found its way into the theses "On the Concept of History," in the passage that deals with the "moment of danger." To articulate the past historically means "appropriating a memory as it flashes up in a moment of danger" (391). Up to this point, the fifth thesis has attracted a great deal of attention. Rather less is it noted that the very danger of which Benjamin speaks here not only comes from without but is also the danger contained in complicity: "The danger threatens both the content of the tradition and those who inherit it. For both, it is one and the same thing: the danger of becoming a tool of the ruling classes" (391).

It is striking that in this fifth thesis Benjamin speaks not only of *tradition* but also of the inheritance that in every age must again be wrested from conformism—without specifying in greater detail what this may mean. Since the following sentence moves the discourse without further ado to that of the Messiah and of that historian who strives to rekindle the spark of hope, tradition quite clearly means the place of the messianic in the understanding of history. Regarding the fact that Brecht's texts lack any sense of messianism yet use Christian iconography and biblical language for their negative theology of capitalism, one can assume that Benjamin scarcely thought of him as he conceived the thought-image of the chess-playing automaton in 1940. Through this puppet, he describes in which ways certainty in the victory of 'historical materialism' ("The puppet, called 'historical materialism' is to win all the time"; 389) is indebted to theology's being taken into service when it is hidden within the mirrored apparatus: the puppet named historical materialism "can easily be a match for anyone if it enlists the services of theology, which today, as we know, is small and ugly and has to be kept out of sight" (389).

# 6

## Jewish Thinking in a World Without God

*Benjamin's Readings of Kafka as a Critique of
Christian and Jewish Theologoumena*

Benjamin's writings on Kafka are symptomatic for his work. The
then-unpublished texts, as well as the notes and correspondence related
to the studies on Kafka that are traceable for a period of at least the thir-
teen years from 1925 to 1938 (Paralipomena, GS II.3/1153–1264), exceed the
amount of work on Kafka published in articles during his lifetime many
times over. The lecture "Franz Kafka: *Beim Bau der chinesischen Mauer*,"
written for a 1931 posthumous volume of Kafka's unpublished work edited
by Max Brod and H. J. Schoeps, was broadcast only once, on *Frankfurter
Rundfunk* on March 7, 1931. A previously "planned book about Kafka,
Proust, etc." (3/379) that had been under contract with the publisher
Rowohlt never materialized. Instead, the notebooks grew: collections of
motifs, attempts at outlines, citations, and the "Dossier of Others' Commentaries and Own Reflections."

Benjamin was only ever able to hold a few of his writings on Kafka
in print in his hands. First, the short article "Cavalier Morals" (*Kavaliers-
moral*), in which he defended Brod's decision to ignore Kafka's request
that his writings be destroyed posthumously, appeared in the *Literarischen Welt* on October 10, 1929. He defends Brod from the "comfort-
able, extremely obvious indictment of a friend's breached obligations"
(IV.1/466). Then, at the end of 1934, two of the four chapters of his essay

---

The title of this chapter is taken from that of a commemorative publication for Stéphane
Mosès (Mattern et al., 2000). The chapter is concerned with the Jewish character of Kafka's
writings, hence the title.

"Franz Kafka: On the Tenth anniversary of his Death" were published in the *Jüdischen Rundschau*: "Potemkin" and "The Little Hunchback." The plan, one he described in a letter to Dolf Sternberger as "interrupted, not ended" (4/487), to revise this work with the intention to "release an expanded version in book form"—as he wrote to Adorno on July 1, 1935 (5/13)—was likewise never realized. His efforts (through Gershom Scholem) to interest the publisher Schocken in the project were not crowned with success, although this intent pervaded his letters like a repeatedly flickering spark of hope as the possibilities for publication in Nazi Germany began to dwindle. Even the critical review of Brod's biography of Kafka, which he sent to Scholem in June 1938 (so that Scholem could give it to Schocken), never found its way into the pages of the *Feuilleton*. Moreover, this criticism of Brod, expanded by "a new perspective, more or less independent of my earlier reflections" (6/110), contains the quintessence of his readings of Kafka, after it had been honed through debates with Scholem, Brecht, and Adorno. In this "terrain," Benjamin himself saw "a number of strategic points that lie in today's thinking," so that the "the efforts to further secure it will not be useless" (BK 99). Not until two decades after the partial publication and fifteen years after Benjamin's death was the Kafka essay known in its full scope through Adorno's two-volume edition of the *Writings* in 1955. The significance of the Kafka complex for his thought was first visible, however, in the extensive "Paralipomena" in the *Selected Writings*.

## Kafka's Significance for Benjamin's Thinking

The efforts made to find a proper reading of Kafka are a key element of Benjamin's theory. It is an attempt to counter the predominantly theological interpretation with one that, without "interpreting Kafka's whole work after a theological pattern" (SelWr 2.806), nevertheless allows multifaceted references to figures and concepts from theology and Jewish tradition. Unlike in many exegeses of the mysterious and enigmatic elements within the tradition, Benjamin is fascinated with literature as asylum for theological content "at their moment of maximum jeopardy, in their most threadbare disguise," as he formulated in his review of Willy Haas's *Figures of the Age* (429). He acknowledges that Haas discovered "a theology on the run" in Kafka (430). By contrast, Benjamin wants to distinguish himself decisively from every kind of Theologoumena—both from "those hideous pacesetters of Protestant Theologoumena" that he referenced in a letter to Scholem on February 28, 1933, and from those "Jewish Theologoumena" that one "wanted to find" in Kafka's work, as he noted in his "Attempt at a schematic of Kafka" (GS II.3/1192). Benjamin's work focuses instead on the "interpreting of a writer from the center of his image world" (SelWr 2.495).

He uses this image world to study the survival of attitudes and concepts that originate in religious and cultic traditions (such as guilt, punishment, Creation, redemption, the last judgment, hope, waiting or *Erwartung*, original sin, or shame) in a world in which knowledge of their origin is forgotten because religious laws and tenets are obliterated—just as the hope for redemption has vanished. With this in mind, Benjamin speaks of a "sickening of tradition" (SelWr 3.326) in the critique of Max Brod. Thus he interprets the world of Kafka's figures less as a type of "'inverse' theology," as Adorno suggested (BA 67), and more as a kind of *negative* or *inverted messianism*. Kafka's characters are those in waiting, who find themselves accused of bearing an unknown guilt and set out in a confused topography. Here "waiting" takes on a completely different meaning than it does in profane illumination (such as in the Surrealism essay), because the stubbornness and squalor of Kafka's personae highlighted by Benjamin correspond to the deferral of their actions and to those endless and aimless paths and deliberations of actors who neither grasp nor master the laws of their existence: "This scurrying away seems to the author the only appropriate behavior for the isolated members of his generation and [his] surrounding world unaware of the law. Yet this absence of law is the result of a process of development" (III/101; SelWr 2.498).

For Benjamin, the outdatedness of Kafka's characters is the sign of their contemporaneity. They are products of a dawning twentieth century that Benjamin described in a 1928 review as follows: "The first decades of this century stand under the sign of technology. Good! But that only means something to those who know that they proceed under the sign of the resurgence of ritual and cultic traditions as well" (III/101). In his 1938 critique of Brod's biography, Benjamin summed up the sign of the era in Kafka's literature similarly:

Kafka's work is an ellipse; its widely spaced focal points are defined, on the one hand, by mystical experience (which is, above all, the experience of tradition) and, on the other hand, by the experience of the modern city-dweller. When I speak of the experience of the modern city-dweller, I mean various things. First of all I'm talking about the citizen of the modern state, confronted by an unfathomable bureaucratic apparatus [ . . . ] But by modern city-dweller I also mean the contemporary of present-day physicists." (6/110; SelWr 3.325)

The interplay of technology and ritual (such as with *In the Penal Colony*) or the simultaneity of the mystical (that is to say, traditional) and the modern (in the form of ungraspable political instances and physical aporias of space, such as in *The Castle*) constitute the framework for Benjamin's interpretation of Kafka's contemporaneity.

### The Creaturely and Higher Order

Coming from ancient, forgotten traditions and rehearsed through physiognomies and gestures, Kafka's characters lack knowledge of the origins of their customs and conduct. Least of all do they possess knowledge of these customs' descent from theology or religion. For Kafka, the "modern man" is "a stranger, an outcast who is unaware of the laws that connect his body to higher and vaster orders" (II.2/680; SelWr 2.497). Because of the lost connection to the "higher orders," he is bound to the being of a creature, namely to mere life, to employ the terminology from "Critique of Violence." Whereas Kafka's characters move in the shadows of a fallen-off culture of religion and forgotten laws, Benjamin's interpretation of Kafka (in that it takes into consideration theological and Jewish aspects without itself producing a Theologoumenon) follows the methodology he developed of a *saving critique*: the illumination of phenomena at the moment of their historical disappearance. As an epistemic constellation, the saving critique represents the counterpart to either *origination* (*Entspringen*), i.e., the moment of appearance in a historical site, or *awakening* as textbook examples of dialectical thinking.

Motifs of a *dialectic of secularization* are again condensed within the Kafka complex, motifs with which Benjamin returns to earlier work. This work was initially focused on language (as in the essay on language of 1916 and the theory of translation from 1921) but thereafter involves not only historical-theoretical and anthropological dimensions but also a critical engagement with political theory and a literature that appears as a crypto-religion (as explicated in the previous chapters). There, it was focused on concepts such as happiness and hope, law and justice, and on indebted life, or rather the "guilt nexus of the living" (II.I/175; GS 1.307) that exists between the poles of natural life (that is, sexuality) and super-natural life. These terms surface again a decade later, complemented by such concepts as law and judgment, witnessing (*Zeugenschaft*) and procreation (*Zeugung*), and Creation and the creaturely. The relationship among guilt, sexuality, and knowledge connects (as the Paralipomena also verify) the Kafka complex with Kraus's position "on the threshold of the Last Judgment" (SelWr 2.443) as in the essay published near the same time. Yet even though Kraus, also without writing from the perspective of a history of salvation, acts as "a deserter to the camp of the creaturely" (II.I/341; SelWr 2.438), Benjamin discovers a world in Kafka's literature populated entirely by creatures. Their hopelessness, however, yields its own beauty (II.2/413). Amid the studies on an "*Urgeschichte der Moderne*" and the theory of optical media, in whose aspects an afterlife of religion plays a rather marginal role, the essays on Kafka and Kraus constitute a unique complex. Linked together through central terms that correspond to theological ones, the name of an author (and thereby literature) stands each time at the center point.

## Before the Library: Benjamin's Dream of a Library

Benjamin's message to Scholem in July 1925 counts as a "first evidence of the engagement with Kafka" (GS II.3/1153) in which he asked for "some things by Kafka that are among his papers" to review. At the same time, he indicates: "Just as I did ten years ago, I still consider his short story 'Before the Law' ('Vor dem Gesetz') to be one of the best German short stories" (BS 279).[1] However, since this text was actually first published in 1919 (in *The Country Doctor*), his memory obviously extended the time of his familiarity with Kafka's text. It cannot be determined how many of his works were actually known to Benjamin at this point, one year after Kafka's death, but it is obvious that his intensive reading of Kafka began no earlier than 1925. From 1927 on, the evidence mounts. In January 1927, he had, for example, not yet read *The Castle*, as shown by his reaction to

1. *The Correspondence of Walter Benjamin and Gershom Scholem, 1932–1940* (Cambridge: Harvard UP, 1992).

Krakauer's review: he wanted to postpone reading Krakauer's text until he "had read and knew *The Castle*" (3/229).

In November of the same year, he sends to Scholem the first known sketch on Kafka, "The Idea of a Mystery." In it, we find a sentence, "there is torture and martyrdom" (SelWr 2.68), that seems to refer to more than the novel *The Trial*. Benjamin read the novel during a bout of jaundice—"I have Kafka beside my bed as an angel of my sickness (*Krankenengel*)" (3/303)—and indeed, as he admits in a letter to the Cohns, he read it while "almost suffering torments (so overwhelming is the inconspicuous plenitude of this book)" (3/312). The torment of reading becomes a topic again in a letter he writes to Scholem in October 1931 about the posthumous volume *Beim Bau der chinesischen Mauer*. Brecht, he writes, "seemed to devour even the posthumous volume, whereas some things in it have resisted my efforts to the present day because of my physical torment while reading" (BS 384). This resistance suggests a mimetic approach to reading with which the "crawling into hiding (*Verkrochenheit*)" of Kafka's "creations from all orders" (GS II.2/681) is transferred to the reader and reading is transformed into physical torment.

These resistances did not end Benjamin's effort to develop his own interpretation of Kafka. For this project there were completely different hurdles to overcome. This is shown by the dream of a library that he relates to Werner Kraft in April 1935, a decade after the first indications of his reading of Kafka:

Recently I had a dream in which I saw someone unknown get up from the desk and take a book out of his library. The sight was shocking for me and my shock cast a sharp light on my situation. / Take this as a small ancillary motif (small, but hardly devoid of conviction) to my wish for books and send me, if possible, the Kafka letters from the *Festschrift* for Brod. (5/70)

The letter, written in a hotel in Monaco-Condamine, is an eloquent piece of evidence for the waning "work equipment" for "*le première critique de la littérature allemande*" (3/502). As a "freelance writer" in exile, Benjamin found himself in an extended struggle for publication opportunities and remuneration (he had been offered 60 Reichsmarks for the Kafka article) from which, writing to Scholem in September 1934, he concludes: "thus you will understand that the continuous engagement with objects of pure literature should have first found its conclusion in the work on Kafka" (4/496). Aggravating above all was the lack of his own library. Conditions such as those during the time he wrote the radio address—times when he could still write a text like "Unpacking My Library"—were long gone. Since his emigration from Germany in March 1933, his residence constantly changed. At times he lived in a hotel in Paris; at times (as in the summer of 1934) with Brecht in Denmark, where he could shelter a part of his library; or with his ex-wife in San Remo the following winter.

Starting in 1928, we find efforts to acquire all of Kafka's publications, especially the early titles. In May 1928, he lacks *The Castle* and *Amerika*, "to say nothing of the rare, out-of-print *Meditation* [*Betrachtung*]. This is the only early Kafka work I still do not have" (CBS 336). In April 1934 he reported to Scholem that some volumes of Kafka also belonged among his books rescued in Denmark. At the same time, however, he laments the "loss of the *Trial* that was stolen several years ago" (433). When he received a contract for delivery of an article on the tenth anniversary of Kafka's death on June 3, 1934, in May of the same year he informs Robert Weltsch, editor in chief of the *Jüdischen Rundschau*, of the "bibliographical difficulties" posed by the inaccessibility of his library and asks if he could be loaned some "works that are almost impossible [ . . . ] to get here—*Trial, Country Doctor, Metamorphosis, Amerika*" (442). A short time later, he writes Scholem in Jerusalem: "If everything else fails, I possibly would telegraph you the titles of the most important books I don't have—i.e., ask you to lend them to me if possible. (Unfortunately, the technical side of the matter is complicated by the deadline.)" (113) Then, in June, he found *The Trial* by chance "in a French bookshop at the original price," but adds, "I don't want to neglect to say that the person who could come up from there [Palestine, S.W.] with a copy of *Betrachtung*, which my library still lacks, would achieve late, if great, honors" (115). Finally he expresses the hope that Schocken would send him an "honorary copy" (*Ehrenexemplar*) from the planned collected works of Kafka. At the beginning of June—when the date of the anniversary of Kafka's death had passed, the preparatory work for the Kafka article was "concluded yesterday," and the departure to Denmark was imminent—Benjamin can finally announce in a letter to Gretel Adorno: "I was successful in assembling all of Kafka's works here, but it required an unbelievable effort" (BG 441).[2] "Here" is Paris. Shortly thereafter, however, he finds himself with Brecht in Skovsbostrand. He begins the epistolary controversy with Scholem over Kafka from there, during which time he asks Scholem

2. *Briefwechsel Walter Benjamin/Gretel Adorno 1930–1940* (Berlin: Suhrkamp, 2005).

to return his manuscript on several occasions. In February 1935, after Benjamin has moved to San Remo, the receipt of the first volume of Kafka's *Collected Works* is an opportunity "to reapply [himself] to [his] manuscript," and to begin "by expanding and reorganizing the second part" (BS 154).

Two months later, on the way from San Remo to Paris, Benjamin is overtaken by the dream of a library. The dream, which he linked to the request for a Kafka book in a message to Kraft, signals that the torment of reading was in the meantime superseded by the anguish of not having his library with him: "I notice, that having worked many years in libraries and having handled, at minimum, thousands of alphabetic characters every week, has created an *almost physical* need, which has now been unfulfilled for a long time. Recently I had a dream [ . . . ]" (70; emphasis S.W.). The dream that then follows is a dream "beyond the pleasure principle" since it reserves the depiction of a fulfilled wish for another person. The latter, however, is located *before the library*, as it were. The history of Benjamin's writings on Kafka spans the same period of time as his Kafka *readings*. Starting from the first sketch in 1927 and continuing up to the critique of Brod's biography in 1938, a trace of Kafka runs for an entire decade through Benjamin's manuscripts, notes, and letters.

## A Historical-Theoretical Thought-Image

The short sketch "The Idea of a Mystery" (1927), which was the result of Benjamin's reading of Kafka's posthumously published novel *The Trial* (1925), initiates a kind of monad and condensed leitmotif for his reading of Kafka: "To represent history as a trial in which man, as an advocate of dumb nature, at the same time brings charges (*Klage führt*) against all Creation and the failure of the promised Messiah to appear" (SelWr 2.68). While the jury flees the court in which the trial is conducted, the only remaining entities are the witnesses for the coming of the messiah (the poet, artist, musician, and philosopher appear as such), and the human accuser. Thus the human voice of the accusation/lament[3] and the philosophical and artistic witnesses of the messianic stand directly opposite each other

---

3. Benjamin here already refers to the interplay between juridical accusation (*Anklage*) and lamentation (*Klage*), as described in the first chapter, by way of using the phrase "Klage führen" in front of a court.

without any judging authority between them. The endlessness of the "new complaints" and "new witnesses" is traced back to the indecisiveness of the court concerning the question of the messiah.

This brief text does not actually offer an interpretation of *The Trial*. The latter is rather an occasion to formulate a *historical-theoretical thought-image* of the notion of history as a process, or the last judgment. Thus, in the first sentence, Benjamin cites the "laconic statement that Hegel took from Schiller: world history is the world's court of judgment (*Weltgeschichte ist das Weltgericht*)."[4] This, however, occurs with a remarkable reversal of positions. In Hegel's *Philosophy of Right* (1821) the world spirit exercises its right over existing minds "in *world history* as the *world's court of judgment*." History thus appears as a courtroom scene in which the world spirit exerts *its* right.[5] Benjamin's constellation differentiates itself from this scene considerably. In his image of a world court, the human comes to the stage as prosecutor, as the one who "brings charges," while standing *on the threshold* of the world court in the sense of Last Judgment, as he wrote in the essay on Kraus, whose preparatory work was undertaken at the same time as "The Idea of a Mystery": "If he ever turns his back on *Creation*, if he breaks off *lamenting* (*Klagen*), it is only to make an *accusation* (*anzuklagen*) at the *Last Judgement* (Weltgericht)" (II.I/349; SelWr 2.443).

In "Goethe's *Elective Affinities*," Benjamin described the *Mysterium* as a breach of a "higher" realm into poetic language (SelWr 1.355). This constellation will be assigned to the concept of history in "The Idea of a Mystery": The description of history *as* a trial (*Prozeß*), not as a process (*Prozeß*), means that the charges brought by humans, who (like Joseph K. in *The Trial*) stand in the midst of history and are subject to secular authorities, are addressed to a Law based on the image of divine justice. This is also why it is impossible for the aforementioned court to come to a verdict. Benjamin thus places Kafka's notions of the trial and the court of law within contexts of a theory of language and history in which their double illumination within a terrestrial *and* divine order is at stake. The twofold position of humans—sharing in "nature" *and* a higher order—is the point of departure of Benjamin's readings of Kafka, to which he returns time and again.

4. Willem Van Reijen and Herman Van Doorn, eds., *Aufenthalte und Passagen. Leben und Werk Walter Benjamins* (Frankfurt/M: Suhrkamp, 2001), 147.

5. G.W.F. Hegel, *Elements of the Philosophy of Right* (Cambridge: Cambridge UP, 1991), 371.

### Literature as Sanctuary for Theological Secrets

"Cavalier Morality," which appeared two years later in the *Literarischen Welt* of October 25, 1929, contrasts an "ethical maxim" toward concealment, one that has been criticized by Benjamin, with a very different concept of secrecy. By highlighting the esoteric-exoteric structure in Kafka's work, Benjamin implicitly places it in the tradition of Jewish secularization. Here, poetry becomes a place for concerns that slip away from theology:

Kafka's work, which is about the darkest concerns of human life (concerns which theologians have time and again attended to, but seldom poets in the way that Kafka has done), derives its poetic greatness precisely from the fact that it carries this *theological secret* entirely within itself, while appearing outwardly inconspicuous and plain and sober. (IV.1, 467; emphasis S.W.)[6]

The reading proposed here, that Kafka's plain poetic language is the place—or shelter—of theological secrets that bear on the "darkest concerns of human life," continues in a remark in Benjamin's review of Haas's *Figures of the Age* (*Gestalten der Zeit*) (1930): the attention of the writer is awakened by works that "grant asylum to theological contents at their moment of maximum jeopardy, in their most threadbare disguise" (SelWr 2.429). Benjamin acknowledges that Haas's stance points the way forward for his own interpretations of Kafka: it points "the way to future exegeses of this writer through an interpretation that energetically presses forward to theological questions at every point" (430).

The title of the subsequent article, "Theological Criticism," published in 1931 in the *Neuen Rundschau*, already signals Benjamin's conflict with the possibilities and limits of theological interpretation. The esoteric nature of Kafka's works, their "theological secret" that is articulated in poetic language without being said, surfaces here again in the *topos* of "productive experiences," experiences "for which he could vouch and that he would never betray, never blurt out" (428). Among the "figures of the age" are two "to whom the author of this book is indebted for such *incommunicable* experiences—experiences that oblige him to testify. These are figures with whom he has kept faith, and who now act as patron saints, presiding over his book on its path through the contemporary world: Franz Kafka and Hugo von Hofmannsthal" (III/275; SelWr 2.428; emphasis S.W.). When Benjamin

6. Translation by Georgina Paul.

mentions the *incommunicable* he refers to his theory of language and the possibility formulated within it that the incommunicable (or the magical, that is to say the mimetic, side of language) can appear through the semiotic armature (*Fundus*) of language. This notion is liberated from a theological nexus of justification and delivered to cultural anthropology, and, in texts written in 1933 in Berlin and Ibiza—"Doctrine of the Similar" and "On the Mimetic Faculty"—the theological element of the incommunicable is discussed again in the context of the Kafka complex. The proximity of theology and semblance (*Schein*) that Benjamin observes in Willy Haas's book (SelWr 2.276) is reminiscent of the concept of the *expressionless* argued for in the essay on Goethe and of the discussion of the "divine ground of the being of beauty" that lies in mystery.

In the review of Haas, the *incommunicable* is, however, linked to witnessing: the writer is a witness to the coming of the messiah and the "theological secret" that he sees concealed in Kafka's stories of trials, courtrooms, and the law. Benjamin thereby describes Kafka in a position that already here sketches out an image of a corporal or literal reversal within the history of Jewish secularization: Kafka "in Prague, in the camp of the degenerate Jewish intelligentsia, where in the name of Judaism he turned away from Judaism, turning his threatening and impermeable back on it" (III/275; SelWr 2.428). This constellation, namely, turning away from the Jewish history *in the name of Judaism*, represented as a return incarnate, gives rise to the figure that plays such a prominent role in the entire essay: that of the return. In turning away from the dominant progression of tradition modeled as a return in the direction of history and prehistory—described in images—is the thought-image of the angel of history prefigured: "because there is indeed a storm that blows from oblivion. And study is the ride that counters it" (II.2/436).

## From the Midst of the Image World

In the radio address "Frank Kafka: *Beim Bau der chinesischen Mauer*," broadcast in July of that year, Benjamin expresses his own method of engagement with Kafka's literature with the formula of an interpretation *"from the midst of his image world"* (II.2/275; SelWr 2.495; emphasis S.W.) and sets this against theological exegesis—or, more precisely, against an interpretation that foists a religious-philosophical scheme onto Kafka's books and thus enacts a "particular way of evading—or, one might almost say, of dismissing—Kafka's world" (SelWr 2.495). At the same time a shift in Benjamin's mode of writing takes place. As already seen in "The Idea of a Mystery," interpretations get substituted in parts by well-known legends that correspond with Kafka's legends; Beda Allemann speaks of this style as a succession of peculiar *Kafka analogies*.[7] Thus Benjamin begins by describing the short story "An Imperial Message" in its entirety, not in order to offer an interpretation ("I will not interpret this story for you") but rather poses the question as one of the author: "You need no guidance from me to realize that the person addressed here is, primarily, Kafka himself. But who, then, was Kafka? He has done everything in his power to bar the way to an answer" (495). Rather than introduce a biographical reading, this question thematizes a failure that would serve to identify the author's name with the *chiffre* K. This symbol tells us no more than the initials on a handkerchief or brim of a hat "and is certainly not enough to enable us to recognize the person who has disappeared" (495). With the key term "recognition," the biographical interpretation is brought into the realm of administrative profiling and litigation. Instead Benjamin presents a legend, followed by two more: one Talmudic and the other the legend of Sancho Panza. Benjamin will expand on both, devoting a chapter to each in his larger essay. The first of these three legends, that which concerns the author, is indeed not a legend about *Kafka* but rather a legend one can construct around Kafka: "It is as if he had spent his entire life wondering what he looked like, without ever discovering that there are such things as mirrors" (II.2/677; SelWr 2.495).

The interpretation of the writer "from the midst of his image world" itself follows a visual narrative procedure and considers Kafka's stories to be images beyond depiction, mimetic representation, or even reflection; they are rather "reflections [ . . . ] in reverse (*Gegensinn*)" (678; 496). This reversal refers to a specific temporal structure in Kafka's narratives: a simultaneity of ages at once contemporary and prophetic, and that reaches back into antiquity.[8] The fear in Kafka's creatures is "at one and the same

---

7. Beda Allemann, "Fragen an die judaistische Kafka-Deutung am Beispiel Benjamins," in Karl-Heinz Grözinger et al., eds., *Franz Kafka und das Judentum* (Frankfurt/M: Jüdischer Verlag bei Athenäum, 1987), 48.

8. On this temporal structure, see Hans Helmut Hiebel, *Die Zeichen des Gesetzes. Recht und Macht bei Franz Kafka* (Munich: Wilhelm Fink, 1983), 138; and Bernd Müller, *Denn es ist noch nichts geschehen. Walter Benjamins Kafka-Deutung* (Cologne: Bohlau, 1996), 11.

time and in equal measure both fear of the primeval, the immemorial, and also fear of what is close by, the immediate future with all its urgency" (SelWr 2.498). Furthermore, the "reversal" refers to the particular status of *symptoms* in the Freudian sense, that is to say, they are signs with inherent disfigurements or displacements. In direct reference to the June 6, 1931, journal entry (the conversation with Brecht about Kafka), Benjamin writes that Kafka's work is full of oddities that the reader can regard as nothing other than "little signs, indicators, and symptoms of the displacements that the writer feels approaching in every aspect of life without being able to adjust himself to the new orders" (II.2/678; SelWr 2.496). It remains for him only to respond with amazement and panicked horror to the *disfigurement of being.* In contrast to Brecht's talk of the "incomprehensible distortion of being" (II.3/1204), Benjamin shifts, in that he conceives of these as "symptoms of displacements," Kafka's imagistic narratives in the realm of Freud's discourse of the unconscious.[9] One cannot imagine any single event that would not be disfigured by the mere act of Kafka's describing or investigation: "In other words, everything he describes makes statements about something other than itself" (SelWr 2.496). In contrast to conventionalized forms of a metaphoric speech—such as parable or allegory—the Freudian *symptom* is defined as a mnemonic symbol (Erinnerungssymbol) whose displaced presentation includes moments of forgetting. Disfigurement (*Entstellung*) and displacement (*Verschiebung*) are—together with condensation (*Verdichtung*)—the most important processes of dreamwork. Benjamin also couples distortion in Kafka with *forgetting*: "For the clearest disfigurement that is characteristic of Kafka's world" results from the fact that due to the inscrutable past, the new presents itself in the figure of atonement so that the unknown guilt must be understood as forgetting. Kafka's literature is full of "configurations of forgetting" (498). The terms *symptom* and *disfigurement*, which surface for the first time here in Benjamin's work on Kafka, are leitmotifs of his further engagement with this literature. Disfigurement, understood as a "shift in the axis of salvation" (II.3/1201; SelWr 2.497 ), will play a central role in the disagreement with Scholem over his inter-

9. Disfigurement (*Entstellung*), as a concept in which Benjamin connects messianism and psychoanalysis, is one of the centerpieces of my earlier book on Benjamin, *Entstellte Ähnlichkeit* (Frankfurt/M: Fischer, 1997), a slightly different German version of *Body- and Image Space* (New York: Routledge, 1995).

pretation of Kafka as an emblem of Kafka's world, one that in Benjamin's reading distinguishes Kafka's world from the world of Kabbalah and the transmission of Jewish tradition. Disfigurement, described as that which is distinguished from revelation, also corresponds to Kafka's unfinished work. In the form of an unspeakable law, the *incommunicable* element within the "theological secret" returns here: "The fact that the law never finds expression as such in Kafka—this and nothing else is the gracious dispensation of the fragment" (II.2/679; SelWr 2.497).

Benjamin therefore claims that the alleged planned end of *The Castle* (in which K. dies as he is finally brought by a messenger from the castle permission to live in the village), rumored by Brod, is not a resolution of a riddle or completion of the novel. He recognizes in it rather a "Talmudic legend," an allegory: a princess (the soul) who finds herself in a village (the body) in exile among a people whose language she doesn't understand, and who pines for her fiancée, discovers through a letter that he (the Messiah) is on his way to her. The soul then prepares a meal for the body, "because she has no other way of communicating her joy, to the people around her who do not know her language" (SelWr 2.497). This legend answers the question "why Jews prepare a festive meal on Friday evening." One more displacement is called for, however, with which this legend can become an "analogy to Kafka": "It needs only a *minute shift of emphasis* in this story from the Talmud to find ourselves in the midst of Kafka's world. Modern man dwells in his body as K. does in the village: as a stranger, an outcast who is unaware of the laws that connect this body to higher and vaster orders" (II.2/680; SelWr 2.497; emphasis S.W.).

The Talmudic legend cited here offers a clarification of the sacred meaning of profane actions in Jewish ritual law. To that end he returns to the paradigm of body-soul duality and compares worship to the experience of linguistic alienation that comes with diaspora. In comparison to this allegoric legend, the "minute shift of emphasis" brings a completely different dimension into play. It is no longer about understanding, but rather a sheer lack of knowledge of the laws of the exercise of religion, since "[he] who lacks knowledge of the laws" is unaware not only of their content but also of their cultic sense in general. To him, the connection the body has to higher orders has been lost—the link between the creaturely (that is, bare life) and higher life. The disfigurement of the Talmudic legend that relocates us in the "midst of Kafka's world" touches on the forgetting of the religious meaning of waiting—just as K. waits in *The Castle* unaware that his waiting binds him to "higher and vaster orders."

This nonknowledge places the human creations in Kafka's world on the same level as other creatures, with animals. Thus one could follow his animal stories for a good while, "without even noticing that they do not deal with human beings at all" (497). Because "without partitions, creatures of every type mix indiscriminately," brought together only by the organ of anxiety. The "unknown guilt" (II.2/681; SelWr 2.497) that can be known to Kafka's characters only in the form of atonement is for Benjamin a symptom of forgetting, unknown laws, inscrutable past, and creatures that have lost a link to higher orders. "What has to be clarified is the relation among three things: law—memory—tradition," he writes in one of the journal entries from this time; "Kafka's work probably builds on these three" (II.3/1200). In this way, he interprets Kafka's literature as an expression of a disfigured tradition into which the misunderstood laws jut. In the debate with Scholem, Benjamin thus says that the law indicates in Kafka the "the dead point of his work" from which "the work cannot be moved in any interpretive direction" (BS 135).[10]

## Inscription in the Concepts of Jewish Tradition and the Primeval World

After the methodological parameters were set, the intensive work on the central Kafka essay began after the radio address. His engagements with available interpretations were now debates with friends, in the course of which Benjamin gave his understanding of Kafka sharper contours. Since the first manuscript (which he had sent before his departure to Svendborg in June 1934 from Paris to Jerusalem) is not available,[11] one cannot reconstruct to what degree the controversy with Scholem shaped the revision of his text. In any case, this debate sharpened "the question of 'theological interpretation'" (BS 128) in the question of Jewish tradition. Benjamin writes Scholem on August 11, 1934, informing him that he

10. See Gasché's investigation of Kafka's law as it is situated between Judaism and Hellenism: Rodolphe Gasché, "Kafka's Law: In the Field of Forces Between Judaism and Hellenism," in *Modern Language Notes*, vol. 117, no. 5, Dec. 2002, 971–1002.

11. The notebooks on this were published in GS II.3/1222–1245.

is putting "the finishing touches on the 'Kafka'" (134) and also responds to Scholem's objections. Yet the fact that he calls the *primeval world* a "historical-philosophical index" (135) of his interpretation can clearly be traced back to his reading of Bachofen during the same period. This plays a significant role in the "revision" written in Denmark. On September 27, the new manuscript went from there to Werner Kraft with a request for "comments on my Kafka" (119). Though the exchanges with Kraft and Adorno about Kafka begin only *after* the essay's completion, its conceptualization and revision was influenced by the debates with Scholem and Brecht as well as by the motifs of those works with which Benjamin was occupied in the interim: the swamp world from his essay "Johann Jakob Bachofen" (1935), the childhood photo of Kafka from the "Little History of Photography" (1931), gestic theater from "What Is Epic Theater?" (1931), and the motif of narration from "Experience and Poverty" (1933). The mode of writing, however, follows the method developed in the radio address, as the four parts of the larger essay present themselves in the form of legends that read Kafka's "fairy tales for dialecticians" (SelWr 2.799) as historico-theoretical images.

Here, Benjamin locates the specific character of Kafka's literature beyond the distinction between allegory and literature: between parable and prose, similar only to *Dichtung*. Kafka's parables unfold "the way a bud turns into a blossom." Their relation "to religious teachings [is] similar to the one Haggadah has to Halachah" (803). In other words, it is similar to the way narratives relate to the laws in Jewish oral tradition. With this comparison, Benjamin translates his previous interpretation of Kafka's texts from a standpoint of the philosophy of art (as the literary veil of a theological mystery, as evidence of incommunicable experiences, and as a disfigured legend of unknown laws) to concepts of Jewish tradition. Because Kafka's parables, however, know no tenet (*Lehre*) but rather allude to one, Benjamin assumes that they are at most *transmission of relics of a tenet* or that they may be considered its precursors. Kafka's literature would thereby be a transmission from something prior to and *beyond the tenet* (after it has been torn apart). Since both biographic-psychological and theological interpretations equally fail to address exactly this twofold place, Benjamin summarizes the critique of the review with the assertion that "[t]here are two ways to miss the point of Kafka's work. One is the natural exegesis; the other is the supernatural one" (II.2/425; SelWr 2.806).

Kafka's own failure is of a very different kind that, as Benjamin assumes, may have motivated the wish to have his manuscripts destroyed: "He did fail in his grandiose attempt to convert poetry (*Dichtung*) into tenet (*Lehre*)." Benjamin connects this failure to the prohibition on images: "No other writer has obeyed the commandment 'Thou shalt not make unto thee any graven image' so faithfully" (SelWr 2.808). Unlike in Brecht, Benjamin's concept of "*Lehre*" is linked to the context of a theological meaning without being synonymous with it.

## The Controversy with Scholem: Revelation and Distortion

The double exposure of the central terms (*Lehre, Entstellung,* and *Umkehr*) that are crucial for Benjamin's interpretation of Kafka is an intersection of the two theoretical disputes: with Brecht on one hand and Scholem on the other. He clearly needed the conflicts in order to more clearly distinguish his own method of reading within the now-familiar economy of arguments with his opponents, who function as antipodes (as discussed in Chapter 5). This is, in any case, indicated by his repeated requests for others' Kafka interpretations and for commentaries on his own manuscripts. It is remarkable how he deploys formulations from the debates and with small displacements uses them for his own interpretation. Whereas in the dispute with Brecht over Kafka both Brecht's position and Benjamin's visibly drifted apart more and more strongly, tensions in the written dialog with Scholem are expressed only indirectly.

Yet the correspondence with Gershom Scholem concerning Kafka[12] is not free from differences of opinion, especially as the discussion is doubly burdened: first, by the postal routes between Jerusalem and Denmark, stretches of which were sometimes delayed by detours through Paris; and second, by the fact that Benjamin must repudiate his friend's demand that he explain his relationship to communism: "Such questions, it seems to me, tend to absorb salt on their way across the ocean and then taste somewhat

12. Pertinent to this, see Stéphane Mosès, *The Angel of History: Rosenzweig, Benjamin, Scholem* (Stanford: Stanford UP, 1994); and Daniel Weidner, "Jüdisches Gedächtnis, mystische Tradition und Moderne Literatur. Walter Benjamin und Gershom Scholem deuten Kafka," in *Weimarer Beiträge* 46, vol. 2, 2002, 234–249.

bitter to the person who has been questioned" (Correspondence 109). Although it is dominated by a less abrasive tone than in the discussions with Brecht, these correspondences will grate on sensitivities on both sides. In addition, the situation was precarious, because Scholem had brokered the contract for the article for the *Jüdische Rundschau*—"I am inclined to believe that a really fine essay on Kafka in this publication could be very useful for you"—and bound it to an expectation: "But you won't be able to avoid an explicitly formulated relation to Jewishness" (106). Benjamin, for whom *implicit* references to Judaism were more in keeping, went back to a "lack of knowledge" in this case. He made use of the suggestion that "for this, pointing fingers from the other side" would be "admittedly indispensable" (141), in order to motivate his friends to confide in him their "own special views on Kafka—emanating as they do from Jewish insights" (113). Scholem initially refused, with lament over a discussion with "*verstellten Fronten*" (which can be read as 'disguised' as well as 'misaligned fronts') (BS 148) and sought support in a rhetoric of distinction—"You will no doubt best follow your line without the mystical prejudices that I alone am in a position to spread" (Correspondence 115). Ultimately, he strengthens the distance through an intimation that must have affected Benjamin, because, in the context of Benjamin's plans to resettle in Palestine, it evokes an unfulfilled promise: Scholem suggests that he could hardly give him something to read, saying that, "in general, my writing is now done in Hebrew" (118). When Scholem sent Benjamin his poem "With a copy of Kafka's *The Trial*" (BS 154–156) a month later, Benjamin was already in Denmark and his manuscript on the way to Jerusalem. Between July and September 1934, a doubly circuitous debate took place in a series of intersecting mailings. In them, the initial and direct controversy was avoided and sensitive issues remained left out—when Benjamin cloaks his reservations about half of the fourteen verses of Scholem's poem in the statement that he could "unreservedly identify" with the seventh to the thirteenth verse (Correspondence 128). After going back and forth many times, however, the differences had to be named.

For Scholem, the struggle to find an appropriate Jewish interpretation of Kafka is a matter of developing an interpretation based on a "*correctly* understood theology" in whose center stands his own thesis of "*nonfulfillability*" (BS 157; Correspondence 126) or "nothingness of revelation" (Correspondence 128): "Kafka's world is the world of revelation, but of revelation seen of course from that perspective in which it is traced back to its own nothingness" (126). Furthermore, he criticizes the strong emphasis Benjamin places on the primeval world and his lack of discussion of what is "Jewish" at those moments where "the main point raises itself so noticeably and bluntly—namely, in the terminology of the Law, which you stubbornly persist in viewing only from its most *profane* side—that one finds your silence about it quite puzzling" (127). In addition, he criticizes passages of the manuscript as being unintelligible, particularly those about the gestic (224).

Benjamin counters that his interpretation also has "its own broad—though admittedly shrouded (*beschattete*)—theological side." The image of the shadow points out the fact that he is interested in theological concepts in view of their effects *in the* profane world, that is, "how one has to imagine, in Kafka's sense, the Last Judgment's *projection* into *world history*" (128; emphasis S.W.). Especially important to him is the figure of an "answer that renders the question superfluous," i.e., the indication of a state of the world "in which such questions no longer have a place, because their answers, far from being instructive, make the questions superfluous" (128). This means that the unfulfilling answers provided by the profane world of Kafka's characters highlight the lack of questions within this world that originate in religion and are cleared away but not sublated in secularization. In contrast to Scholem, for whom the concepts of *revelation* and *law*[13] are most important, redemption is, for Benjamin, key: "I endeavored to show how Kafka sought—on the nether side of that 'nothingness,' in its inside lining, so to speak—to feel his way toward redemption" (129). Just as he will describe redemption as "the best" in the revised essay (II.2/434), this concept appears (in the profane variant of *hope*) in the first place in his seven points of objection to Scholem's "dissents" in the notes on the letter to Scholem (BS 166). The messianic aspect of revelation that Benjamin explains as "disfigured" in the fifth point (Correspondence 135) marks the clearest difference between him and Scholem. The latter's "nothingness of revelation" declares itself from the central position of the *nothingness* in his cabbalistic theory of language: the name of God, unsayable and itself with-

13. Stéphane Mosès has pointed out that, for Scholem, revelation stands in for the Hebrew word *Tora*; "in accordance with the polysemy of the term, this also involves the notions of Law and Doctrine. Thus, the 'nothingness of Revelation' denotes a paradoxical moment in the history of tradition, that of a decisive (but not definitive) break in which the law has already lost the principle of its authority, but in which its shadow continues to stand out on the horizon of our culture" (Mosès 2008, 156).

out any concrete meaning, is the origin of all meaning.[14] If literature then emerges as the inheritor of theology, it is because he regards it as an echo of the "lost word of Creation."[15] In contrast to this, Benjamin conceives of the difference between the "state of the world" (that is, history) and revelation in the figure of distance and displacement. This structure is analogous to his theory of translation in which the foreignness of languages marks its difference from "pure language." In this respect, he interprets the figure of redemption as the adjustment of a disfigurement.

This misunderstanding is indirectly addressed in the legend of the great rabbi without alluding to the underlying framework of Scholem and Benjamin's[16] divergent linguistic theories in their correspondence. In his essay Benjamin writes: "the inmate of the disfigured life [ . . . ] will disappear with the coming of the Messiah, who (a great rabbi once said) will not wish to change the world by force but will merely make a slight adjustment in it" (II.2/432; SelWr 2.811). Scholem then claims authorship of this legend: "[t]he great rabbi with the profound dictum on the messianic kingdom who also appears in Bloch is none other than *I* myself; what a way to attain honour!" (BS 154; Correspondence 123). He then appeals to an earlier version of his: "[e]verything will be as it is here—only slightly different" (Correspondence 123). The difference between "only slightly different" and "disfigured" that Scholem disregards here can be read as a symptom of the disagreement over a concept of revelation grounded in linguistic theory. When Benjamin likewise construes disfigurement as a form—one that the "things assume in oblivion" (SelWr 2.811)—the gap between history and revelation is first recognizable to him through the framework of memory.

This, exactly, is the intersection of his disputes with Brecht and with Scholem. The date of his objection to Scholem (August 11, 1934) lies between his second and third conversations with Brecht and thus Benjamin's figure of the reversal (*Umkehr*) that he gained from the perspective

14. Gershom Scholem, "Der Name Gottes und die Sprachtheorie der Kabbala," in *Judaica 3: Studien zur jüdischen Mystik* (Frankfurt/M: Suhrkamp, 1973), 69.

15. Ibid., 70.

16. See my investigation of Scholem's literary theory, which he developed from the concept of *Kina*, in contrast to Benjamin, "Gershom Scholems Gedichte und seine Dichtungstheorie—Klage, Adressierung, Gabe und das Problem einer Sprache in unserer Zeit," in Stéphane Mosès and Sigrid Weigel (eds.), *Gershom Scholem—Literatur und Rhetorik* (Köln: Böhlau, 2000), 16–47.

of memory, through which life turns into writing, is already of significance in this letter: "Kafka's messianic category is the 'reversal' or the 'studying'" (BS 135). This also explains Benjamin's thesis on the "problem of scripture" (135) that touches on a particularly sensitive point, as Scholem's comment signals: "It is about this text that we will have to reach an understanding" (127). Regarding Scholem's comment that Scripture is not lost but cannot be deciphered, Benjamin replies:

Whether the pupils have lost it or whether they are unable to decipher it comes down to the same thing, because, without the key that belongs to it, the Scripture is not Scripture, but life. Life as it is lived in the village at the foot of the hill on which the castle is built. It is in the attempt to transform life into Scripture that I perceive the meaning of "reversal" (*Umkehr*), which so many of Kafka's parables endeavor to bring about—I take "The Next Village" and "The Bucket Rider" as examples. (BS 167; Correspondence 135)

This means that for Benjamin the status of what has been read *as* Scripture is not assumed as given. Rather, it has always already, even in the tradition, depended on a specific exegesis whose key has been lost in modernity. On the other hand, for Scholem the always already enigmatic writing of the 'tradition' continues in modern times in literature. Thus he will be able, in his *Ten Unhistorical Aphorisms on Kabbalah*, to discover "the secularized representation of the cabbalistic world feeling unknown also to him" in Kafka's writings.[17] In this respect the discrepancies between the two are also grounded in their different positions on secularization. Although Scholem regarded literature as a secularized form of the tradition and the heir to Kaballah, theological concepts come into view for Benjamin only from the perspective of having been forgotten—that is, in reversal. The attempt to transfer *Dichtung* into *Lehre* leads to a—necessary—failure.

## Reading Legends

In contrast to the rigorous composition of the Kraus essay (a triptych made up of three pieces: *Allmensch, Dämon, Unmensch*, as discussed in the first chapter), the four-part essay "Franz Kafka: On the Tenth Anniversary

17. Gershom Scholem, "Zehn unhistorische Sätze über Kabbalah," in *Judaica 3* (Frankfurt/M: Suhrkamp, 1973), 271; *Gershom Scholem: Modern Critical Views* (New York: Chelsea House, 1987), 121.

of his Death" unfolds a complex network of motifs, legends, characters, concepts, and *citations*. These come from Kafka's own texts, available interpretations (like those from Brod, H. J. Schoeps, Hellmuth Kaiser, Haas, Kraft, Denis de Rougement),[18] from the work of other writers (Goethe, Robert Walser, Dostoevsky, Pushkin, Hamsun), from writings of cultural history and philosophy (Lao-Tse, Rosenzweig, Cohen, Lukács, Bloch, Bachofen, Léon Metchnikoff, among others), and folk songs. The essay does not interpret individual titles but rather refers to passages from the novels (*The Castle, The Trial, Amerika*), a range of stories ("The Judgement," "Der jüngste Tag," "Before the Law," "The Cares of a Family Man," "The Great Wall of China," "Meditations," "The Country Doctor," "The Metamorphosis," "Silence of the Sirens," "A Hunger Artist," "The Wish to Be an Indian," "In the Penal Colony," "Up in the Gallery"), and Kafka's diaries, from which Benjamin weaves a dense web of motifs. Some places, such as the judicial and administrative offices and the Nature Theater of Oklahoma, acquire a special role.[19]

In the process, Benjamin confronts several available interpretations; he rejects, for example, Soma Morgenstern's claim that Kafka is a founder of religion (II.2/425). Other citations attain the status of commentaries, comparable to the legends that he places alongside Kafka's parables, which he thereby transfers to a *Talmudic form*. The readings of legends acquire a compositional function, insofar as each of the four chapters is grouped around such stories. The posthumously published notebooks confirm this role. The *Story of Potemkin* opens the first chapter; the *Talmudic legend* of the body as a stranger to the soul (from the radio address) comes at the end of the second chapter, "A Childhood Photograph"; the *story of Knut Hamsun* introduces the third chapter, "The Little Hunchback"; and the fourth, "Sancho Panza," begins with the *tale of the Hasidic beggars*.

The mythic names, such as Ulysses and Sisyphus, with whom Benjamin compares the author, Kafka, play a completely different role. With them, he depicts Kafka's historical perspective by means of an image: as a glimpse of prehistory and of the underbelly of history. Under the mantra of an "other Ulysses," he comments on Kafka's world as the world of

18. Cf. the *Bibliographie zu Kafka* (GS II.3/1247) compiled by Benjamin.

19. On the subject of exterritoriality, see Samuel Weber, "Exterritorialité et théâtralité chez Benjamin et Kafka," in Nicole Fernandez-Bravo, ed., *L'Exterritorialité de la littérature allemande* (Paris: Harmattan, 2002) 91–106.

the un-divided, still without orders and hierarchies. It is a world that is older than myth, and Kafka did not follow up on the promise that myth would redeem the world. In this way, he sees Kafka, similar to Ulysses, "on the threshold dividing myth and fairy tale" (II.2/415; SelWr 2.799) there, where through guile and reason mythical power ceases and at the same time creates the fairy tale to be a "traditional story of the victory over these forces" (SelWr 2.799). The talk of Kafka's "fairy tales for dialecticians" emphasizes the difference between him and his classical "ancestors," so that the silence of the sirens corresponds to the "other Ulysses," as which Benjamin presents Kafka. When he describes the fact that according to the tradition mythic violence has been overcome as a fairy tale, his "fairy tales for dialecticians" invents a reversal of this reflection through which the historico-theoretical interpretation of the tradition becomes question-able, i.e., *worthy* of being questioned. To this end, Benjamin's reading of Kafka occupies an exact counterposition to the *Dialectic of Enlightenment*, in which Ulysses appears as an allegory for self-preservation and the origin of art that arises from its dissociation from physical work.

The comparison to Sisyphus also creates a perspective related to that of the "other Ulysses" that looks back to the primeval world, literally *before the law*—or, to the underside of history. Subsequent to the observation that shame, Kafka's "strongest gesture," is not a personal one but a "sophis-ticated social reaction" that is explained in his texts by the constraint of a (unknown) family, Benjamin writes:

Doing the family's bidding, he moves the mass of historical happenings the way Sisyphus rolled the stone. As he does so, its nether side comes to light; it is not a pleasant sight, but Kafka is capable of bearing it[. . . . ] Kafka did not consider the age in which he lived as an advance over the primordial beginnings of time. (808)

Thus to make the primeval world visible *in the present* seems to be the most difficult work. This explains the slowness and heaviness of movements that mark the characters in Kafka's literature. While in Benjamin the legends are *analogies to Kafka's texts* that correspond to his world, Benjamin's *compari-sons to Kafka* are thought-images that illuminate his historical-theoretical perspective of Kafka's world.

In order to discuss the specific relationship into which the primeval world and profane powers of the present day come together as a constella-tion, Benjamin once more takes up his "mirror simile"—but not without slightly adjusting it. In place of the "reflections [ . . . ] in reverse" (II.2/681; SelWr 2.496), he now presents a mirror scene in which the correspondences between past and future become discernable: "In the mirror which the *prehistoric world* held up to him in the *form of guilt*, he merely saw the *future* coming into sight in the *form of judgment*" (427; 807; emphasis S.W.). This is a thought-image *par excellence* that emphasized the historical asynchrony between the concepts of guilt and jurisdiction that Benjamin has analyzed in "The Critique of Violence": "Kafka, however, did not answer the question how one has to imagine this [the judgment—S.W.]. Wasn't it the Last Judgment? Doesn't it turn the judge into the defendant? Isn't the trial the punishment?" (427; 807) If Kafka's world is governed by litigations, court officials, accusations, punishments, unknown guilt, and shame, then Benjamin shows that mythical and theological terms (such as guilt, original sin, and the Last Judgment) overlap with the terms of human jurisdiction.

Without knowledge of their Christian origin, "inherited sin" appears as a nexus of guilt in life and puts a "perpetual trial" in motion. Where history presents itself as natural history, the father represents the accused *and* punished alike. The *family*, as the origin of "this inherited sin—the sin of having produced an heir" (796), thus appears as the source of sin and at the same time as an instance that sits in judgment upon it, as a place in which the prehistoric world and the present meet. Thus Benjamin describes "Kafka's world" as a "middle world" (*Mittelwelt*; II.2/416) or "in-between world" (*Zwischenwelt*; 430), that is to say, located on the threshold of nature and culture, and of the organic and inorganic simultaneously in a state of becoming and of decay. It is populated by both the "unfinished and the clumsy" (II.2/415; SelWr 2.799) and the sunken and the rising, a mixture of "that which never came into being (*Ungewordenem*) and overripe" (424; 799).

## The Structure of the Kafka Essay

The *first chapter* presents a quasi-archaeology of a cycle of characters (*Gestaltenkreis*) from "Kafka's world." It introduces Pushkin's stupefied Potemkin as the

first ancestor of those holders of power who in Kafka's works live in the attics as judges or in the castle as secretaries. No matter how highly placed they may be, they are always fallen or falling men, although even the lowest and seediest of them, the doorkeepers and decrepit officials, may abruptly and strikingly appear in the fullness of their power. (410; 795)

For Kafka, the world of officials is the same as that of the fathers: "The similarity does not redound to this world's credit; it consists of dullness, decay, and dirt" (SelWr 2.796). Corruptibility and "unchastity in the family's bosom" complement the comparable "conditions in offices and in families" (II.2/413; SelWr 2.797). Conversely, in order to discuss the fate of the unsuspecting accused, who are deemed guilty without their knowledge, Benjamin returns to his thoughts in "Fate and Character" (1919), in which he situated the concept of fate (*Schicksal*)—beyond a religious order, or an "empire of justice"—in a "legal order" arising from myth, namely as "guilt nexus of the living" (II.I/175; SelWr 1.307). The only "cycle of characters" among Kafka's protagonists that is not yet completely "disbanded from nature's womb (?)" (SelWr 2.798—transl. mod.) consists of the adjuncts (*Gehilfen*), messengers, students, and fools—inhabitants of a type of "middle world," i.e., a "world of creatures" that live under a dismal law: "to them and their kind, the unfinished and the clumsy, the hope is allotted" (II.2/415; SelWr 2.799).

The *second chapter* is dedicated to the various incarnations of K. in Kafka's novels and to the scene of the Nature Theater in Oklahoma. Introduced with a "childhood photograph" of Kafka, its passage on the "nineteenth-century studios" cites from Benjamin's "Little History of Photography" (1929). The "immensely sad eyes" of the six-year-old boy are here a point of departure to connect the deep "Wish to be an Indian" (416; 800) from Kafka's eponymous text with the novel, *Amerika*, in which Karl Roßmann "attains the object of his desire" in the Nature Theater of Oklahoma and on Clayton's racetrack. For Benjamin "the mysterious place and the entirely unmysterious, transparent, and sincere figure" belong together. He describes Roßmann as a man "simply without character"[20] (417ff.; 801) because he lacks exactly that which Benjamin had defined as "character" fifteen years prior in the essay "Fate and Character": the "answer of genius" to "this mythical enslavement of the person in the guilt context" (SelWr 1.205). Whereas the concept of character there originates in the context of tragedy, here, the human without character is at home in a *gestic the-*

20. This reference to the "ordinary men" who are themselves without mystery, but whose world is full of it, is connected to references to the Chinese cultural sphere, which Benjamin repeatedly makes: with citations from Rosenzweig's *Stern der Erlösung* (1921) and Léon Metchnikoff's *La civilization et les grands fleuves historiques* (1889).

*ater*: "[o]ne of the most significant functions of this theater is to dissolve events into something gestural." Kafka's entire body of work is a "code of gestures," but without a definite symbolic meaning, as it exists "in ever-changing contexts and experimental arrangements. The theater is the assigned place for such experimental arrangements" (II.2/418; SelWr 2.801).

The interpretation of the Nature Theater as a gestic theater and an experimental arrangement of meanings is part of Benjamin's way of reading Kafka's world as *world theater*: "For him, man is on stage from the very beginning" (II.2/422). In this way he presents gesture and bodily expression in the "center of the action," similar to Brecht's epic theater, which he also considered a gestic and experimental arrangement. Whereas in Brecht's work the citability of the gesture (i.e., its facilitation of a reflection of conventional symbolism) is at stake (II.2/529), Benjamin rather interprets Kafka's gesture as the "cloudy part of the parables" (SelWr 2.808).[21] Since "he divests human gesticulation (*Gebärde*)[22] of its traditional supports, and then has a subject for reflection without end" (802), the gesture (as a kind of imitation appearing as an escape or evasion) here constitutes an attitude that corresponds to the stage as a place of last refuge. For Benjamin, this does not preclude the possibility that this place refers to salvation: "Salvation is not a premium on being, but the last way out for a man, whose path, as Kafka puts it [ . . . ] 'is blocked . . . by his own frontal bone'" (II.2/423; SelWr 2.804). The search for a way out, for a last evasion, would thereby be interpreted as the form salvation acquires in a world in which in tradition has become a theater. The chapter closes with Talmudic legend (borrowed from the radio address), which leads "right into Kafka's world," a legend about the body that has become a hostile stranger to the present-day human. Awakened as vermin,[23] the strangeness has become his master,

21. On the subject of gestures in Kafka, see Werner Hamacher, "The Gesture in the Name: On Benjamin and Kafka," in *Premises: Essays on Philosophy and Literature from Kant to Celan* (Stanford: Stanford UP, 1998).

22. Benjamin uses both *Geste* and *Gebärde*, whose difference is difficult to translate. Whereas *Geste* is more or less a coded gesture (often specific to different cultures), *Gebärde* denotes a bodily expression, as for example in *Ausdrucksgebärde*, expression of emotion for which Aby Warburg invented his 'pathosformula'.

23. "Vermin" here denotes the German *Ungeziefer*, the same word used to describe Gregor Samsa's condition at the beginning of *The Metamorphosis*. It is a word without clear imagery; it is collective and can denote any verminlike pests, not necessarily a roach or beetle as it is often translated.

it says in an allusion to Kafka's story "The Metamorphosis" (SelWr 2.806). Thus Benjamin reads Kafka's texts as stories of humans without character who are subjected to the fate of an unknown guilt and are placed into ever-new test arrangements, at the center of which stand their gestures.

The figure of disfigurement in the *third* and *fourth chapters* is connected to this reflection on gestures: disfigurement is "the form which things assume in oblivion," as in the example of the little hunchback who is the archetype of disfigurement and the body as "most forgotten strangeness" (811). Against the backdrop of Jewish commemorative tradition that Benjamin invokes with a quote from Willy Haas—"the holiest [ . . . ] act of [ . . . ] ritual is the purging of sins from the book of memory" (II.2/429)— the forgotten in Kafka is placed within a double frame of reference. On the one hand, the forgotten references redemption: "but forgetting always involves the best, for it involves the possibility of redemption" (SelWr 2.813). On the other hand, it will be linked to the "forgotten of the prehistoric world" (810) and the idea of the "swamp world" (808) borrowed from Bachofen: "The fact that this stage is forgotten does not mean that it does not extend into the present. On the contrary: it is present by virtue of this very oblivion" (809). When the radio address introduces disfigurement as a symptom, the meaning of this concept is enriched in a variety of phenomena. Aside from the physical symptom, the physiognomy of those who are loaded, stooped, or bent (as if all burdens are always laid upon their backs) brings the "shift in the axis of salvation" into play, by which Benjamin develops the superimposition of the messianic and psychoanalytic sense of redemption on each other. The legend of the great rabbi that played such an important role in the Scholem controversy now receives an important addendum: "no one says that the disfigurement which it will be the Messiah's mission to set right someday will affect only our space; surely they are disfigurements of our time as well" (II.2/433; SelWr 2.812).

The closing passages of the essay are dedicated to a clan, a species among Kafka's creations that "reckons with the brevity of life in a peculiar way": the adjuncts (*Gehilfen*), whose spokesmen are the students (SelWr 2.813). For Benjamin, their gestures point to an "age of maximum alienation" (814), what he (with recourse to his concept of the "optical unconscious," 512, in the "Little History of Photography") discusses by means of the example of experiments with film and gramophone in which humans do not recognize their own gait or voice: "The situation of the subjects in such experiments is Kafka's situation; this is what leads him to study" (814). Yet the study is described as a monstrous effort: "It is a tempest that blows from forgetting, and study is a ride that counters it" (II.2 436; SelWr 2.814). Through this image the position of the students is placed in proximity to mythic heroes. By citing Plutarch via Bachofen, Benjamin illustrates the students' position with Plutarch's assumption of "'two particular primary essences and two opposing forces, one of which points to the right and straight ahead, whereas the other turns around and drives back.' Reversal is the direction of study which transforms being into script" (815). As one of Kafka's characters that literally embodies the ride back, Benjamin cites Bucephalus from the story "The New Advocate." In the story, Bucephalus has become a human being, free of the burden of his master, Alexander the Great, just as Kafka's Sancho Panza rid himself of his devil, Don Quixote. With Bucephalus, who is also a reader who turns "the pages of our old books," this story at the same time discusses law again in its descent from justice: "The law which is studied but no longer practiced is the *gate* to justice" (815; emphasis S.W.).

The subsequent passage adopts the thesis, formulated during the Scholem controversy, that reversal and study are Kafka's messianic categories, and it explicates the difference between Kafka's world and the world of revelation: "The gate to justice is study." This sentence concerns the biblical origins of the concept of justice, whose meaning opens up in study, even if this cannot be conceived of in the continuum of tradition. Thus, Benjamin continues: "Yet Kafka doesn't dare attach to this study the promises which tradition has attached to the study of the Torah. His adjuncts are sextons who have lost their house of prayer; his students are pupils who have lost the Holy Writ" (815). Along with the figure of the reversal (*Umkehr*) that is so central to Benjamin's thought, a movement against the storm, the vanishing point of a double derivation is presented—from both Athens and Jerusalem. In any case, it does not provide a return.

## Kafka's Complementary World in Terms of Modern Physics

The debates with Kraft and Adorno over Kafka never entered the essay, but rather the "Dossier von fremden Einreden und eignen Reflexionen." Whereas for Werner Kraft the matter was one of a critique of an esoteric form of representation (II.3/1167), Adorno emphasized above all how Benjamin's writings conformed to his own thinking. His own *Aufzeichnungen zu Kafka* were written only after Benjamin's death and published in 1953. Benjamin's "Dossier" makes clear that Adorno's commentaries interested him mainly in respect of the reflections on media images, first of all, those on film and on gestures: not only the formulation that Kafka's work is "a photograph of our earthly life from the perspective of a redeemed life" (BA 66) but also the thesis that Kafka's texts are "the last and disappearing connecting texts of the silent film" (70). The work on his final text on Kafka (his discussion of Brod's biography of Kafka) was a welcome opportunity for Benjamin to return "with great interest to study Teddie's letter on Kafka of 17 December 1934" (260).

The criticism of Brod's book, initially inserted in a letter to Scholem in June 1938 (6/105–114) in order to then make a review out of it (one of the many articles that were never published), amounts to a scathing review in which Benjamin could not pass up the opportunity to throw a rhetorical punch. With regard to the combination of Brod's intimacy and sacralization of a dead friend, Benjamin writes: "Intimacy with the saintly has its own special religio-historical signification: pietism. Brod's attitude as a biographer amounts to a pietistic stance of ostentatious intimacy—in other words, the most impious attitude imaginable " (6/106; Correspondence 220). In order to characterize Brod's rejection of other interpretations of Kafka, Benjamin presents a Brod who does not only brush aside all other interpretations but is also keen "to belittle any future writing on Kafka" (Correspondence 222). What is more important about Benjamin's renewed reading of Kafka, which was motivated by Brod's biography, is the fact that he further develops his own interpretation in the second part of the letter. The remark that this interpretation differs from his own previous reflections pertains to the perspective of modern physics.

The last contribution that Benjamin wrote on Kafka not only shifts his interpretations more strongly toward motifs from the "*Urgeschichte der Moderne*"[24] but as well emphasizes the ever-more-pronounced motif of failure and delimits itself from an "apologetic feature" of his text from four years prior. The second part of this text, which argues beyond the scope of the review of Brod, begins with the previously cited thesis that Kafka's

24. Cf. Michael Jennings, " 'Eine gewaltige Erschütterung des Tradierten': Walter Benjamin's Political Recuperation of Franz Kafka," in *Fictions of Culture*, ed. Steven Taubeneck (New York: Peter Lang, 1991), 199–214.

world is an *ellipse*. Benjamin certainly means this less as a rhetorical trope that comes about through ellipses in the sentence structure than as an epistemic configuration: the two poles of it are named mystical experience, on one hand, and the contemporaneity of "today's physics," on the other. From this elliptical perspective of the work, then, the thesis is developed that Kafka lives in a complementary world, and he does this by way of a long passage from the book of an English physicist, A. S. Eddington's *The Nature of the Physical World* (1928, German transl. 1931). *Complementarity* thus appears as the very form in which the ways of knowing that originate in both poles can be expressed simultaneously in *life*. Although the term does not itself appear in the citation of Eddington, it can be inferred from it. Since the thesis that Kafka lives in a complementary world is the summation of a transfer that begins with the "Kafka-*gestus*," to be compared to the "physical aporia" described by Eddington, the physicist's writing thus enters Benjamin's writing as an analogy to Kafka:

I know of no passage in literature which displays the characteristic Kafka-*gestus* to the same degree. One could easily juxtapose any point in this physical aporia with just about any sentence from Kafka's prose pieces; and there are more than a few indications that many of his most "incomprehensible" sentences would be at home here. (6/111; SelWr 3.325)

The significance of the natural sciences for Benjamin's thought (which traces back to his years in college, and especially to conversations with Scholem, who was notoriously involved with mathematics and number theory)[25] belongs to the as-yet-unwritten chapters in the reception of Benjamin's work. The passage from Eddington concerns a description of space from the last chapter of *The Nature of the Physical World* in which the physicist takes, under the heading "Science and Mysticism," the "strange new conceptions of the physical world" as a point of departure for a discussion of the philosophical consequences of relativity and quantum theory and pursues these deliberations in the "wider aspects of human experience, including religion" (Eddington 1931, V). The passage concerns the complicated and difficult enterprise of entering a room when one is aware of and takes into account all

25. The reading of Natorp's *Grundlagen der exakten Wissenschaft* (1910) is attested to, for example, in the correspondence with Scholem; and Benjamin's "Verzeichnis gelesener Schriften" includes Ernst Bartel's *Die geometrischen Grundbegriffe* (1916) as well as books on scientific theory and epistemology.

the physical conditions involved (such as atmospheric pressure, the speed of the Earth's rotation, and the spherical shape of the planets). The passage ends with this image:

> Verily, it is easier for a camel to pass through the eye of a needle than for a scientific man to pass through a door. And whether the door be barn door or church door it might be wiser that he should consent to be an ordinary man and walk in than wait till all the difficulties involved in a really scientific ingress are resolved. (Eddington 342; SelWr 3.325)

Eddington describes the physicist as standing *before the law* of physics, so to speak, incapable of acting, in a way similar to Kafka's character. There is an obvious association to the story "The Next Village," about a young man's intention to ride to the next village, which seems remarkable when one considers the shortness of life and the laws of mortality. However, although the physicist makes the world into an enigma through the conceptions of modern physics, the situation in Kafka's stories is the reverse. When he further expands his comparison, Benjamin assumes that the "absolutely new world of experience comes to him by way of the mystical tradition" (SelWr 3.325). From opposing points of departure, both ways of perception move toward one and the same position.

The comparison is continued implicitly when Benjamin stresses that Kafka's perception of the earliest world of experiences, one based in the mystical tradition (analogous to the questioning of the iron laws of physics), would not have been possible without catastrophic events *within* this tradition, whose power, at the same time, had to be evoked in order to confront "an individual (here, Franz Kafka) [ . . . ] with the reality that presents itself as ours—theoretically in physics and in practice by military technology" (6/111 f.; SelWr 3.326). The mystic tradition, as well as its erosion, becomes a presupposition and at the same time the medium for a confrontation with a present that is characterized by the ubiquity of physics and military technology. In literature, this complex interrelationship of the mystic and the modern is presented as a complementary constellation. The concept of the complement comes into play precisely at the point where Benjamin describes Kafka's prose as a type of simultaneity of catastrophe and the world of angels:

> I would say that this reality is now almost beyond the *individual's* capacity to experience, and that Kafka's world, often so serene and pervaded by angels, is the exact

*complement* of his age, which is preparing to do away with considerable segments of this planet's population. In all likelihood, the public experience corresponding to the private one of Kafka's will be available to the masses only on the occasion of their elimination. (6/112; SelWr 3.326)

Through Benjamin's reading of Eddington, the concept of *complementarity* that comes from the Copenhagen school's (Niels Bohr and Werner Heisenberg) interpretation of quantum theory, which deals with the justification of varying, contradictory, or even mutually exclusive yet complementary images, is thus transferred to Kafka's world in two steps. Once the historical index of texts by Eddington and Kafka was established as an interrelation between the mystical and the modern (modern physics and technology), the term 'complementarity' is used explicitly for his readings of Kafka's prose. The *complementary* world thereby becomes the condition of possibility for a unique perception in modernity that Benjamin places alongside "Klee, whose work is just as intrinsically *isolated* in painting" (SelWr 3.326): a perception of that which is coming and "what is today." From such a perspective, one of complementarity turned into a historico-theoretical concept, Benjamin extrapolates the *"play*-space" (*Spielraum*) of Kafka's literature, which he describes as the space of a unique knowledge: "Kafka's gestures of horror are well served by the glorious play-space of which the catastrophe will know nothing" (326). Benjamin thereby attributes to it an insight into that which is coming and which contains no trace of the prophetic. It is similar to what he will formulate two years later in his theses "On the Concept of History."

The new perspective developed in Benjamin's reading of Kafka in this short text includes recognition of the fact that the concepts of *Agada* and *Halacha*, from Jewish tradition, are replaced by *wisdom* and *truth*:

Kafka's work represents a sickening of tradition. Wisdom has sometimes been defined as an epic side of truth. Wisdom is thus characterized as an attribute of tradition; it is truth in its haggadic consistency. / This consistency of truth has been lost. Kafka was by no means the first to be confronted with this realization. (326)

Benjamin had largely let go of concepts such as *truth*—namely, in the course of the "complete upheaval" of his multitude of thoughts and images, "one that comes from the remote period" of his "actual metaphysical, indeed theological thinking," had to pass through, as he wrote to Werner Kraft in June 1935 (5/88). That he again employs such terms in his last text on Kafka likewise identifies it as an effect of his engagement with modern physics. In the wake of the theory of relativity, it cannot, in any case, pertain to an idea of absolute truth. At most, could it concern a relativity of truth—relativity in the exact sense of dependency on a perception of respective time-space relations—in whose wake terms such as 'vagueness' and 'uncertainty' were introduced in *Das Naturbild der Physik*.[26] Benjamin derives the idea that Kafka discloses the truth, from the actual loss of *consistency* of truth, through a detour that compares Kafka to Eddington's physical aporia. Though other authors react to the loss of the consistency of truth by renouncing transmissibility, what is new and of genius in Kafka's stance is that he *reveals* the truth in order to hold on to transmissibility—that is to say, to the haggadaic element.

Scholem takes a very similar thought, one that bears on the impossibility of reconciling tradition and truth, as the point of departure for his *Ten Unhistorical Aphorisms on Kabbalah*, published in 1938, the same year Benjamin's reflections on Brod's biography appeared in the *Festschrift* for Daniel Brody. The first paragraph of Scholem's text reads:

> The Kabbalist claims that there is a tradition on truth that can be transmitted. An ironic claim since precisely that truth which is the issue here is anything but transmittable. It can be recognized, but not transmitted and precisely that which is transmittable in it, it no longer contains. Authentic tradition remains hidden; only the deteriorated tradition refers to a subject matter and only in decay does its greatness become visible.[27]

They each stress different sides of the same problem. Although Scholem focuses on the intransmissibility of truth and on the concealment of tradition, and Benjamin emphasizes Kafka's adherence to transmissibility in the abandoning of truth, both thinkers edged their way to the same point in their readings of Kafka. It is a movement similar to the image of the two opposing arrows that advance each other and thus similar to the configuration that represents a structuring thought-image in Benjamin's writings.

Yet from his assessment that literature is the medium of transmissibility in the abandonment of truth (or study) it follows that Benjamin must problematize the status of Kafka's stories as allegories (such as the Talmudic legend). He therefore takes his reflections on the problem of the

---

26. Werner Heisenberg, *Das Naturbild der heutigen Physik* (Hamburg: Rowohlt, 1955), 33.
27. Scholem (1987), 65.

allegorical one step further than in the essay "von Haus aus Gleichnisse." Kafka's writing is indeed more than such a house, because they do not bow to teaching (*Lehre*), but rather raise a hand against it. Thus for Benjamin, the only things that remain in Kafka are products of the decay of wisdom (such as rumor, "a type of theological news whispered down the lane" [6/113], and folly). As it presents the products of wisdom's decay, Kafka's literature—in its failure—delivers infinitely more than all attempts to rescue teaching for a profane world:

> To do justice to the figure of Kafka in its purity, and in its particular beauty, one should never lose sight of one thing: they belong to a figure who failed. The circumstances of this failure are manifold. Perhaps one might say that once he was sure of ultimate failure, then everything on the way to it succeeded for him as if in a dream. Nothing is more remarkable than the fervor with which Kafka has underscored his failure. (6/114; SelWr 2.327)

As opposed to "Goethe's *Elective Affinities*," in which hope and the expressionless were still connected to a "divine ground of the being of beauty" (351), Benjamin discovered another, quasi-*ahuman* beauty, serenity, and hope in Kafka's works: "So, as Kafka says, there is an infinite amount of hope—only not for us. This statement truly contains Kafka's hope. It is the source of his radiant serenity" (327). This serenity clearly owes itself to the play space opened up by the complementary world. If the stage and world theater (the images for Kafka's gestic experience in the essay) have become a play space, then this image stands in a series of *topoi* with which Benjamin describes Kafka's world as a signature (but not likeness) of modernity. These *topoi* are topographical figures that enhance the figure of the gap and distance between history and Creation. They are, in principle, differentiated from a mirror image. In the radio address, it is a *reversed mirror image* (or a mirror that reflects in the reverse sense); in the 1934 essay it is *disfigurement* and *symptom*; and in the 1938 text it is *complementarity* and play space.

FROM THE MIDST OF HIS IMAGE WORLD

# 7

# Translation as the Provisional Approach to the Foreignness of Language

*On the Disappearance of Thought-Images*
*in Translations of Benjamin's Writings*

In the editions of Benjamin's writings available to date in languages other than German, one encounters many real errors of translation. This often happens when the complex syntactic structure of Benjamin's sentences, for example, leads to negative statements being given a positive thrust and vice versa. However, as regards the task of the translator of Benjamin's texts, those sections are of greater importance where, when attempting to correct erroneous translations, one encounters elements that are impossible to translate. These are instances where neither a literal translation nor a paraphrase would accurately capture the word or linguistic phrase. As a result the translations necessarily morph into a commentary or resort to footnotes in order to provide additional explanations. But the more serious problem in the prevailing conventions of translation is the fact that in most cases this phenomenon of (un)translatability remains covert due to distinct *decisions* made by the translator. Yet since these cases are obscured by the demands inherent to the process of translating, this grave problem seems to me to be the result of the conventions of translation.

What is at stake, as previously stated, is less the problem of 'erroneous translations' and more the failure to recognize the shift between different registers of language and signifying systems intrinsic to the process of translation, a shift that disappears in seamless linguistic conversion, a process in which language is reduced to its signifying function. A letter

Sigmund Freud wrote to Fließ on December 12, 1896, contains this remark: "The failure (*Versagung*) of translation, now that is what is clinically
termed 'repression.' The motivation for this is always a release of the displeasure that would arise through translation, as if this displeasure were
to prompt a disturbance of thought that the work of translation does not
allow."[1] What Freud calls *translation* here, in the context of his elaboration
of the reinscription and reordering of the material of mnemonic traces that
occurs in memory, is the necessary translation of psychological materials
from one epoch in life into another within the sequential and superimposed scriptures. Although Freud conceives of a site for script in his concept of memory, the process of translation he describes should be taken
literally. The *Versagung*[2] of this translation refers to a possible disturbance
that would then originate from the material to be translated.

If the decisions made in the translation of a text are geared to prevent a disturbance within the translation, then in the case of Benjamin's
writings the process relates first and foremost to his thinking in images,
namely those linguistic constellations through which his use of language
is to be located beyond the opposition of concept and metaphor: "Where
thinking comes to a standstill in a constellation saturated with tensions—
there the dialectical image appears. It is the caesura in the movement of
thinking" (Arcades, 475). If, however, Benjamin's thinking in images (images, both read and written) becomes indiscernible in the translated text,
then the specific character of his thought gets lost in translation: namely
the work on and with language itself, by means of which he inverts the
regular detachment of the concept from the word in order to remind us
of the word's emergence from the act of nomination and of the names
concealed in the words. By contrast, linguistic operations that render language a mere signifying system elide those linguistic elements that either
go beyond conventional meaning and lexical conversion or break into

1. *Sigmund Freud, Briefe an Wilhelm Fließ 1887–1904*, ed. Jeffrey Moussaieff Masson
(Frankfurt/M: Fischer, 1986), 219. I have Andrew Benjamin to thank for drawing my at-
tention to the quotation, in Alfred Hirsch, *Übersetzung und Destruktion* (Frankfurt/M:
Suhrkamp, 1997), 232.

2. The standard translation for Freud's *Versagung* is "frustration," which is critically discussed in Laplanche/Pontalis's article on "Versagung" (Frankfurt/M. 1972), 601. Freud's explanation to Fließ in which he connects *Versagung* with *Verdrängung* makes clear that there
is a sort of resistance involved.

them. These moments, as is well known, are at the very heart of Benjamin's theory of language.

## Translation and Foreign Words

This elision is the consequence of a practice of translation required by many English-speaking publishers in particular. It is geared toward a goal of the complete assimilation of the foreign into a "comprehensible" idiom in the target language. Even those words that cannot be found in a German dictionary (Benjaminian neologisms) are translated, as if the foreignness of a foreign word needed to be rendered harmless. And only in exceptional cases do we encounter parenthetic inclusions that provide information on Benjamin's original formulations. Although a critique of faulty or even erroneous translations is measured against an assumption of the possibility of complete translatability, at stake here is the fact that a translation policy of total assimilation hinges on a fundamental misunderstanding of the *problem* of translation. It causes the elision of those traces that point to the *task of the translator*. The importance of Benjamin's essay of the same name does not consist in a discussion of the criteria that make for a better translation, but rather in elaborating *translatability* as an essential feature of specific works (SelWr 1.254). Above all, however, he addresses the role that the problem of translation plays in a philosophy of language.

As shown in relation to his approach to secularization in the first chapter, Benjamin's "Task of the Translator" opens up a space for reflection on the way in which language is imprisoned within the demand for communication, meaning, and intention. His essay deals with the difference of languages and their distance to "pure language," which, as long as we find ourselves in history, will always remain virtual. Translation is thus of immense importance in terms of a theory of language, primarily because it constitutes a test of our knowledge of the distance to revelation. If Benjamin understands translation as the test (*Probe*) of "how far removed is their hidden element [of languages] from revelation? How contemporary may it become by the knowledge of this remoteness?" then this test refers to the presence of the hidden element *in awareness* of the distance to complete cognition or legibility. And if, as regards the task of the translator, Benjamin emphasizes the literalness of word and syntax and the way in which they produce meaning, as opposed to what is meant (*das Gemeinte*), then *what is meant* is also defined here as what is hidden in languages. Translation thus marks the unavoidable distance to revelation and keeps that remoteness open. As a somehow "provisional way of coming to terms with the foreignness of language" (257), translation is always imperfect. In this respect, the practice of translation always hinges on the legibility of the historically conditioned imperfection of translation and the recognizability of the foreignness of language, without bridging the gap through familiar formulations. Translation's role as a test and as an awareness of the distance to revelation should thus clearly not take perfection as its measure or standard, but should seek to pinpoint its own imperfection and provisional character, rendering *différance* recognizable: opening up a linguistic space in which thinking with and in the traces becomes possible. Most of the existing English translations of Benjamin's writings block that space; they practice translation as *closure*. What is at stake here is nothing less than the question of how to approach the *belatedness* of any translation.

This also relates to the legibility of difference to a text written in one's own language (as the original). The practice of assimilation in translation focuses on the goal of giving the translated text the semblance of having been written in the mother tongue, thus smoothing over and adapting the foreignness of the foreign. This practice thus shies away from the important effect of confrontation with a foreign language or with words from a foreign language. Although the act of nomination and designation in a text written in one's own language remains largely concealed by the fact that the language seems to be natural, it is precisely the words arriving from the foreign world, as the title of Adorno's essay *Wörter aus der Fremde* (1959, *On Foreign Words*) would have it, that render this process visible again. In keeping with an image from Benjamin's *One-Way Street*, in which he writes of the silver rib of the foreign term that the author inserts into his handwriting, Adorno reflects in that essay on the "use of foreign words":

instead, each newly posited foreign word reveals again the truly primordial act of naming in its moment of appearance. And in each one, genius escapes anew from mythic bondage to a life that is merely natural.

This is why, historically, foreign words are the points at which a knowing consciousness and an illuminated truth break into the undifferentiated growth of the aspect of language that is mere nature: the incursion of freedom.[3]

3. Theodor Adorno, *Notes to Literature*, vol. 2 (New York: Columbia UP, 1992), 289. (Translation modified.)

In his comparative analysis of the history of languages, Adorno discusses the impact of the fact that the integration of different layers of language in the German case took place quite late in history in comparison with the French and English (the Gallic and Roman strands in France, the Saxon and Norman in England) where it occurred both far earlier and far more thoroughly than in German. Here the elements of Latin and the older popular language remained socially disparate, and to this extent the foreign words stand out in more acute contrast and thus more clearly as unassimilated components in the dictionary. In this light, the foreign words function as the memory of linguistic differences and, in the mother tongue, occupy the access to the trace of *différance*. Or, put differently, "Foreign words are citations" (645), as Adorno goes on to say, clearly alluding to Benjamin's above-mentioned theory of citation as put forward in the essay on Karl Kraus, "In front of language, both realms—origin and destruction—reveal themselves in citation" (II.1/363; SelWr 2.454).

This meaning of foreign words becomes more obvious in instances where a word from the mother tongue returns, as a quasi-foreign word or as a foreign proper word, to one's own language after a detour through a translation of a foreign-language text into which the word had initially been adopted without having translated. The asterisk serves to mark such an event, that little star placed after a word (often together with italics), a feature encountered especially often in German translations of Derrida's writings and the meaning of which is then stated in the footnote: "German in the original," as, for example with the words *Bild\**, *Bildung\**, *Einbildung\**, *Übersetzung\**, *Setzen\** in Derrida's essay on the theology of translation.[4] Absent this mark, these words would lose their status as foreign words in the original text and would by means of *twofold translation* return seemingly unchanged as proto-innate words. The asterisk, however, prompts one to pause while reading and ensures the words from the reader's mother tongue return as words from a foreign language. The asterisk thus serves to mark a *différance* and a belatedness, showing that in the case of words taken from texts by German authors (in the fields of philosophy and psychoanalysis) an alteration has taken place through their twofold translation. Conversely, commentaries and parenthetic insertions are used to insert language games from the original into

---

4. Jacques Derrida, "Theologie der Übersetzung," in Alfred Hirsch, ed., *Übersetzung und Destruktion* (Frankfurt/M: Suhrkamp, 1997).

the translated text, thus interrupting it. They signal that the translation is provisional and at the same time render the inclusion of *différance* in the same word legible: for example, "l'à traduire," which in terms of the sound of its pronunciation can be read as to translate, to de-translate and to translate it (the language).[5]

### Ungereimtheit: Sound, Inconsistency, and Citation

These language games relate to a theory of linguistic consistency (*Stimmigkeit*) that is not just a matter of reason and logic but also one of sonority.[6] These games or word play touch on the covert affinity within words that cannot be discerned from their function as signs but can be recognized in the memory of and with recourse to the status of words as names. For Benjamin, writing is always *citation* (and "to quote a word is to call it by its name" [SelWr 2.453]) as well as *translation*—and to translate is to awaken the echo of the original language in the other and find a linguistic site "where at a time the echo of one's own language is able to give the reverberation of a work in the alien one" (IV.I/16; SelWr 1.258ff.).

In the context of his short theory of citation (found in the essay on Kraus), this other *Stimmigkeit* is not conceived of by Benjamin as a sort of *Gereimtheit* (meaning both sonorous consistency and being rhymed) but rather appears as a language that he terms "*nicht ungereimt*," and thus sonorous, congruous; the citation appears "with rhyme and reason, sonorously, congruously, in the structure of the new text" (SelWr 2.454). If the word *ungereimt* were to allude here not to the literal but to the metaphorical meaning of 'not being rhymed,' i.e., indicative of inconsistency in a logical sense,[7] only then

5. See the note by translator Alexander Garcia Düttmann on Jacques Derrida: *Babylonische Türme. Wege, Umwege, Abwege*, in Hirsch, 136.

6. German *stimmig* means consistent both in terms of being coherent and sounding harmonious, similar to the sound in the double meaning of reasonable and to resonate. In the semantic field of *Stimme*/voice and *Stimmung*/atmosphere, mood plays a central role in German philosophy (cf. Nietzsche) and cultural science (Auerbach, Spitzer), respectively. See now also Gumbrecht, *Stimmungen lesen: Über eine verdeckte Wirklichkeit der Literatur* (München: Hanser, 2011).

7. "Unrhymed, Middle High German: ungerîmet, since the 15th century metaphorical for 'inconsistent, absurd,'" in Hermann Paul, *Deutsches Wörterbuch 9*, vollständig neu bearbeitete Auflage (Tübingen: Niemeyer,1992), 941

would this correspond to the English phrase "without rhyme and reason." Through the negative structure of *nicht ungereimt* (not un-rhymed), Benjamin's original text rejects the metaphorical meaning in order to return it, via the operation of a double negation, to the literal meaning of 'rhymed' (associated with voice/sound and not with logos/reason) with the intention of gaining a different sense of *Gereimtheit* (rhyme/consistency) that is not only rooted in logic. The addition of *"klingend, stimmig"* acknowledges the fact that this appears in or through sound. This struggle with the meaning of *ungereimt* is part and parcel of Benjamin's method of transforming metaphors and transferred meanings into *dialectical images*: he begins with the familiar metaphorical meaning and squeezes from it the dialectic ossified within.[8] Indeed, in the description of the citation he accordingly uses language *as* citation, because the citation "summons the word by its name, wrenches it destructively from its context, but precisely thereby calls it back to its origin" (454). In this way, the original (that is, the text from which the citation comes) is always already distinguished from the origin.

In the English translation of the collection, *One-Way Street*, "nicht ungereimt erscheint es, klingend, stimmig" is translated as "It appears, now with rhyme and reason, sonorously, congruously in the structure of a new text" (OWS 286). Since the expression for "un-rhymed" in the sense of logic (i.e., the metaphor "without rhyme and reason") here appears in a positive formulation, Benjamin's double negation is eliminated. In other words, the entire project of work of transposition within one language has been forfeited. Along with the double negation, the specific method— namely the destruction of the metaphorical meaning and the rekindling of a literal reading situated at the origin—is likewise forfeited. This means that in the process of translation the simultaneous nonsimultaneity of origin and destruction that Benjamin identifies as the property of citation is also lost. In this way, translation from one language into another obscures a mode of writing that is already performed as a type of translation within one and the same language, i.e., as reversal from the metaphorical to the preceding literal meaning of language.

8. For greater detail on this method, see the chapters on "Dialectical Images" and on gender images in my previous Benjamin book, and my article on Eros: "Eros and Language: Benjamin's Kraus Essay," in *Benjamin's Ghosts: Interventions in Contemporary Literary Theory and Cultural Theory*, Gerhard Richter, ed. (Stanford: Stanford University Press, 2002).

Sound is also involved when Benjamin suggests that Karl Kraus's "theory of language" should be understood as a "contribution to the rules of court for language (*Sprachprozeßordnung*)." With this disfiguration from *Strafprozeßordnung* (rule for criminal proceeding) into *Sprachprozeßordnung* (rule for linguistic procedure), Benjamin designates neither a use of language similar to that in court nor linguistic norms for jurisprudence. Rather, as stated in the first chapter, what concerns him is that for Kraus language itself, with reference to the "image of divine justice as language," constitutes a sphere of law and justice, while the juridical system is accused of being "the law's high treason against justice." In other words, language litigates against the legal system precisely *not* placing itself in the latter's service. It is exactly this thrust of Kraus's theory of language that is misunderstood if we understand "the word of someone else in his mouth only as a *corpus delicti*, and his own only as a judging word" (II.I/329; SelWr 2.443; emphasis S.W.). For Benjamin, such a misunderstanding goes hand in hand with interpreting Kraus's language as quasi-juridical practice, as transposition of legal logic into and onto language, whereby language is applied as a *means* of indictment and thus functions as a *corpus delicti*. Here, Benjamin once again discusses Kraus's language against the backdrop of the caesura between the immediacy (*Unmittelbarkeit*) of the Adamitic language and the language of judgments and signs—otherwise stated, between "justice as language" and the intermediacy (*Mittelbarkeit*) of language, on which he elaborated in his early theory of language.

His neologism *Sprachprozeßordnung* is constructed by means of a disfigured sonorous similitude.[9] This word, which is also a foreign body within the German language, is not cited in the English translation but instead assimilated into so-called natural English and translated as "linguistic rules of court," a phrase which means something quite different from rules of court for language. Therefore it is no coincidence that the word's role as *corpus delicti* and as judging word in the English translation is rendered as the precise opposite of the original, for it is given a positive spin. Benjamin's sentence about Kraus's *Sprachprozeßordnung* is cited here in its

---

9. See the relation between Benjamin's well-known concept 'unsensual similitude' and the more obscure concept of a 'distorted similitude,' which I have examined in my former book on Benjamin with the title *Entstellte Ähnlichkeit* (Frankfurt/M: Fischer, 1997), a slightly different German version of *Body- and Image Space* (New York: Routledge, 1995).

entirety—first in the German original, secondly in my own translation, and finally the version from *One-Way Street*:

Man begreift seine "Sprachlehre" nicht, erkennt man sie nicht als Beitrag zur Sprachprozeßordnung, begreift das Wort des anderen in seinem Munde nur als corpus delicti und sein eigenes nur als das richtende. (GS II, 349)

One does not understand his "theory of language" if one does not conceive it as a contribution to the rule of a court for language, but rather understands the word of someone else in his mouth only as a *corpus delicti*, and his own only as a judging word. (GS II, 349)

It is to misunderstand his theory of language to see it as other than a contribution to the linguistic rules of court, the word of someone else in his mouth as other than a corpus delicti, and his own as other than a judging word. (OWS, 272)

For Benjamin it is a misunderstanding of Kraus to think that he deals with words as *corpus delicti* (that is to say, as a piece of evidence in front of the judge) but not the other way around. A misunderstanding of the linguistic image leads in this case to the exact inversion of the statement and its implications for a theory of language.

This is also the context of the misunderstanding of the linguistic constellation in which the dis-synchrony of lament (*Klage*) and indictment (*Anklage*) is described: the lament is addressed to Creation, while the accusation is lodged before the *Weltgericht* (world's court / Last Judgment):[10] "Kraus is not a historic Genius." Benjamin claims that Kraus "does not stand on the threshold of a new age," in order to interpret the threshold at which Kraus does stand as a *different* one, namely as the threshold between the world and language of Creation on the one hand and history as the 'world's court' on the other: "If he ever turns his back on creation, breaking off the lamentations (*Kehrt er der Schöpfung je den Rücken, bricht er ab mit Klagen*), it is only to accuse at the world's court (*so ist es nur, um vor dem Weltgericht anzuklagen*)" (II.I/349; SelWr 2.443). As opposed to the figure of redemption, which coincides with the end of history, the indictment before the "world's court" coincides with the end of laments that acquire meaning only in the presence of divine justice. Here, thanks to the reference to Creation, the term 'world court,' which has been used to designate world history ever since Schiller's renowned state-

10. See note 3 in Chapter 1.

ment that "World history is the world court," brings to mind the older, differing meanings of the court: on one hand, secular courts and the divine court sitting in judgment upon the world, on the other, namely the 'Last Judgment.'[11] In other words, it points to the double reference of history to both human law and divine judgment. Both entail judgment and the distinction between good and evil, while the world of Creation does not (yet) know of this difference. The decision made in the English translation elides ambiguity and opts for "Last Judgment," while at the same time abandoning the dialectic of lament and litigation: "If he breaks off *in* lamentation, it is only to file a complaint at the Last Judgment" (SelWr 2.443). The inconsistencies in such examples that fail (in the above-mentioned Freudian sense) on the level of the phonetic and scriptorial image in the translation are based in the illusion of universal translatability. Derrida describes such problems of translation as a paradox: "I do not wish to litigate against the translators. I simply wish to emphasize a paradox: *the concept of the principle translatability is tied poetically to natural language and resists translation.*"[12]

Since it evidently cannot be stressed often enough: these examples of the problems of translation taken from the English versions of Benjamin's works are by no means intended as a complaint or a trial. By highlighting passages that are impossible to translate, they make the case for the necessity of a different practice of translation, one that includes a reflection on the manifold processes of transposition innate in translation. The misreadings cited here mainly concern Benjamin's mode of writing and thinking in images and are to be encountered not only in translations of his writings into other languages, but—and this is just as serious—in the usual transpositions of his thought into customary discourses within German, for example when his linguistic work on images is transposed into the conceptual frame of sociology or critique of ideology. Many German readings and interpretations of Benjamin's writing tend to homogenize his linguistic images just as much, either in *concepts* or in *metaphors.*

11. See the entry "Weltgericht" in Jacob and Wilhelm Grimm, *Deutsches Wörterbuch* (Munich: Bertelsmann, 1991), Bd. 28, 1583ff.

12. Derrida, 20.

## (Pro-) Creation and Testimony (*Zeugung* and *Zeugnis*)

One of the main and most important effects of Benjamin's usage of language is demonstrated by the way he engages modern secular concepts in relation to and tension with their religious, mythical, or pre-modern ancestors. This is an effort to make an echo of the former audible or perceivable in the present. Many examples of this have already been mentioned, specifically *Erlösung*/salvation and *Lösung*/solution, *Klage*/lamentation and *Anklage*/accusation. In addition, Benjamin repeatedly addresses the relationship of history and genealogy to language through dialectical images that refer to the visual field of reproduction (*Zeugung*). The project of *Babel*, in which the human attempt to "make a name for themselves" by building a city and a tower that reached to heaven failed, marks the equi-primordial outset of the increase in languages and the scattering of peoples (Gen. 11). This biblical scene also pinpoints the split in the unity of human genealogy and history of language, of corporeal and intelligible reproduction, of *sōma* and *sma*—all these splits being repetitions of the caesura of the Fall, which symbolizes the simultaneous emergence of knowledge and sexuality in cognition. From here, a practice arises in which multivarious transpositions move back and forth between the field of language/thought and that of corporeal reproduction.

We can encounter such transpositions in Ancient Greece as well. They are to be found not only the in model of the Socratic Eros, which Benjamin, in his *Anti-Socrates* (1916), considered demonic because it degraded Eros to the status of a mere means and thus conflated the spheres of intellectual and corporeal reproduction.[13] In an essay on "Shem," which interprets narratives on the house of Shem in the Biblical context of the Babel myth as a dispersal of "Shem," Thomas Schestag studies different words entailing *sēma*, among other *sēmen* and *sēm*: sign and tomb, word and seed. Similar associations are also evoked by the Greek word *spermologos*: the seed, the word, someone or a bird who gathers seeds. In the metaphorical sense it denotes a babbler,[14] and is thus a metaphor that evidently functions through the surfeit of words or seeds. This linkage of word and seed can likewise be shown to exist in countless Biblical metaphors where the seed is, for example, used to describe God's word.

13. For more detail, see "Eros and Language: Benjamin's Kraus Essay."
14. Thomas Schestag, "Sem," in Hirsch, 71ff.

Benjamin's obsessive and deconstructive work on the comparison of *Zeugung* or (pro-) creation and *Zeugnis* (testimony) concerns such a linkage of language and reproduction. Because of Kraus's reference to the creature, which contains an implicit thematization of social relationships as natural relationships and, further, as the "temple of the creature," Benjamin characterizes Kraus's discourse as one that produces its own ideal follower in the form of a "devoted creature" because his discourse calls it into being in the first place. In a passage already discussed in the first chapter, Benjamin condenses his thoughts on this quite complex constellation into one short sentence: "Bestimmen kann sein Zeugnis nur die, denen es Zeugung nie werden kann" (II.1/341; "His testimony can determine only those for whom it can never provide [pro-] creation"; SelWr 2.438, transl. mod.). This statement means that those who have been created (only) by his words (those who are mere spiritual characters) cannot at the same time function as receivers of his words intended as a testimony, especially because the concept of testimony is based on evidence or experience that can by no means be a matter of production: either it exists or not.[15] Although for Benjamin the double transferal from the realm of artifacts into the realm of the natural is here at issue, the language game of *Zeugnis* and *Zeugung* proves to be an image that needs to be read. It draws on the tradition of the aforementioned comparison between body and language and explodes it in the figuration of asynchrony in order to shed light on the abyss between *Zeugnis* and *Zeugung*. On this point, the *task of the translator* would thus be to contend with the translation of a deconstructed transposition, that is to say, with the translation of a dialectical image that refers to the comparison and destroys it. In this instance, the translation again fails to take the word by its name and misunderstands the sense: "His word can be decisive only for those whom it did not beget" (OWS, 265). Yet Benjamin's sentence has nothing to do with a word that begets but rather with words as the products of a quasi-natural or quasi-physiological production in language. In *Selected Writings* it is translated as "His testimony can determine only those for whom it can

---

15. For a more intense discussion of the concepts of testimony in historiography, justice, the narrations of survivors, and fiction, see Sigrid Weigel, "Zeugnis und Zeugenschaft. Klage und Anklage. Zur Geste des Bezeugens in der Differenz von *identity politics*, juristischem und historiographischem Diskurs," in *Zeugnis und Zeugenschaft. Einstein Forum Jahrbuch 1999* (Berlin: Akademie-Verlag, 2000).

never become generative" (SelWr 2.438). This translation gets much closer to the meaning, but it also deprives the English reader of Benjamin's creative work with the etymological affinity between *Zeugnis* und *Zeugung*, testimony and (pro-) creation.

In part, Benjamin's essay on Kraus presents his elaboration of an idea that is preempted by a note in *One-Way Street*, namely in a sentence that involves the most extreme moment of possible untranslatability in Benjamin's writings. Under the heading "For Men" he writes, "Überzeugen ist unfruchtbar" (IV.1/87). A purely literal translation of these three words is: convincing is infertile. This sentence, however, is a thought-image *par excellence*, in which *überzeugen* can also be read as *über-zeugen*, which literally means to *over*-procreate, and thus as a reflection of the transposition of an economy of sexual reproduction into language, denoting the practice of *convincing* as generating rhetorical zealousness. The focus here is on an economy of intermediacy that is geared toward procreation, progeny, or results, an economy inscribed into the comparison between a wealth of words and seed(s), and which essentially has no effect. The act of 'convincing' as over-production is likewise reflected on as an excessive fulfillment of a positivist stance, as a mode of thinking dependent on testimony and what has been testified to—that is to say, as an impossible stance that in the final instance comes off as empty to the extent that it cannot count on (and thus reckon with) the hoped-for result.

Instead of adding a parenthetic note after the translation of *convince* in order to outline the language game, the English translation shifts the game of meaning onto the second part of the sentence by rendering it as "To convince is to conquer without conception" (OWS, 47; SelWr 2.2, 446) and thus ends up with a kind of sexual allusion, while Benjamin's work on the field of images around reproduction and creation specifically sets out to burst mere allusions asunder. What follows from this analysis is the awareness that reading Benjamin in English does not only mean to read Benjamin's work in another language but to read a different Benjamin.

## The Authentic and the *Un-eigentliche*

Benjamin's thinking-in-images primarily seeks to counter the function of metaphors, comparisons, and allusions in language, memory, and discourse. For example, in his essay on surrealism he expressly delimits the concept of *image* from those of metaphor and comparison, and proceeds to posit the discovery of "a hundred-percent image space" (II.1, 309). In the meantime, it should have become clear that this image space is by no means "a sphere *reserved* one hundred percent *for* images" as the English translation would have it (OWS, 239; emphasis S.W.). Benjamin instead construes *Bildraum* as a space *of the* image, the space of thought-images, images both written and read. The specific treatment of images in Benjamin's mode of writing thus relates more than the manner in which metaphors are read and transcribed into dialectical images. If the image is "that wherein what has been comes together in a flash with the now to form a constellation" (Arcades 462), then it also bears on a sphere of the image space that cannot be grasped in terms of the opposition between concept (*Begriff*) and metaphor, of so-called authentic and inauthentic designation. And precisely here one again encounters instances where no translation is possible, instances that remain covert due to the decision in favor of either concept *or* metaphor.

One of the most frequently cited sentences from Benjamin's writings, a quote within a quote, relates to this sphere and again rebuffs any notion of complete translatability: "Articulating the past historically does not mean recognizing it 'the way it really was'" (SelWr 4.391). The German citation of 'wie es denn eigentlich gewesen ist' is rendered here as 'the way it really was' and supplemented by a footnote referring to Leopold von Ranke as the author (398), wherein the vernacular phrase, the *on dit*, is transformed into a proper citation. However, the "eigentlich" not only oscillates among the possible English equivalents of *really*, *actually*, and *in fact*; it also cites the *Eigentliche*, equivalent to *authentic* or *actual*. He thus calls by name a concept that has been discussed intensely in philosophy, for example by Hans Blumenberg, who studied the *Eigentliche* in the context of his elaborations of the sphere of the 'non-conceptual,' with reference to Heidegger, among others. According to Blumenberg, the philosophical negation of the authentic originates in a sphere of 'being' that cannot be grasped by metaphor. Blumenberg interprets the "inauthenticity of our existence" (*Uneigentliche unserer Existenz*), which Heidegger conceived of within the conceptual frame of his history of Being (*Sein*) as "an episode of being-as-concealed (*Seinsverborgenheit*), or rather of being-concealing of Being (*Seinsverbergung des Seins*)," as a response to the metaphorical failure of the attempt to grasp authenticity (*Eigentliche*): "The fact that existence (*Dasein*) is being-in-the-world means precisely that the world of this being-in does not consist of 'objects,' but neither can be grasped by metaphors."[16]

Benjamin, by evoking this meaning in his citation, at the same time posits a *different* response to the necessarily failed authenticity. His negation of *eigentlich* does not infer a reference to the inauthentic: neither to that conception offered by metaphor—as opposed to concepts, i.e., the language of so-called actual denomination (*eigentliche Benennung*), and thus understood as inactual denomination (*uneigentliche Benennung*)—nor to that innate in an ontological rewriting of the inauthentic via concealed being. Instead, he returns to the literal level and origin of the nonauthentic, by reemphasizing, evoking, or quoting the image character of words as is concealed in the concepts. This procedure is comparable to a return to those primordial tropes from which philosophical discourse arose and which then, in the course of philosophy's dissociation from myth and through the disavowal of its image character, mutated into a language of the authentic. From concepts of authenticity, metaphors were then split off as impure, inactual, and inauthentic, as Derrida has outlined in his essay *White Mythology*.[17] Benjamin's use of language and his attitude toward the image, which goes back before this split into concept and metaphor, can be understood as an answer to their dialectical development. His method reminds us that in every image a heterogeneity of the intelligible and the sensory converges in a constellation, i.e., the image preceding any distinction between visual and verbal images and any materialization in different media.

One of Benjamin's most famous figures for both his language theory and his manner of engagement with language is what he terms "calling on the word by its name." By doing so, the word approximates a proper name and thus enters a level of language in which, as a result of the simultaneity of literalness and meaning, the law of translatability comes up against genuine untranslatability. In a study of Biblical names, Stéphane Mosès has shown that the logic of these names, which is inscribed into the very structure of the Hebrew language, is "by definition untranslatable." Though this is true of the divine name per se, Mosès also demonstrates the

16. Hans Blumenberg, "Ausblick auf eine Theorie der Unbegrifflichkeit," in *Theorie der Metapher*, Anselm Havekamp, ed. (Darmstadt: Wissenschaftliche Buchgesellschaft, 1996), 452.

17. Jacques Derrida, "White Mythology: Metaphor in the Text of Philosophy," in *Margins of Philosophy* (Chicago: University of Chicago Press, 1982).

coexistence of literalness and meaning, taking the example of such names as jiZH'aK (Isaac). This coincidence regularly gets lost in translations of the Bible in moments when a choice must be made between semantic and onomatopoetic translation.[18]

In the closing passage of the essay on the translator, at the threshold between Hölderlin's translations of Sophocles and the Holy Scripture, Benjamin mentions the possibility of not collapsing into the abyss of meaning by expressing that there is a *Halten* (IV.1/21). Where the word *Halt* signifies both 'stand still' and 'support,' and would, if used, have elided the difference of pausing, stopping, and retaining, Benjamin's *Halten* opens up a different track. For the word *halten* also conceals an historically prior meaning in the sense of to guard, heed, observe. Oscillating between different meanings, Benjamin's *Halten* is thus likewise legible as *hüten*, i.e., a caring and protective act of attention or beholding, and proves to be a stance owning the possibility for a specific perception.

Since I could continue this consideration of Benjamin's use of language *as* thinking in images *ad infinitum*, in order to bring the never-ending series of examples to a halt I shall seek support in the translation of "Aber es gibt ein Halten" with its insufficient but now apposite: "There is, however, a stop" (SelWr 1.262).

18. Stéphane Mosès, " 'Ich werde sein, der ich sein werde.' Zur Unübersetzbarkeit der biblischen Gottesnamen," in *Zwischen den Kulturen. Theorie und Praxis des interkulturellen Gesprächs*, Carola Hilfrich-Kunjappu and Stéphane Mosès, eds. (Tübingen: Niemeyer, 1997).

# 8

# The Study of Images in the Spirit of True Philology

*The Odyssey of* The Origin of the German Mourning Play
*Through the Kulturwissenschaftliche Bibliothek Warburg*

Mannerist painting comes into the picture in *The Origin of the German Mourning Play* with the section on the dramas of tyrants and martyrs, where the matter at hand is the state of exception and sovereignty. Benjamin references the compositional techniques of mannerist painting in order to focus attention on the expressive gestures of the theatrical figures, in which the sovereign's conversion into a tyrant and martyr is legible, a movement proper to the Janus head of sovereignty in the Baroque period. He uncovers the Tyrant's *inability to decide* as a result of the "antithesis between the power of the ruler and his capacity to rule" (Origins 70), which he considers to be one of the main characteristics of Baroque sovereignty. His interpretation is demonstrated to the reader by way of a comparison to painting:

The prince, who is responsible for making the decision to proclaim the state of exception, reveals, at the first opportunity, that he is almost incapable of making a decision. Just as compositions with restful lighting are virtually unknown in mannerist painting, so it is that the theatrical figures of this epoch always appear in the harsh light of their changing resolve. What is conspicuous about them is not so much the sovereignty displayed in the stoic turn of phrase, as the sheer arbitrariness of an emotional storm that can shift at any moment and in which the figures of Lohenstein especially sway about like torn and flapping banners. (I.I/250ff.; Origins 71)

For Benjamin, the impassioned gestures (*erregte Gebärden*) and streaming figures are signs of an a-sovereignty and reinforce his thesis that it is through the *inability to decide* that the sovereign becomes a tyrant. The reference to painting thus is not part of a discourse that engages in a *paragon* and is thus less concerned with visual argumentation. Benjamin rather conceives of the expressive gestures of Baroque theater as a symptom of a specific concept of sovereignty that is based in the "disproportion between the unlimited hierarchical dignity, with which he is divinely invested and the humble state of a human being" (250; 70). Benjamin describes the disproportion between the political and mortal body of the king, between a godlike position and that of the creaturely, as a conflict inherent to the political theology of the Baroque concept of sovereignty. This is expressed in the affects of the sovereign as a "conflict between the impotence and depravity of the person, on the one hand, and, on the other, the extent to which the age was convinced of the sacrosanct power of his role" (Origins 72). The direct relation between politics and the modulation of affect allows the term *Trauerspiel* within contemporary consciousness to designate the dramatic genre and at the same to describe the historical conditions. As a result, the expressive gestures of theatrical figures are understood as the unmediated representation of the historical problematic: the theatrical figures *are* the images of the Baroque age.

## Pathos Formulas

When Benjamin cites individual images or paintings, it often concerns gestures (*Gesten*), gesticulations (*Gebärden*),[1] and bodily expression within the image space. Such pathos formulas are indispensible 'material' for his physiognomic gaze. The expressive gestures are not only regarded as a mimetic-physical indication of affects and memories but also read as a physiognomic signature of the time. The affinity that this approach has to the pathos formulas in Aby Warburg's writings helps explain Benjamin's interest in the work done at the Kulturwissenschaftlichen Bibliothek Warburg (KBW), a degree of interest that far exceeds what is obvious through the number of direct quotations of and references to the KBW in the section on Dürer's *Melancholia* in his Baroque book. The expressive gestures constitute an intersection between Benjamin's physiognomic treatment of history and Warburg's work on the iconographic memory

1. See note 19 in Chapter 6.

(*Bildgedächtnis*) of Europe's cultural history. It is significant, therefore, that the cultic and religious origin of culture constitutes a central premise of both writers' thought.

The manner in which Warburg and Benjamin treat the gestures, however, is neither a translation of image formulas into text nor vice versa. The classic works of antiquity, rather, provide a common reference point in their conceptions of rhetoric, tragedy, and poetics—all of which are grounded in affect. Thus Warburg can describe the pathos formulas as, among other things, "migrating (*wandernde*) antique superlatives of gestural language" and "immigrated antique rhetors" and thereby indicates the formulas' origin in ancient rhetoric.[2] For the most part, when he speaks of pathos formulas he does so in terms of a "pagan" culture that emulated an expressive gestural language of enhanced affects. He studied the formulas primarily in the culture of the Italian Renaissance, using as examples both paintings and the dramas that were performed as song and dance pieces and that represent one of the early forms of opera.[3] These expressive gestures also play a central role in Benjamin's *The Origin of the German Mourning Play*, as well as in numerous works on modernity up through the *Arcades Project*—including bodily expressions, countenances, verbal gestures, and the voice and costumes of various genres, media, and cultural practices. In the process, he finds worthwhile correspondences between the baroque and modernity.

In his essay on Karl Kraus, for example, Benjamin references baroque altar painting in order to show readers how the entirety of world history closes in on Karl Kraus with a single phrase. The perspective typical of Baroque ceiling painting (with its shortened proportions) thereby becomes the image of a "wholly uncontemplative moment (*Nu*)" (SelWr 2.443), a

2. On the epistemological function of Warburg's term *Wanderung* and the genealogy of the term *pathosformula*, see the extensive commentaries in my edition of Aby Warburg's *Writings* (Warburg 2010). For the connection of pathos formula to the concept of catharsis within ancient rhetorics, see Ulrich Port, "'Katharsis des Leidens.' Aby Warbugs 'Pathosformeln' und ihre konzeptionellen Hintergründe in Rhetorik, Poetik und Tragödientheorie," in *Deutsche Vierteljahrschrift für Literaturwissenschaft und Geistesgeschichte*, 1999, Vol. 73, 5–42; and *Pathosformeln. Die Tragödie und die Geschichte exaltierter Affekte (1755–1888)* (Munich: Wilhelm Fink, 2005).

3. On the significance of drama and opera to the development of Warburg's concept of the pathos formula, see Sigrid Weigel, "Pathosformel und Oper. Die Bedeutung des Musiktheaters für Aby Warburgs Konzept der Pathosformel," in *KulturPoetik 6*, Vol. 2, 2006, 234–253.

full, compendious moment that becomes evident in the composition of paintings:

> Just as, in the most opulent examples of Baroque altar painting, saints pressed hard against the frame extend defensive hands toward the breathtakingly fore-shortened extremities of the angels, the blessed, and the damned floating before them, so the whole of world history presses in on Kraus in the extremities of a single item of local news, a single phrase, a single advertisement. (2.443)

The structure of argumentation, "as in painting—so in Kraus," highlights the common vanishing point of an unnamed, enduring linguistic image in the idiom: that something *einstürzt* (literally collapses, falls down) on somebody. In this locution, painting and metaphor meet in one image and become a constellation. Yet there is more to it. The reference to altar painting brings to mind pictorially the kind of baroque heritage that for Benjamin provides the ambivalent heritage of Kraus's thoughts, as already discussed in the first chapter. He writes: "This is the heritage that has come down to him from the sermons of Abraham a Sancta Clara" (443), and with this statement Benjamin places Kraus's polemics and critiques in a line of succession to the baroque court chaplain, regarded as the most powerfully eloquent Catholic preachers in German language.

Several paragraphs later, with reference to the correspondences between expressionism and miniatures from the early middle ages, he thematizes the "bend" in the bodies of the figures in the pictures of *Vienna Genesis*: "as if falling sickness had overtaken them thus, in their running which is always headlong, they lean toward one and other" (445). In this case, the example of the Vienna Genesis introduces the scene of a detailed ekphrasis of the miniatures that takes up almost the entire page and continues the discussion of a sense of guilt after the First World War in reference to the body language in the images. In his work on Baudelaire, by contrast, he mentions only briefly the "expressiveness of Giotto's *Iracondia* at Padua," with which Benjamin characterizes Baudelaire's "violent temper" and "passion for gambling" in *Les Fleurs du mal* (SelWr 4.332). There he cites a figure out of the history of art as the pictorial embodiment of a specific image of affect, thus using the iconography of the renaissance as a comparative register for the poetic speech of modernity: the afterlife of the renaissance's pathos formulas in modernity (Illustrations 1 and 2).

Exactly those more incidental references to images within the history of art make clear that Benjamin does not regard painting as an object of art-historical observation, be it epochal, stylistic, or formal analyses of history. He is obviously more interested in the language of affect, which is represented by means of the expressive movements and gestures in images. For him, these pathos formulas are connected to the gestures of speech and the figures and metaphors of poetry and literature. What the *body* is in *painting*, the *voice* is in *language*—one only has to think of the enfeebled humming and armed pathos, the two poles of Kraus's linguistic expression discussed in the first chapter. What *expressive gestures* of *images* are, that is the *imagistic character* of *writing*. For this reason, figures from painting reach out to figuration in language and create a common repertoire of expressive or affective gestures. The interaction of bodily-linguistic and pictoral-scriptoric gestures in painting and literature plays a central role in Benjamin's writings, at the latest with the work on baroque mourning play. They are certainly not to be confused with that beloved phrase "the language of art," with which the semiotic function of nonverbal forms of art such as painting, sculpture, architecture, and music is understood as a system of meaning analogous to the linguistic system. This is a point of view that the young Benjamin still

ILLUSTRATION 1:   *Wiener Genesis* (series 5r)
*Wiener Genesis*, folio 5r, in Barbara Zimmermann, *Die Wiener Genesis im Rahmen der antiken Buchmalerei. Ikonographie, Darstellung, Illustrationsverfahren und Aussageintention*, Wiesbaden 2003, illus. 9.

ILLUSTRATION 2: *Ira*, detail from *Le Virtù e i Vizi*, around 1305, Fresco, Padua, Cappella degli Scrovegni

Giotto, *Ira*, Ausschnitt, in *Le Virtù e i Vizi*, ca. 1305, Fresco, Padua, Cappella degli Scrovegni; in Alberto Busignani, *Giotto*, Florenz 1993, p. 156.

shared at the end of the essay on language from 1916, where he speaks of a "language of sculpture or painting," writing: "For an understanding of artistic forms, it is of value to attempt to grasp them all as languages and to seek their connection with natural languages" (SelWr 1.73).

## Philosophy of Art, Art Criticism, and Science of Art (*Kunstwissenschaft*)

This kind of reference to art forms as "language of the arts" recedes into the background (paradoxically) at that moment when Benjamin's reading goes beyond the repertoire of literary and linguistic objects and turns to other media and arts as well as phenomena within the history of culture, a reading from which the project of the "*Urgeschichte der Moderne*" (an urhistory or archaic history of modernity) emerged. On this threshold, one that Benjamin himself reflected upon as a complete upheaval (*Umwälzung*) of his entire "mass of thoughts and images" (5/89 ), he formulates a "Doctrine of the Similar" ("Lehre vom Ähnlichen"; 1933) in which he considers language to be the "highest application of the mimetic faculty" and language and writing as "the most perfect archive of nonsensuous similarity" (SelWr 2.697). This archive is owed to a cultural-historical process in which the mimetic faculty has "migrated" into language (722). Only from the perspective of this linguistic theory may other phenomena (such as physiognomy, facial expressions, scriptorial pictures, and sound patterns) be considered as revenants of previous mimetic practices and as phenomena of a distorted similarity. In them the past survives within the semiotic world of modernity and juts into it. Reflections that Benjamin developed in his readings during the previous years (not the least during his work on the *Trauerspiel* book) also appear in the phrasings in his "Doctrine of the Similar."

Although until the middle of the 1920s Walter Benjamin's writings are embraced by the paradigms of the philosophy of art, *Kunstwissenschaft*[4]

4. Benjamin's relationship to art history was systematically investigated for the first time thirty years ago by Wolfgang Kemp; see Kemp, "Fernbilder. Benjamin und die Kunstwissenschaft," in *Walter Benjamin im Kontext*, ed. Burkhardt Linder (Frankfurt/M: Syndikat, 1978). Since then, Benjamin has indeed frequently been used for art-theoretical and artistic projects; his engagement with the science of visual art (or art history) has thereby played a role only at the edge, such that in this regard the state of knowledge has not essentially changed. Although Michael Jennings, for example, has analyzed the significance Alois Riegl has for

hardly played a role in his work to that point. Subsequent to his dissertation, "The Concept of Criticism in German Romanticism" (1920), he had, as shown in Chapter 1, developed a programmatic concept of art criticism. In "Goethe's *Elective Affinities*," he demonstrated a philosophy of art in an emphatic sense, where the language of art recognizes its own "virtual possibility of formulating" (SelWr 1.334) as the limit of art's own discourse: "the task of art criticism is not to lift the veil but rather, through the most precise knowledge of it as a veil, to raise itself for the first time to the true view of the beautiful" (351). Benjamin thus did not develop his theory of the "true work of art" (334) out of reflection on works of visual art but rather from the reading of Goethe's novel. When the essay on Goethe was published in the *Neue Deutsche Beiträge* in two parts on April 1924 and January 1925, Benjamin had long since taken up his work on *The Origin of the German Mourning Play,* and with it discovered his "passion for Baroque emblematics" (2/433). The interrelation between the two projects (the Goethe essay and the *Trauerspiel* book) more concretely illuminates the transformation in Benjamin's interests and theorems in terms of the relation between writing and image. Although in the paradigms of 'art criticism' and the 'philosophy of art' the various arts were still embedded in a broad concept of the *artwork*, Benjamin now directs his attention (with his interest in the scene of cultural history in Baroque emblematics) to the pictorial form of writing and the script of pictures in particular: "at one stroke the profound vision of allegory transforms things and works into stirring writing" (Origins 176).

  In the context of his work on the *Trauerspiel* book, Benjamin again took up his readings in visual arts history from which he had already profited in his time as a student. As it says in the *Curriculum Vitae* that he prepared, "Decisive stimuli [Anregungen] came to me during my years of study at university from a series of texts that in part lay far outside my narrow field of study" (VI/225). The fact that Alois Riegl is the most important name among the titles and authors he lists is due to the retrospective orientation of the text. This confirms that Riegl remained indeed so vital,

---

Benjamin's literary theory ("Walter Benjamin and the Theory of Art History," in *Walter Benjamin*, Uwe Steiner, ed., Berlin: Europäischer Verlag der Wissenschaften, 1992), the eminent role authors of art history had in the development of Benjamin's image theory has been left obscured. Only recently has Heinz Brüggemann discussed the young Benjamin's reflections on color and imagination in a comprehensive study. See Brüggemann, *Walter Benjamin. Über Spiel, Farbe und Phantasie* (Würzburg: Königshausen & Neumann, 2007).

as he writes in his review "Bücher, die lebendig geblieben sind" ("Books that Remain Alive," 1929), where he acknowledges Riegl's *The Late Roman Art Industry* (*Spätrömische Kunstindustrie*, 1901) as an "epoch-making work" (III/170). When Benjamin first encountered the work of Riegl is not entirely clear, however. Werner Kraft, who knew Benjamin since 1915, indicates that Benjamin wrote to him about Riegl's *Spätrömische Kunstindustrie* from Bern:[5] thus it can be assumed that he had studied this book during his stay in Bern in connection with work on his dissertation, the "Concept of Criticism in German Romanticism." Yet during his years at various universities, it was Heinrich Wölfflin instead who belonged to the canon read by Benjamin. During his semester in Munich in 1915–16 he attended Wölfflin's lecture "Denkmäler mittelalterlicher Zeichnung" ("Monuments of Medieval Drawing"). Yet to a great degree, Wölfflin's name stands for a story of disappointment. While twenty-year-old Benjamin still counted Wölfflin's *Classic Art* among the most useful works that he had read "on visual art (*in concreto*)" (1/58), he reversed his opinion three years later. In November 1915, Benjamin writes to Fritz Radt that an experiment conducted in concert with Grete Radt in the *Munich Pinacotheka* confirmed that Wölfflin's lecture was actually a poor one (289). Two weeks later, he confirms the bad impression and summarizes his disappointment: "Now I am aware that in this case one encounters the most disastrous impact that I have encountered at German universities. A man of by no means overwhelming talent, who by nature has just as little relationship to art, like any other" (1/296ff.), and who compensates for this lack only by exaltation.

## The Spirit of Philology and Significance of the Insignificant

Fifteen years later, Benjamin wrote "Strenge Kunstwissenschaft," an article outlining his fundamental principles, as a review of the first issue of *Kunstwissenschaftliche Forschungen* (1931),[6] which could only be published

5. Werner Kraft, "Über Benjamin," in *Zur Aktualität Walter Benjamins*, ed. Siegfried Unseld (Frankfurt/M: Suhrkamp, 1972), 59–69. Here, 62.

6. *Kunstwissenschaftliche Forschungen. Erster Band*, ed. Otto Pächt (Berlin: Frankfurter Verlags-Anstalt, 1931). The comprehensive volume (246 pages) contains Hans Sedlmayr's essay "Zu einer strengen Kunstwissenschaft"; a contribution "Sophienkathedrale von Konstantinopel" by Andreades; an article by Otto Pächt about Michael Pacher; and the longest contribution by Carl Linfert, "Die Grundlagen der Architekturzeichnung."

under his pseudonym, Detlef Holz, in July 1933 in the *Frankfurter Zeitung* after quite a few difficulties. The article not only signaled that this field had moved into the center of his attention but also proposed, from the distance of a quasi-historical evaluation, a milder judgment of Wölfflin:

> And, in fact, Wölfflin did not succeed in his attempt to use formal analysis (which he placed at the center of his method) to remedy the bleak condition in which his discipline found itself at the end of the nineteenth century and which Dvořák later in his obituary on Riegl had characterized so precisely. Wölfflin had identified a dualism—a flat, universalizing history of the art of "all cultures and times," on one hand, and an academic aesthetic, on the other—without, however, being able to overcome it completely. (III/370; SelWr 2.666)

Because of opposition to the publication of his article from the Feuilleton editors at the *Frankfurter Zeitung*, Benjamin (supported by diplomatic mediation and correspondence with Carl Linfert)[7] revised the manuscript, and in the process retracted or formulated more mildly several critical remarks from the first version—in particular, the further characterization of the nineteenth century's legacy within the academic discipline, such as work "with objects of pleasure, with formal problems, with modeled experiences (*Erlebnissen*),[8] or any other clichés inherited from a belletristic consideration of art" (SelWr 2.667). Conversely, the revised version of the article sharpens the contours of a positively evaluated new art history. Thus at the same time Benjamin, in the critique of Wölfflin, also designates the field to which another, *new Kunstwissenschaft*[9] must adapt: it lies beyond the dualism of universal history and academic aesthetics.

---

7. See the letter from Linfert from 12/13/1932 (III/653–657) and the letter from Benjamin from 7/18/1933 (5/260–262).

8. The difference between *Erfahrung* und *Erlebnis* (both rendered as experience in English) is crucial for Benjamin and the philosophical context of his time. *Erlebnis* is one of the key terms of *Lebensphilosophie* and, after the First World War, became a pathos formula in autobiographical writings of the generation of First World War soldiers. See, for example, Benjamin's critique on Ernst Jünger in his "Theories of Fascism" (1929). Benjamin later, in the Baudelaire complex, refined the tension between *Erlebnis* and *Erfahrung* as providing an epistemological paradigm to examine phenomena of modern culture. See Chapter 10 in this volume.

9. The fact that Benjamin chooses the term *Kunstwissenschaft* instead of art history (*Kunstgeschichte*) is significant for his commitment to visual art, and it anticipates current critical analyses on the paradigm of art history, a name that refers to both the subject mat-

The positive counterpart to Wölfflin is Alois Riegl, who enters the picture at precisely this point. Benjamin describes him as the progenitor of a "new type of *Kunstwissenschaft*": "It is the detailed interpretation of the *individual work of art* that, without anywhere denying itself, meets with the rules and problems of the evolution of art in general" (372; emphasis S.W.). The methodology of this new type of research had to focus on the close relation between meaning-content (*Bedeutungsgehalt*) and material content (*Sachgehalt*) of the work, leading to a relation in which the more inconspicuously and intimately these are bound, the more crucial the works are. It was a matter of the reciprocal illumination of historical changes and the accidental, external aspects of the artwork:

For if the most meaningful works prove to be precisely those works whose life is most deeply embedded in their material contents—one thinks of Giehlow's interpretation of Dürer's *Melencolia*—then over the course of their historical duration these material contents present themselves to the researcher all the more clearly the more they have disappeared from the world. (SelWr 2.669)

In this passage Benjamin takes up the two terms *commentary* and *critique* once more, which provided the basis of "Goethe's *Elective Affinities*," wherein he distinguishes commentary (an analysis of the material content of a work) from critique (the analysis of its truth content). After his work on the allegorical gaze in the *Trauerspiel* book, his work undergoes a significant shift. While in the context of his philosophy of art, *material content* and *truth content* stand opposite one and other, now the category of the *truth content* has been supplanted by that of the *meaning-content*. Traces of the *Trauerspiel* book are discernible in the substitution of 'meaning' for 'truth.' Inasmuch as the gaze of the allegorist turns everything into writing, the question as to the manner in which things and images receive meaning becomes central. As already mentioned, in 1935 Benjamin diagnosed, in the form of a self-reflection, the "process of complete upheaval that a multitude of thoughts and images had to undergo, ones that come from the remote period of my actual metaphysical, indeed theological thinking so that they could nourish my current disposition with all the force they contained" (Correspondence, 486). With this transformation, terms and con-

---

ter and the discipline. See Didi-Huberman, *Devant L'image. Question pose aux fins d'une histoire de l'art* (Paris: Editions de Minuit, 1990); and Hans Belting, *Das Ende der Kunstgeschichte?* (München: C.H. Beck, 1983).

cepts derived from metaphysics (such as 'truth') fade into the background while the rules of signification are now emphasized first and foremost—in particular, the interplay of writing and images, and thus also of rhetoric and iconography. The scene of this upheaval is the work on the *Trauerspiel* book, primarily in the section on melancholy and the second part on "Allegory and Trauerspiel." Here, the authors discussed in *Strenge Kunstwissenschaft* are explicitly cited: Alois Riegl and *Die Enstehung der Barockkunst in Rom* (1923), and Karl Giehlow with his study of Dürer's *Melencolia I* (1903) and *Die Hieroglyphenkunde des Humanismus in der Allegorie der Renaissance* (1915). In this way, Benjamin's review not only contains a discussion of the first volume of *Kunstwissenschaftliche Forschungen* but at the same time also concludes the sum total of an intensive engagement with the literature of art analyses that he had assembled for work on the *Trauerspiel* book. In this article, structured as an inventory of the discipline of *Strenge Kunstwissenschaft*, he describes the "new study of art" as a manner of approaching art that arises from the "spirit of true philology." One of its most important principles is the significance of the seemingly insignificant:

Also characteristic of this manner of approaching art is the "esteem for the insignificant" (which the Brothers Grimm practiced in their incomparable expression of the spirit of true philology). But what animates this esteem, if not the willingness to push research forward to the point where even the "insignificant"—no, *precisely* the insignificant—becomes significant? The bedrock that these researchers come up against is the concrete bedrock of past historical existence (*geschichtlichen Gewesenseins*). The "insignificance" with which they are concerned is neither the nuance of new stimuli nor the characteristic trait, which was formerly employed to identify column forms much the way Linné taxonomized plants. Instead it is the inconspicuous aspect [ . . . ] which survives in the works and which constitutes the point where the content reaches the breaking point for an authentic researcher. And therefore, due to their historico-philosophical braces, it is not Wölfflin but Riegl to be the first ancestor of this new type of *Kunstwissenschaft*. (III/371ff.; SelWr 2.668)

In this way, Benjamin acknowledges the new study of art since it does not identify itself as a discipline on a certain subject matter but as a specific approach. In its methodology the seemingly insignificant receives a similar epistemological significance as the *detail* in Warburg's and his own works (which will be discussed more intensely in the last chapter).[10]

10. On the epistemological status of the detail in Warburg, Freud, and Benjamin, as one of the epistemological centerpieces of *Kulturwissenschaft*, see also chapter 1, "Die Entstehung

## The Boundary Case:
## Overcoming the Territorial Character of Scholarship

In addition to the significance of the inconspicuous, an eye for which grows out of the spirit of philology, the new *Kunstwissenschaft* is marked by its engagement with the *boundary case* of artworks and genres. An example of this orientation can be found in Benjamin's review of Linfert's contribution on architectural drawing.[11] Here, Riegl is again named as the model, in whose *The Late Roman Art Industry*, according to Benjamin, the boundary case has already proved to be "a starting point of the most significant overcoming of conventional universal history" because it is "in the investigation of the boundary case," rejected by universal history,[12] "that material contents reveal their key position most decisively" (669). What particularly interested Benjamin in the plates accompanying Linfert's drawings, was the fact that they do not represent likenesses or depictions but rather emblems of their epoch, as it were:

one cannot say that they *re*-produce architecture. They *perform* it in the first place, and this less often benefits the reality of planning than it does dreams[. . . . ] How the architectural prospects open up in order to take into their core allegories, stage designs, and monuments! And each of these forms in turn points to unrecognized facts which appear to the researcher in their full concreteness: Renaissance hieroglyphics; Piranesi's visionary fantasies of ruins; the temples of the Illuminati, such as we know them from *Die Zauberflöte*. (373; 669ff.)

What follows is a programmatic statement in which Benjamin's critical stance toward academic disciplines solidifies and in which he posits work in boundary domains: the touchstone of the new spirit of research is "to be at home in boundary domains."

---

der Kulturwissenschaft aus der Lektüre von Details. Übergänge von der Kunstgeschichte, Medizin und Philologie zur Kulturtheorie: Warburg, Freud, Benjamin," in Weigel, *Literatur als Voraussetzung der Kulturgeschichte. Schauplätze von Shakespeare bis Benjamin* (München: Wilhelm Fink, 2004).

11. In this article, Benjamin would have been pleased that Linfert refers—as Kemp has already pointed out (Kemp 1978)—to Benjamin's conception of allegory.

12. Work on boundary cases might be the reason that Benjamin (along with Riegl in a curriculum vitae) names Carl Schmitt, "who in his analyses of political structures undertakes an analogous attempt at the integration of phenomena that can only seemingly be isolated by disciplines" (VI/219).

Benjamin's study of the allegorical treatment of objects relies on Linfert's rereading of iconology, which treats it as pictographic script of the Renaissance, and in turn incorporates it into his review as evidence of a dream structure in this pictographic script. Their legibility is, however, owed to the historical index of the *Arcades Project*, with which Benjamin was already occupied at the time he wrote the review. There, the trace of the Renaissance's afterlife in modernity is taken up again when Benjamin describes the architecture of Second-Empire Paris as images of fantasies and dreams of the collective: "The most hidden aspect of large cities: this historical object of the new metropolis with its uniform streets and immeasurable rows of houses has materialized the dreamed-of architecture of ancient Greece: the labyrinth" (V.2/1007), as he writes in the early drafts of the *Arcades Project*. His essay on the artwork in the age of mechanical reproducibility, written shortly thereafter, also attests to how directly Benjamin was able to apply his discoveries from the scholarship of *Kunstwissenschaft* to his media-historical investigation of modernity, for example when, in the context of his theoretical arguments on film, he works out the thesis that human sense perception is not only natural but also historically determined and bases this on, of all things, Wickhoff's work on the medieval miniatures and on Riegl's interpretation of late-Roman art. He thus bases his thesis on two authors who, as he stresses, were the first to employ their respective (art) objects of study, which had lain buried in the classical tradition, to gain insights into historically specific perception:

The era of migration of peoples, an era which saw the rise of the late-Roman art industry and the Vienna Genesis, developed not only an art different from that of antiquity but also a different perception. The scholars of the Viennese school Riegl and Wickhoff, resisting the weight of the classical tradition beneath which this art had been buried, were the first to think of using such art to draw conclusions about the organization of perception at the time the art was produced. (SelWr 3.104)

Benjamin thus places the entire weight of the *neue Kunstwissenschaft* in the balance in order to discuss film in terms of *aisthesis* (Gr. perception), that is to say, in terms of perceptions shaped by the historical index. The question of whether photography and film are art forms did not move Benjamin, as will be seen in the following chapter. He is instead interested in examining the cultural techniques of perception in order to show how cinematic pictures inherit the cultic value of art.

In his résumé of the above-mentioned review, in which Benjamin solidifies his esteem for the "neue Kunstwissenschaft" in a critique of the ponderous mediocrity of the *Gründerzeit* (the industrial expansion of the late nineteenth century), with its demand for the "great whole," he affirms his appreciation that the new spirit of research is "at home in marginal domains" as its programmatic opposite. Herein he brings into play names that have nothing to do with the reviewed volume of *Kunstwissenschaftliche Forschungen*. Yet for Benjamin, they embody a movement: work done in marginal realms is that with which "the contributors to the new yearbook secure their place in the movement that today fills marginal areas of historical study, from Burdach's German studies to the studies in the history of religion at the Warburg Library, with fresh life" (III/374). Benjamin had already cited both authors (Burdach and Warburg) in the book on *Trauerspiel*: Burdach, from the book *Reformation, Renaissance, Humanismus* (1918); and Warburg, from the study on *Heidnisch-antike Weissagung in Wort und Bild zu Luthers Zeiten* (1910), the latter in addition to works from the Warburg Circle, most importantly, the book on melancholy by Erwin Panofsky and Fritz Saxl (1923). He had discovered it during the writing of the *Ursprung des deutschen Trauerspiels* and immediately recommended it as a "capital book" in a letter to his friend Scholem (2/509).

He soon seized the opportunity to produce an evaluation of Warburg that had no place in the review of the *Kunstwissenschaftlich* yearbook. For it, he made use of his essay "Johann Jakob Bachofen," written in 1934 under contract with the *Nouvelle Revue Française*, but never published. Here, Warburg (who died five years prior) ranks as a *grand seigneur* of scholarship and of the noble and notable spirits of the time: "The type of magisterial scholar splendidly inaugurated by Leibnitz deserves to continue in our day as it still engenders certain noble and remarkable minds like Aby Warburg, founder of the library that bears his name and who has just left Germany for England" (II.1/224). Whereas an affinity between Bachofen and Warburg is justified by their mutual contempt for established borders between academic disciplines, Warburg's name also stands in relation to the already described network of names in which Alois Riegl and Franz Wickhoff also appear—the latter as scholars this time, who would have prepared the way for expressionism with their scholarly work.

What primarily interested Benjamin in the new scholarship was the work being done on marginal cases and through the transgression of disciplinary borders (be it German studies or art history), namely the work done at those thresholds and transitions from where the new school of *Kulturwissenschaft*[13] arose at the turn of the century. Benjamin wanted to understand his own work as part of this approach, as evidenced by a *curriculum vitae* whose date of origin is unknown. In it, Benjamin names Benedetto Croce as a model for him, for Croce's "destroying the doctrine of art based in formal analysis" and efforts to uncover "the way to the individual concrete work," efforts to which Benjamin saw himself connected:

I have thus far directed my efforts at opening a path to the work of art by destroying the doctrine of the territorial character of art. What our approaches have in common is a programmatic attempt to bring about a process of integration in scholarship—one that will increasingly dismantle the rigid partitions between the disciplines that typified the concept of the sciences in the nineteenth century—and to promote this through an analysis of the work of art. Such an analysis would regard the work of art as an integral expression of the religious, metaphysical, political, and economic tendencies of its age, unconstrained in any way by territorial concepts. (VI/218ff.; SelWr 2.78)

It is precisely this attempt that he undertook in *The Origin of the German Mourning Play*, one that is linked to both Riegl's methodology and the contemporary investigations of Carl Schmitt, which are likewise dedicated to an "attempt to integrate phenomena." As he writes: "Above all, however, any such approach seems to me to be a precondition for any effective *physiognomic* apprehension of artworks that make them incomparable and unique. To that extent, I believe it is closer to an *eidetic* way of observing phenomena than to a *historical* one" (78; emphasis S.W.). From this juxtaposition of eidetic and historic approaches, Benjamin will develop a central principle for the "*Urgeschichte der Moderne*," namely (as he formulates in the *Arcades Project*), the maxim that the relationship of what is to what has been is "not temporal in nature but like an image (*bildlich*)"[14] (Arcades Project 464).

13. Not to be confused with Cultural Studies, *Kulturwissenschaft* is the name for works done by authors like Warburg, Freud, Simmel, Cassirer, Benjamin, and others who were working beyond disciplinary restrictions and were interested in the afterlife of religion, cult, and magic meanings within the cultural and social phenomena of modernity. This intellectual constellation is a crucial point of reference for the so-called cultural turn in present-day German humanities. See Weigel, *Literatur als Voraussetzung*.

14. This is one of the examples of untranslatability because the translation must choose between different types of images: 'figurative' is wrong because Benjamin does not refer

A Missed Elective Affinity:
Benjamin and the Warburg School

Benjamin's description of the "new spirit of research" as a movement that feels at home in boundary zones highlights that in his writings
he also conceived of an intellectual topography in which he could himself
feel "at home," all the more so since he no longer had any actual specific
residence. The disappointment over futile attempts to concretize this topography with a personal epistolary network of correspondence and contacts must have been so much the bitterer. Thus the elective affinity that
he felt toward the Kulturwissenschaftliche Bibliothek Warburg was particularly sincere because Benjamin's own method of reflection converged
closely with that of Aby Warburg at more than a few places. The proximity of Benjamin to Warburg is especially striking in the greater context of
the creation of *Kulturwissenschaft* by going beyond disciplinary methodologies, a movement that grew stronger at the first decades of the twentieth century. Above all, they share an emphasis on meaningful details as
regards the significance of the 'insignificant,' an interest in the traces of
excitement and gestures as an expression of affect, in the writing of images and image memory, in the origins of art in cultic and religious history, and in the development of technology and new media. They share a
concept of history that—although conceiving of the progression of cultural history as being *eidetic*, that is to say, following the thread of image
memory—takes into particular account phenomena of an afterlife of artistic and cultural forms of expression from preceding epochs in order to
configure multiple correspondences: between antiquity and the Renaissance, between antiquity and modernity, or between the Renaissance or
the Baroque and modernity.

Thus Benjamin's statement about the grounds of a historical 'has-
been' (*Gewesensein*), from which the significance of the insignificant and inconspicuous accrues, references not only his own allegorical procedure but
also the phrase that came to prominence through Aby Warburg: "God is in

---

here to metaphorical language, and 'pictorial' would put too much emphasis on the visual aspect of images. Benjamin instead deals with a broad concept of the *Bild* defined as a
constellation in which heterogenic elements meet to form a condensed image in the sense
of having a momentous meaning. As regards the role of visual images within this concept,
see the next chapter.

the detail."[15] The similarities could hardly be more significant and densely coupled. In the corpus of Warburg's writings, the concepts of *"bewegtes Beiwerk"* (flowing accessories, mainly hair, scarf, and cloth) and the *"erregte Gebärden"* (excited gestures, which in the history of the reception of the Warburg School are inextricably linked to his name) already appeared in his dissertation on Botticelli (1893) thanks to his sense for detail. This sense assigns meaning to the insignificant, literally to the "nothing but."[16] From this sensitivity to marginalia in respect of motifs and themes, the key Warburgian concept was born: the pathos formula. Benjamin, having studied the manner in which details and fragments in baroque emblematics became "stirring writing" (Origins 176) in his work on the *Trauerspiel*, examined (as will be shown) the significance of the inconspicuous, above all in the media-historical signature of modernity, in photography and film: "image worlds, which dwell in the smallest things—meaningful yet covert enough to find a hiding place in waking dreams, but which, enlarged and having become capable of formulation, make the difference between technology and magic visible as a thoroughly historical variable" (II.I/371ff.; SelWr 2.512).

Formulations like those that can be found in Benjamin's "Little History of Photography" (1931) would have pleased Aby Warburg, had he had the opportunity to read them. The same is true for Benjamin's theory of awakening, since the state of the figures in Botticelli's paintings, as Warburg described them, is as if they have "just woken from a dream to become aware of the world around them; however active they may be in that world, still their minds are filled with images seen in dreams."[17] This state anticipates the threshold of awakening between consciousness and dreaming that Walter Benjamin later assesses in the *Arcades Project* as the "textbook example of dialectical thinking" (V.1/59). Yet nothing illustrates Benjamin's thesis that the *neue Kunstwissenschaft* has emerged out of the spirit of philology more vividly than Aby Warburg's Nymph Project. For Warburg, it is not only the afterlife of antiquity in particular that con-

---

15. See Wolfgang Schäffner, Sigrid Weigel, and Thomas Macho, eds., *"Der Liebe Gott steckt im Detail." Mikrostrukturen des Wissens* (Munich: Wilhelm Fink, 2003).

16. Aby Warburg, "The Birth of Venus and Spring," in *The Renewal of Pagan Antiquity: Contributions to the Cultural History of the European Renaissance* (Los Angeles: Getty Publications, 1999), 107.

17. Ibid., 14, 1.

denses in the figure of the classical nymphs he rediscovered in several renaissance paintings, but also the language of pathos formulas that are
found in their striding gait, fluttering hair, and billowing garments. Yet
even though the tone of the proposal by his friend, André Jolles, to carry
on a correspondence on nymphs was of a fascinated reverence, Warburg
abandoned the project in order instead to focus "the philological gaze to
the ground on which they alight."[18] Instead of committing himself to his
friend's desire for images, Warburg turned toward a different project, a
study of images drawn from the spirit of philology. Though the conventional view of art gave the written tradition the status of a model or source
material for works of art, for Warburg it was now a matter of the *reading
of images* themselves in which details were given equal importance as the
expressive gestures of classical works of art. The ground onto which Warburg's philological gaze is directed is exactly the same as the one Benjamin
describes as the basis of "becoming historical" in which the inconspicuous
gains its significance.

Benjamin could not have read Warburg's sentence that refers to the
"philological gaze to the ground" since it was located in the extensive papers among Warburg's unpublished manuscripts. On the other hand,
traces of an actual reading of Warburg are found in the *Trauerspiel* book.
Thematically, they concern the image memory of the Renaissance (the subject of Warburg's essay on Luther) from which Benjamin quotes a significant Warburgian terminology:

European antiquity was divided and its obscure after-effects in the middle ages
drew inspiration from its radiant after-image in humanism. In a congenial mood
Warburg has given a fascinating explanation of how, in the Renaissance 'heavenly manifestations were conceived in human terms so that their demonic power
might be at least visually contained.' The renaissance stimulates the image memory
(I.I/395; Origins, 221).

The elective affinity that Benjamin diagnoses in respect to Warburg's relation to the divided aftereffect of antiquity applies at least as much to the
author of the *Trauerspiel* book in his relation to Warburg. At the time when
Benjamin writes this, and in his citation of Warburg emphasizing with a

---

18. Weigel, "Aby Warburgs Göttin im Exil," in *Vorträge aus dem Warburg-Haus, Vol. 4*,
2000, 77. The letter from Jolles's and Warburg's manuscripts is now published in Warburg
2010.

hyphen in the typeface the word formations that have 'after,' he had already long ago developed his own theory of the afterlife of a work: "The concept of life is given its due only if everything that has a history of its own, and is not merely the setting for history, is credited with life" (SelWr 1.255), as he writes in "The Task of the Translator" (1921), a text in which the figures of translation, imitation, and echo are converted into one and other.

Yet a comparable echo (like that which Benjamin found for his theory of allegory in art critic Carl Linfert's monograph on architectural drawing) was not granted to Benjamin in the writings of the Warburg School. Although "in respect of the interpretation of the stone, he went further into the store of allegorical symbols of the melancholy than Panofsky and Saxl,"[19] Benjamin's contribution to the decryption of the iconography of Dürer's *Melencolia I* found no attention in the extensive revision of the book that both authors undertook together with Raymond Klibansky. Panofsky had merely incorporated a quotation of Lohenstein from the *Trauerspiel* book, not, however, in the book on melancholy but in his essay "Et in Arcadia ego."[20]

Walter Benjamin's efforts to recommend his book on the *Origin of the German Mourning Play* to the scholars in Hamburg are well known. These efforts demonstrate how intensively he labored through Gershom Scholem and Hugo von Hofmannstahl to come into contact with the circle of scholars at the Kulturwissenschaftliche Bibliothek Warburg (GB 3/308, 320, 346, 369, 405).[21] Yet this interest also ended in disappointment—though of an utterly different type from the one he experienced at the beginning of his interest in *Kunstwissenschaft*, a disappointment marked by the name Wölfflin. His opinion of Warburg's scholarship, however, was not disappointed. Even *after* futile efforts at an intellectual exchange with the Warburg circle, Benjamin still drew the image of a *grand seigneur* of scholarship from Warburg. Rather, the hoped-for recognition of an elective affinity and the

---

19. Kemp, 241.

20. Erwin Panofsky, "Et in Arcadia ego. Poussin und die Tradition des Englischen," in *Sinn und Deutung in der bildenen Kunst* (Cologne: DuMont, 1975), 375, 35.

21. Wolfgang Kemp first reconstructed apparent traces in Benjamin's correspondence (Kemp 1978). His view here can be expanded on the basis of the Warburg circle's correspondence, gathered and tagged by Dorothea McEwan in the Warburg Institute in London, and the edition of the letters of Panofsky, edited by Dieter Wuttke (Panofsky 2001ff.). The documentation in the appendix is developed from research at the Warburg Institute in London.

realization of the latent relationship through their obvious epistemological correspondences were disappointed. As familiar as Benjamin's endeavors to make contact with the Warburg School are, until now the reasons they never reciprocated remained unknown. The odyssey taken by the *Trauerspiel* book, however, can be reconstructed with relative accuracy. Instead of including Benjamin's book in the library, it was sent from one person to the next within the Warburg Institute: from Aby Warburg in Hamburg to Fritz Saxl in London and back to Hamburg to Erwin Panofsky.

"Too Clever":
The Failure of the *Trauerspiel* Book in the KBW

In detail, the treatment of the book is as follows: The KBW had been sent a review copy of Benjamin's *Ursprung des deutschen Trauerspiels* from Rowohlt publishing house. Subsequently, a secretary of Warburg, Clara Hertz, on January 28, 1928, sent a check for twelve Reichsmarks by post to the publisher, because "the Professor does not, on principle, accept sample copies that come with the obligation to write a review, although this book interests him and fits within the framework of the library." Afterward, she must have given the copy to Aby Warburg, because on June 4, 1928, he himself sent Benjamin's book, furnished with a dedication,[22] to Saxl, who had just taken sojourn in London to undertake research in the archives. The book was already recommended to Saxl in a letter from Scholem from May 24, 1928, in which the latter inquires about the state of the second edition of Saxl and Panofsky's book on melancholy:

A chapter on the problem of melancholy, which I believe to be very brilliant and quite obviously approaches your own purposes from a completely different angle, has just recently appeared in the significant work, *Ursprung des deutschen Trauerspiels* by W. Benjamin. Perhaps this suggestion is completely unnecessary (I have strongly recommended to the author to send a review copy to the Warburg library.) But it is possible that this escapes your attention because of the seemingly unrelated title. The author of this book is my best friend and I regret very much that I did not tell you of him in Hamburg, because I believe that you seldom find many people who bring with them such an extraordinary understanding of the

22. The title page bearing Warburg's handwritten dedication is reproduced in Brodersen 1991, 90.

problems of history that concern the Warburg circle as this man does, who came upon you from such a completely different starting point.

With his recommendation, Scholem believed he would be able to build on existing contacts, since he had been in contact with Hamburg for several years. What Scholem certainly could not know, however, was the fact that they would appreciate his knowledge of the history of mysticism and Juda-ism beyond measure, and were also interested in including an article of his in the KBW's yearbook, all the while striving to keep his person at a polite distance. After Scholem's visit to Hamburg, for example, Saxl reported to Warburg (who was in Rome at the time) in great detail and concluded his picture of Scholem's intellect and character with the sentence, "If one asks him regarding a concrete topic, he responds effervescently and ends with the stereotypical sentence: I could easily give an excellent lecture about this here" (29.10.1927). Considering this, Scholem's attempt at mediation was perhaps not the most providential. However, in his written reply to Scholem, Fritz Saxl asserted his interest and also stressed the importance of the book for the revision of the study on Dürer. Nevertheless, he too sent the book along. He responded to Scholem as follows:

Benjamin's book interested me very much, although it is actually not easy to read. But the man has something to say and knows his material. Today I again sent it on to Panofsky so that it can be incorporated into the second edition. Benjamin's material is quite interesting particularly for the late period, for which we have no material. I also sincerely hope to meet Mr. Benjamin in person some time. Where does he live? (17.6.1928, cf. also 3/407ff.)[23]

Another letter in which Saxl thanked Warburg for the delivery of the book and for the dedication speaks more frankly: "Many thanks for the dedication in Benjamin's book. I was delighted by the presence of the dedication. To me, the book is *too clever*" (6.6.1928; emphasis S.W.). This distinction between Warburg's dedication and Benjamin's book is partic-ularly interesting, since in the same letter Saxl commented ironically on certain roles in the division of labor between him and Warburg. Although Warburg, at whose "power of divination in historical matters" he marvels, is able to provide the great theories of interpretation, it remains "gracious-ly left to [Saxl], as often before [ . . . ] to gather up the stuff for it"—that

23. The letter is located in Scholem's posthumous papers in Jerusalem; it is now also re-produced in Panofsky 2001, 275ff.

is, to do the positivistic hard graft: "I do not yet know how I still have the stamina for this undertaking, yet it does not interest you and the others." Retreating into the role of adjunct worker, he is legitimized to reject the "too clever" book.

In rejecting this "too clever" book, Saxl could indeed find a way to go along with Erwin Panofsky. As he received the book from Saxl, the matter was not completely new to him, because he had already held Benjamin's theses on melancholy in his hands (in the form of an advance copy of the chapter on melancholy that was published in the *Neue Deutsche Beiträge* and that Hofmannstahl had sent to him) and obviously rebuffed them harshly. In any case, Benjamin told Scholem on January 1, 1928, that he had received "a cool letter, full of resentment from Panofsky in answer to this letter." He added, "Can you make sense of this?" (3/325) This diplomatic detour via Scholem to Saxl, initiated by this rejection, ended up again, of all places, at Panofsky's address. Although Panofsky reacted no more receptively to receiving the book for the second time, he felt embarrassed about his previous explicit rejection, as becomes clear in his written reply to Saxl on June 21, 1928:

First of all: I have already read the Benjaminian book as well; it also seems to me to be too clever, but nevertheless I also learned much from it. One of the descriptions of melancholy by a 17th century baroque poet is, after all, though B. has not noticed, pretty much in accordance with Ripa: toss the cat in whatever manner you like, it always lands on its well known iconographic hind legs. By the way, this Benjamin is, what is to me very embarrassing ex post, the same one about whom Hofmannsthal had then written to me (I believe I told you about that), and of whom, unaware of his book at that time, I wrote back that I did not know him and I am also not aware of having sent the proposal he received from me.[24]

From this correspondence it is evident that the authors of the study on melancholy from the Warburg circle had certainly "learned" a number of things from Benjamin's contribution on cultural history and the emblematics of melancholy, particularly from the corpus of texts investigated by him that did not coincide with their sources. Therefore it remains all the more surprising how strongly they rejected the book and snubbed the author's interest in an intellectual exchange.

24. Panofsky, *Korrespondenz 1910 bis 1968*, Vol. 1, ed. Dieter Wuttke (Wiesbaden: Harrassowitz, 2001), 289.

With the odyssey of Benjamin's *Trauerspiel* book through the War-burg circle as a backdrop, one may read Benjamin's assessment, published a few years later, as something of an evocation: his claim that the *neue Wissenschaft* exists beyond the "territorial character" of the disciplines and is thus a "movement," one that he attributes to Riegl as well as Burdach and Warburg. That Benjamin, in the *Trauerspiel* book, demonstrates his theory of the "loyalty to things" (*Treue zu den Dingen*) as being the at-titude of melancholy with, of all possible sources, a quotation from Abû Ma'sar—one he cited from Panofsky and Saxl's study on Dürer from 1923 (I.1/334)—makes the phantomic function of his "movement" even clearer. Since the *phantom* is, according to Nicolas Abraham (1991), the fantasy that replaces and covers over the lack in the stories of relatives—although in Benjamin's case this concerns elective relatives.[25] The disregard of his in-terpretation of melancholy presumably had profane motives that can be found in a defense of disciplines, yet such motives point to the gap that lies between the epistemological meaning-content of the term "territorial character" and their material content that partakes in the politics of schol-arship. Benjamin had already (with reference to Goethe) reflected upon the fact that the writing on *elective affinities* feeds itself on an experience of neglect (*das Versäumte*) in his essay on Goethe's novel.

25.  See Nicolas Abraham, "Notes on the Phantom: A Complement to Freud's Metapsy-chology," in Nicolas Abraham and Maria Torok, *The Shell and the Kernel: Renewals of Psy-choanalysis* (Chicago: U of Chicago P, 1994), 171–176.

# 9

# The Unknown Masterpieces
# in Benjamin's Picture Gallery
*On the Relevance of Visual Art for Benjamin's Epistemology*

## Concept of the Image and Art

Given the importance that images have in Walter Benjamin's thought and writings, it is astonishing that he accords comparatively little space to the topic of painting in his oeuvre. Although the concept of the *image* forms a kind of leitmotif in his writings—whether as the image of memory, a thought-image, or dialectical image; or in his use of the terms "image worlds," "image space," or "dream image"—paintings, artworks, and other material images are not a main subject in his thought on the philosophy of art and cultural theory. Nevertheless, painting, the history of art, and a discussion of modernist art play foundational roles for his way of thinking. To date, this fact has not been paid due attention. There is one exception: only a few of the studies devoted to Walter Benjamin have managed to be published without an illustration of or quotation from one of the two artworks that, as pivotal elements in Benjamin's oeuvre, occupy a crucial place in his texts: Albrecht Dürer's engraving *Melencolia I* (1514) in the chapter on melancholy in his book on the German mourning play, and Paul Klee's *Angelus Novus* (1920) in his reflections "On the Concept of History." Yet little notice has been taken of the innumerable, usually terse or condensed, but occasionally wider-ranging remarks on other pictures from the history of art and contemporary painting. Naturally, this is all the more remarkable when it comes to Benjamin's reception by art scholars.

Reports on visits to exhibitions and commentaries on individual artists and paintings occupy quite some space in the large body of his correspondence. Additionally, a dense network of quotations from and remarks on pictures runs through his oeuvre, as do discussions of individual art currents and artists. These range from remarks on the Viennese Genesis via Giotto, Andrea Pisano, Konrad Witz, Matthias Grünewald, Hieronymus Bosch, Raphael, Rembrandt, Hans Holbein the Elder, Hokusai, Charles Meryon, Hans von Marées, Antoine Wiertz, Gustave Courbet, Arnold Böcklin, Odilon Redon, Constantin Guys, James Ensor, and Franz Overbeck through to Paul Cézanne, Otto Gross, Wassily Kandinsky, Marc Chagall, Giorgio de Chirico, Salvador Dali, Paul Klee, and many others. Even the fact that individual sections of the *Arcades Project* are dedicated to Honoré Daumier and Grandville has to date hardly motivated closer studies of Benjamin's analysis of these artists. Only the photographic and filmic images, in particular those by David Octavius Hill, Félix Nadar, Eugène Atget, August Sander, Karl Blossfeldt and Man Ray, which Benjamin discusses in his essays on media history (to be addressed in the final chapter), have been considered in any greater depth. This neglect may seem astonishing, but the reception of Benjamin's concept of art has thus far taken place almost without any reference to art in the narrow sense, that is to say, to painting and other visual genres.

In fact, Benjamin's interest in individual paintings and in certain modes of representation goes far beyond the *expressive gestures* discussed in the last chapter. Indeed, this interest can, as a less prominent line of thought, also be discerned in his writings prior to his programmatic discussion of *Neue Kunstwissenschaft* and even before his book on the baroque. Though his *oeuvre* does not include any art historical essays in the narrow sense, nor contain a coherent, elaborated theory of painting, Benjamin's reflections on and memories of pictures he has seen nonetheless serve as incubators of a sort for his images of thought, so that the imaginary viewing of paintings functions as *latency* for *dialectical images*. This function of art plays a key role for him that is expressed in his scattered and not infrequent commentaries on the color, composition, gestures of figures, or technical details of individual pictures that he mentions essentially *en passant*. In this way his imaginary picture gallery finds an important place in his *aisthetic* conceptualization of history. The programmatic sentence in the epistemological section of the *Arcades Project*, where he says that the relationship of the past to the present "is not temporal in nature, but like an image (*bildlich*)" (*Arcades*, 463), may also apply to images from art history. Engravings, paintings, and prints by artists are, alongside photographs and films, in fact indispensable to Benjamin's epistemology.

Its specificity is due in no small part to the fact that his historical perspective was trained through viewing, observing, and contemplating pictures: he favors synchronicity over continuity, setting (*Schauplatz*) over sequence, gestures over statements, and similarity over convention. In short, he prefers images to discourse. Visual and material images play more the part of nonsensory similarity in Benjamin's dialectical conception of language (in the broader meaning of the term "language"), in the context of which the magical or mimetic elements of nonsensory or distorted similarity appear as the bearer of the semiotic (SelWr 2.722); this does not exclude the fact that in the context of his allegorical methodology they can be transformed into stirring writing. The question thus arises as to whether and how the countless citations of pictures in Benjamin's writings differ from his use of texts and quotations from literature and how they correspond to his theory of citation.

The concepts of *art, the philosophy of art*, and *art criticism* that lie at the heart of Benjamin's theory have, in the reception of his writings, largely been addressed without additional and more intensive consideration of the works of art history themselves—with the exception of the two icons within Benjaminian criticism, namely Dürer and Klee. Countless contemporary artists took Benjamin's images of thought and figures as a challenge that stimulated their own output—with widely varying results. And his theories on the concepts of the *aura* and the *artwork in the age of its mechanical reproduction* have triggered controversial debates in art history about the consequences they have for the discipline (above all owing to the abbreviated if not erroneous reading of them, as I shall try to show in the next chapter). His engagement with the art scholarship of his day and with the cultural studies of the Warburg school have repeatedly been examined as well. However, no one has as yet undertaken a systematic study of his consideration of artworks and the role that the many quotations from art play in his writings.[1] It is as if the concentration on his *image thought*, his

---

1. This even includes studies such as that by Howard Caygill on the significance of color in Benjamin's writings: *Walter Benjamin: The Colour of Experience* (New York: Routledge, 1998). Even the volume Andrew Benjamin edited on *Walter Benjamin and Art* (2005) hardly considers Benjamin's observations on actual artworks.

work to create and to use thought images, written images, and dialectical images, and the discussion of the interlinkage of linguistic images and pictorial script in his theory has obstructed attention being paid to the countless times he quotes real, material pictures and images.

The important role painting already played in Benjamin's days as a student has recently been analyzed by Heinz Brüggemann in his study on *Spiel, Farbe und Phantasie* (2007), in which, among other things, he reconstructs the dialog with Scholem on painting, composition, color, and cubism in the context of the time they spent together in Berne and the debates in art theory of the day. The edited writings of Benjamin also include notes he made in the years prior to the time in Berne and in which he deals most explicitly with painting. Even before writing the essay on language and before he became acquainted with Scholem, Benjamin had, in 1915, written *Der Regenbogen. Gespräch über die Phantasie* (VII.1/19–26, *The Rainbow. Conversation on Imagination*), which takes the form of a dialogue (a method not unusual in the writings of Benjamin's youth), as well as *Malerei und Graphik* (II.2/602ff., Painting and Graphic) and *Über die Malerei oder Zeichen und Mal* (603–607, On Painting or Sign and Marking). The latter text systematically studies signs, marks (physical marks, memorial landmarks), and painting in terms of the relationship of materiality/spatiality to semiotic or symbolic meaning. Moreover, a convolution of notes has survived on the complex of the imagination and color, penned in 1915 and 1919–20 (VI/109–126). They reveal how considerations on the material conditions of painting (cultural techniques and bodily conditions) progress to the interest in expressive gesture, found for example in *Erröten in Zorn und Scham* (Rubescene in Anger and Shame). Imagination and perception, fantasy, impression, and expression form a common complex of themes the young Benjamin addresses. Although in these fragments he is more interested in the anthropological conditions of painting than in their basis in theories of perception and expression (he hardly mentions any actual artworks or individual paintings), his letters of the day attest to his ongoing interest in art, as witnessed above all in reports and commentaries on visits he made to museums and exhibitions.

Benjamin also encountered the two paintings by Dürer and Klee that were to be so important for his later work at an early date. Before investigating his remarks on other pictures, I shall initially look once more at Dürer's *Melencolia* and Klee's *Angelus Novus* in Benjamin's oeuvre to bring to mind the meaning these pieces have for his reflections.

## History of the Fascination[2] with Seen Pictures as the Latency of Thought Images

Both pictures accompanied Benjamin for many years before finding their way into his texts. As a twenty-year-old, Benjamin already spoke of Dürer's *Melencolia* as one of his "greatest and most perfect impressions." After a visit to a museum in Basel in July 1913, he wrote in a letter to Franz Sachs, "Only now do I have an idea of Dürer's power and above all the Melancholy is an immensely deep, highly expressive piece" (1/143). Yet the engraving first appeared in his writing more than a decade later, in his *Habilitationsschrift* on the *Origin of the German Mourning Play*, written in 1925 (though admittedly this work he had first drafted nine years earlier). There, *Melencolia* plays a leading role on the stage where allegorical contemplation and the knowledge of melancholy encounter each other. Benjamin viewed Dürer's engraving (not unlike the thinkers he cited as authorities: Karl Giehlow, Aby Warburg, and Fritz Saxl/ Erwin Panofsky) as taking the Saturnine dialectic even further in the tension created between gravity and spirituality and thus prompting a reinterpretation of Saturnine melancholy in the Renaissance. In the course of this reinterpretation, the traditional symbols of Classical and Medieval astrological knowledge were in flux, and this is what Dürer's engraving signifies: "expressing the visionary concentration of the mind in the Saturn like features of the face," as Benjamin wrote following Karl Giehlow (I.1/329). To this extent, we find not only a specific constellation of cultural history in the engraving but also the perspective of an "allegorical profundity" (*Tiefblick*) on which Benjamin focused all his analytical attention; thanks to the Dürer, things became transformed into "stirring writing" all "at one stroke" (Origins 176). In his book, Dürer's *Melencolia* is quite literally a thought image—the site for a way of viewing things that turns conventional iconography into script in order to shed light on its meaning. Benjamin later, in his review on the journal *Kunstwissenschaftliche Forschung*, cites Giehlow's interpretation of Dürer's *Melencolia* as an example of the new art scholarship.

2. On the concept of the history of fascination, see Klaus Heinrich, *Das Floß der Medusa. 3 Studien zur Fazinationsgeschichte mit mehreren Beilagen und einem Anhang* (Basel: Strömfeld, 1995).

ILLUSTRATION 1: Albrecht Dürer, *Melencolia I* (1514), engraving

Albrecht Dürer, *Melencolia I*, 1514, engraving, print room at the Berlin State Museums—Prussian Cultural Heritage Foundation.

ILLUSTRATION 2: Paul Klee, *Angelus Novus* (1920), oil crayon printed on water-
color
Paul Klee, *Angelus Novus*, 1920–32, oil transfer printed on watercolor; in Johann Konrad Eberlein,
*"Angelus Novus." Paul Klees Bild und Walter Benjamins Deutung*, Freiburg i.Br. 2006, p. 42.

Things are different in the case of Klee's *Angelus Novus*, which appears in Benjamin's reflections "On the Concept of History." There we read: "The angel of history must look like this" ("*Der Engel der Geschichte muß so aussehen*").[3] This "certainly looks like" emphasizes the distance between the artwork and an imaginary figure, between the picture and the imagination, the difference between representation and notion. Benjamin does not discuss here "how the angel of history must look" (SelWr 4.392), as the translation in the standard English edition of Benjamin's works puts it, since the angel of history is not a subject for depiction; rather it is the case that Klee's picture calls the idea of the "angel of history" into mind, the "*muß so aussehen.*" Unlike as is often assumed, Klee's picture is by no means to be seen as the embodiment of the dialectical image on the angel of history. Instead its expressive gesture—its eyes staring wide open and gaping mouth—forms in Benjamin's text the counterpart to the wish for a return to the origin, as is indicated by the motto from a Scholem poem Benjamin quotes at the outset: "I would like to turn back." It is only this tension between the lyrical wish for return and the image of affright that gives rise to a counterstriving constellation in the storm of progress: between the "angel of history" and "us," between *his* gaze at the ruins of the catastrophe and the chain of events that "we perceive."[4] So here Klee's *Angelus Novus* is the medium and the reflective image for Benjamin's written image, for the creation of a thought image on the concept of history.

This appearance of an image in Benjamin's text likewise had been preceded by a long latency, in this case more than two decades. For as early as October 1917, when he sent a letter to Scholem (who was staying in Jena at that time) from Berne in order to explain his notes *On Painting* with considerations on cubism, Benjamin mentioned the painter Paul Klee as an example of the incompatibility of great art with such "scholastic concepts" as Cubism (1/394). Henceforth, Klee's name (and first and foremost

3. The phrase "muß so aussehen" expresses an assumption on something that has no access to a positive knowledge and can't become a matter of proof, i.e., a sort of statement owing only a relative certainty based on one's own notions.

4. On reading this image not as an allegorical but as a dialectical image in which Klee's *Angelus* can be identified neither with the motto from the Scholem poem nor with the "Angel of history," see my previous book on Benjamin: *Body- and Image Space: Re-Reading Walter Benjamin* (London: Rutledge, 1996). Cf. also my entry "Angelus Novus" in *Enzyklopädie jüdischer Geschichte und Kultur*, ed. by Dan Diner. Vol. 1, A–Cl (Stuttgart, Weimar, 2011), 94–100.

the *Angelus Novus*) served as a memory trace in the letters and poems the two friends sent back and forth, until finally, in 1940, Benjamin translated the *Angelus Novus* into a thought image. With the *Angelus Novus*, he discusses the central concept not of *art* history, but rather of the epistemology of historiography, the *concept of history*. And, although Benjamin owned the Klee watercolor, the picture was for most of the time not part of his real picture gallery but rather of his imaginary one, as the circumstances of his life permitted him to hang it up in his apartment only for short periods; that is, he had few opportunities to contemplate it in real time. For most of the time it was Scholem who cared for the picture, and it was also Scholem to whom it was bequeathed in Benjamin's will (drawn up in 1932). The preeminent importance of the watercolor becomes particularly clear if one bears in mind that Benjamin borrowed the title of his failed project for a journal in early 1920, *Angelus Novus*, from it.[5]

## Angelus Novus as the Third Party in the Bond of Friendship Between Scholem and Benjamin

The picture had an almost magical significance for the friendship between the two distinct and dissimilar intellectuals, serving as a kind of guarantee of concurrence between them, something all too often sorely put to the test. Comparable to the subtle controversy over their different interpretations of Kafka (discussed in Chapter 6), the differences in how they viewed the Jewish tradition were often not negotiated directly but, as it were, through a third party, the *Angelus Novus*, and then usually in a covert fashion. After acquiring the picture in Munich, where it came to hang in Scholem's apartment, Benjamin spoke of the *Angelus Novus* in a letter to his friend as the "protector of the Kabbalah" (June 16, 1921, 2/160). When Scholem thereupon sent a poem on occasion of Benjamin's thirty-ninth birthday, *Greetings from Angelus July, 15th 1921*, whose lyrical first person takes an angel's perspective to present Scholem's own reading of the Klee picture, Benjamin answered by draping his distance from Scholem's interpretation in the colors of thanks: "I do not know whether I said anything

---

5. See the article *Literaturkritik, Avantgarde, Medien, Publizistik*, by Uwe Steiner in *Benjamin-Handbuch. Leben-Werk-Wirkung*, Thomas Küpper et al., eds. (Stuttgart: Metzler, 2006) 301–310.

to you about the 'greetings from him.' For all its wonderful beauty, the language of angels has the disadvantage that you cannot respond to it. And all that remains for me, is to ask you, instead of the Angelus, to accept my thanks" (2/173). By addressing the thanks explicitly to Scholem "instead of the Angelus," he rejects both Scholem's identification with the angel and the identification of Klee's figure with Scholem's interpretation. It is not only the wish to return that Scholem placed in the mouth of Klee's *Angelus* with the words "My wing is ready for flight, I would like to turn back," which run counter to Benjamin's awareness of the distance between history and Creation. It also will not have missed Benjamin's sensitive philological eye that Scholem's poem on the one hand states that the angel has no meaning: "I am an unsymbolic thing / mean what I am / in vain you turn the magical ring / I have no meaning" (175). On the other hand, it proposes a hegemonic interpretation of Klee's picture by borrowing authority for first-person-singular voice in the poem from the Angelic voice and thus ascribing a very determinate meaning to him. In this way the *Angelus* becomes the embodiment of a heavenly being, which, in the tone of an annunciation, condemns the time of the living *per se* to be less happy: "for if I also remained living time / I would have little happiness."[6]

Presumably written in the same year, and possibly motivated by his irritation with Scholem's poem, Benjamin writes instead that the "rhythm of messianic nature, is happiness" (SelWr 3.306) in the "Theological-Political Fragment." To this extent, he and Scholem's angelic poetry are worlds apart. Only when bearing these historico-theoretical differences in mind in addressing the "protector of the Kabbalah" can one decipher the rhetorical subtlety of Benjamin's response in his letter to Scholem. Yet however subtle, he also very clearly expresses the main disagreement to Scholem when he states that the difference between the language of angels and that

---

6. Scholem often used his poems to formulate confessions of belief. And it was also his habit to address poems like letters to his friends. On the role of Scholem's poems, see Sigrid Weigel, "Gershom Scholems Gedichte und seine Dichtungstheorie—Klage, Adressierung, Gabe und das Problem einer Sprache in unsere Zeit," in Stéphane Mosès and Sigrid Weigel, eds., *Gershom Scholem—Literatur und Rhetorik* (Cologne: Bohlau, 2000). On angels as a symptom of a fundamental problem of representation within the history of knowledge, see Weigel, "Die Vermessung der Engel. Bilder an Schnittpunkten von Poesie, Kunst und Naturwissenschaft in der Dialektik der Säkularisierung," in *Zeitschrift für Kunstgeschichte*, Vol. 84, 2007, 480–494.

of human being is too fundamental to be able to communicate with them. In the famous theory of citation that appears in his essay on Kraus, Benjamin returned to this idea. It is not that there he understands quotation as the language of angels, but rather he assumes that quotations reflect the language of angels, "in which all words, startled out of the idyllic context of meaning, have become mottoes in the book of Creation" (SelWr 2.454). Against the backdrop of these thoughts on citations it becomes clear that Benjamin, as I hope to show, uses quotations of art differently from those from literature or texts.

The status of Dürer's engraving and Klee's painting in Benjamin's writings, however, goes well beyond that of quotations from art, and not just in quantitative terms. Because the language of pictures is so different, they become media of reflection for him, the embodiments of meanings with which he struggled in his thoughts: the picture becomes a partner in an inner dialogue that Hannah Arendt in her *Thought Diary* once called the "soundless dialog of thinking," as a "two-in-one."[7] For Benjamin, artworks are mnemonic images that in the process of perception remind us of *something* that cannot yet be expressed in language. The picture, once seen and then remembered, not only precedes the thought image but also functions as a crucial drive toward the differentiation and precision of knowledge. In this way, Benjamin uses the genuine perceptual and cognitive mode of images from art to elaborate his theoretical ideas.

Not until twenty-three years after Benjamin had written a letter telling Gershom Scholem that, among the new painters, Klee had "touched" him (Oct. 22, 1917, 1/394) and two decades after acquiring the *Angelus Novus*—which is to say, after a long period of fascination—did the picture then take center stage within the context of his theoretical work "Theses on the Concept of History." It is an artist's picture that initiates a contemplation from which an imagined image (the figure of the "angel of history") gains clearer contours. Here, the picture is a kind of vis-à-vis that leads to the generation of the thought-image. The moment of being *touched* at first sight and the long-lasting concealment and absence (in the dual sense of the word: the absence of the picture for its owner Benjamin[8] and its invisibility within his published writings) are followed by being cast in a cen-

7. Hannah Arendt, *The Life of the Mind* (New York: Mariner, 1981), 193.
8. The picture hung only briefly and temporarily in his room, for example in 1931 in Berlin, where "Angelus Novus is hanging for the first time in the right way" (4/64).

tral role in Benjamin's concept of history. After a decade as the *protector* of the Kabbalah and its metamorphosis into the only "*ambassador of the* Kabbalah" among the "saintly images" on the walls of Benjamin's room[9] (4/62; emphasis S.W.), Klee's *Angelus* whiles away another decade before emerging as the image that reflects a counterposition to the concept of progress, itself bereft of language and movement. It is a mnemonic image that reflects the position of a turn toward both history's ruins and the dead while the distance from Creation becomes ever greater. The thought-image of the "angel of history," created by contemplating the *Angelus*, quite literally embodies a Messianic position *in the* history that is irreconcilable with the latter. At the cost of "use (*Einsatz*) at the historical level," which Scholem was later, in 1959, to analyze as the "price of Messianism" in his text *The Messianic Idea in Judaism*,[10] the angel of history turns away from the direction of history. Yet its stance, with its back to the future, is not open to human beings who move in and with history—that is to say, as actors in history. The image of the angel, however, reminds them of concern for the dead and the ruins of history.

Similar to being *touched* by Klee, Benjamin's first encounter with Dürer's *Melencolia* in Basel entailed a comparable intensive *impression* that, after long being concealed, was elaborated as an example of "gaze of allegorical profundity" in the *Trauerspiel* book. The traces left by both pictures in Benjamin's writings form an analogous constellation among *initial encounter* (fascinated contemplation of the piece and impression/touch) *latency* (the picture in the mind as the imaginary vis-à-vis for reflection), and *thought-image* (discussion of the picture and generation of a dialectical image in theory formation). What, then, is the status of the other pictures that Benjamin did not discuss as extensively as those by Dürer and Klee?

9. "The old Three-Headed Christ, which you must know, a representation of a Byzantine relief in ivory, a trick image (three different representations of saints, depending on your angle of vision) from the forests of Bavaria, a Sebastian and, as the sole ambassador of the Kabbalah, the Angelus Novus, not to mention the 'Vorführung des Wunders' that is also by Klee." Thus he writes from the same situation in a letter to Scholem (4/62). Benjamin's wife, Dora, gave him the *Vorführung des Wunders* as a present in 1920, meaning before the *Angelus Novus*.

10. Gershom Scholem, "Zum Verständnis der messianischen Idee im Judentum," in *Judaica 1* (Frankfurt/M: Suhrkamp, 1986); English translation collected in *The Messianic Idea in Judaism: And Other Essays on Jewish Spirituality* (New York: Schocken, 1995).

Quotations from Art as the Lighting Flash for the
"long echoing thunder" of the Development of Theory

In the same letter in which he recounts his visit to the museum in
Basel and his encounter with Dürer's *Melencolia*, Benjamin also reports
how impressed he was by Grünewald: "Finally, the largest of the paintings there, Grünewald's Christ on the Cross, which seized me much more
strongly this time than last year" (1/143). "Seized" here is meant less in the
sense of being "overcome with emotion" than the beloved phrase for the
enjoyment of art in museums would have it. It seems instead to articulate something that was only later to become tangible, namely the way in
which the image had seized his mind and thought. This time it took three
years until the impression left by Grünewald's painting emerged in one of
his texts. In "Socrates" (1916), a brief article in which the twenty-four-year-
old student struggled with the relationship between 'sexuality' and 'intellect,' Benjamin argues against using Eros as a mere means to an end in the
attainment of knowledge *qua* pedagogic Eros—using, among other things,
the juxtaposition (discussed in the first chapter) of the saintly and the Socratic question. The second section starts with a quotation of a painting:

"Grünewald painted the saints with such grandeur by means of the colors in the
paint *their halos loomed (tauchte) out of the greenest black*. The radiant is true only
where it is refracted in the nocturnal; only there is it great, only there is it *expressionless*, only there is it asexual and yet of supramundane sexuality. The Thus Radiant One is the genius, the witness to every real spiritual creation. He guarantees its
asexuality." (II.I/130; SelWr 1.52ff.; emphasis S.W.)

In this short passage Benjamin describes an aesthetic praxis of semantici-
zation through colors, thanks to which the sacred directly arises from the
material properties of the image. Many years later he was to return to this
idea in his essay on Goethe's *Elective Affinities* and elaborate on it for the
language of literature, using the phrase (explored in Chapter 4) "something from beyond the poet that breaks into poetic language." Analogous
to this constellation in the language of poetry, in *Socrates* he outlines a
specific treatment of color in painting as something radiant that emerges
from the nocturnal. This is not a matter of drawing an analogy between
*image* and *language*, but rather one of identifying two related aesthetic
approaches that are expressed quite differently in their respective media:

in the one the use of rhythm, rhyme, etc., and in the other the use of color, composition, etc.

Benjamin calls Grünewald's painting to mind in only one sentence within his discussion of the relationship of Eros and knowledge. He was no doubt thinking of the *Isenheim Altar* in Colmar, with which he was very familiar. Scholem relates that for many years Benjamin had a reproduction of "Grünewald's altar paintings from Colmar" hanging in his study, for which "[i]n 1913 as a student he had made a special trip to Colmar to see the original."[11] At that time he was studying in Freiburg. In several notes from the following years, the young Benjamin was occupied with theoretical issues relating to the visual arts, painting, symbol and sign, color and imagination, etc. In the fragment, "Imagination," there is a sentence on paintings by Hans von Marées in a similarly erratic vein. They show, as Benjamin puts it, "gray Elysium" in which he was interested as a third kind of "pure semblance," alongside the two forms of passing away and becoming, in the images of dusk (*Abendrot*) and dawn (*Morgenrot*) respectively.

Reflections on eternal transience and infinite dissolution prompt him to reflect on this with the image of dusk. He suggests that eternal passing away is "like the dusk above the deserted arena of the world with its deciphered ruins. It is the infinite dissolution of the purged beautiful semblance, bereft of all temptation" (VI/115). In continuation of the comparison of "passing away" and dusk, dawn is then chosen as the image for becoming, which Benjamin likewise sees as pure semblance: "Thus, there is also a pure semblance in the matutinal age (*Morgenalter*) of the world, it is the nascent semblance. It is the gleam that lies over things in Paradise." The reference to the art first comes into play, however, when Benjamin introduces a third mode of semblance, one that takes him beyond the conventional metaphors of becoming and passing away: "At long last, a *third* pure semblance, less than, doused or subdued: gray Elysium, as Marées' pictures show. These are the three worlds of pure semblance that are part of the imagination" (emphasis S.W.). So the painting here is a supplement to the metaphors of nature introduced in order to present a third term beyond both the *concepts* (becoming and passing away) and the *metaphors* (dawn and dusk).

Benjamin's "Conversation on Imagination" with the title of "The Rainbow" (presumed to have been written in 1915), is part of the same

---

11. Scholem, *Walter Benjamin: The Story of a Friendship* (New York: New York Review of Books, 2003), 47.

thematic complex. There he takes the rainbow—a medium and as a non-material pure property—as the image for the color of the imagination and thus as the "primordial image of art." Consequently, a year before the text "Socrates," Grünewald had already played a role in Benjamin's writings, namely in a passage on the color of imagination: "Finally, religion transposes its *holy realm* into the clouds and its *blessed realm* into Paradise. And Matthias Grünewald painted the haloes of angels on his altar in the colors of the rainbow, such that through the holy figures, the soul shines through as the imagination" (VII.1/ 25; emphasis S.W.). Here, color is construed as a medium through which, in the material of art, something emerges that is yet removed from it—whether it be given the name of the soul, the imagination, the saint, or the radiant.

This context explains the importance the quotation of Grünewald has in the discussion of "cognitive creation" in "Socrates." There, color is the element that quite literally gives rise to the sacred moment of the artwork. The phrasing that their halos "aus dem grünsten Schwarz *tauchte*," rather than emerged (*auftauchte*), itself resembles the image of an *epiphany*. Thus, from Benjamin's viewpoint it is not the themes and objects in the picture that constitute the sacred element of Grünewald's images[12] but rather the use of color and light. Without further explicating it, in the following sentences Benjamin transposes the halo into the "Radiant One," the greenest black into the "nocturnal," and their constellation into the *expressionless*. In a kind of immediate transposition, the concepts arise from the arena of the artwork itself.

In the theoretical considerations on the relationship of gender/spirit (Geschlecht/Geist) and Eros/knowledge (Eros/Wissen) that appear immediately after the Grünewald quotation, Benjamin develops a critique of the widespread metaphors of "spiritual creation" or "spiritual conception." This forms a starting point for one of the leitmotifs of his thought that runs through his entire oeuvre. It relates to his theoretical effort to illuminate the meaning of the 'human' that, as shown, stems from the dialectic of reference to two spheres, the creaturely and the supernatural: be it in relation of "mere life" to "just being" ("Critique of Violence"), of "natural" to "supernatural life" ("Goethe's *Elective Affinities*"), of sexuality and mind, or procreation and testimony ("Karl Kraus"), etc.

12. Grünewald crops up another time, when Benjamin mentions him together with El Greco in his essay on Bachofen as artistic witnesses for expressionism (II/220).

To the extent that this trace involves a dialectics of secularization, it is no coincidence that Benjamin takes a sacred image to set the initial scene. In this respect, we can construe the significance of the quotation of the work of art as a flash of insight that triggers a long-lasting theoretical effort: "In the fields with which we are concerned, knowledge comes only in lightning flashes. The text is the long roll of thunder that follows," as he writes in the section on the theory of knowledge in his *Arcades Project* (Arcades 456). One could compare this lightninglike flash of insight with the *punctum* in Roland Barthes's *Camera Lucida*, the "punctum of a photography" that grabs or seizes the viewer and that Barthes rates as the disturbance and interruption of the *studium*.[13] But for Benjamin the first encounter with paintings that touched him triggered a sort of study that can by no means be considered an aimless interest or semidesire, which are

13. Roland Barthes, *Camera Lucida: Reflections on Photography* (New York: Macmillan, 1994), 42.

ILLUSTRATION 3:  Matthias Grünewald, *Isenheimer Altar* (1515), first panel
Matthias Grünewald, *Isenheimer Altar*, ca. 1515, first panel, oil on wood, reproduced with the generous permission of the Musée d'Unterlinden, Colmar.

ILLUSTRATION 4:   Panel of the Resurrection, high altar
Matthias Grünewald, *Auferstehung*, ca. 1515, Hochaltar; in Max Seidel (ed.), *Mathis Gothart Nithart. Grünewald. Der Isenheimer Altar*, Stuttgart 1973, p. 162.

ILLUSTRATION 5:    Concert of Angels
Matthias Grünewald, *Engelskonzert*, um 1515, oil on wood, in Max Seidel (ed.), *Mathis Gothart Nithart. Grünewald. Der Isenheimer Altar*, Stuttgart 1973, p. 146.

the terms Barthes uses to describe the *studium*. Rather, the linguistic image of the long echo of the roll of thunder indicates that the energy of the flash on impact continues to discharge in the text, too, and leads to a truly charged study. The meaning of images for the initial scene is, in the case of Grünewald, not unlike that in the cases of Dürer and Klee. Although there the images crop up again in Benjamin's texts after a long period of latency, here the phenomena and concepts resulting from the flash of insight become the subject of long-standing study.

## Clouds and Waves Among Religion, Nature, and Modernity

The Grünewald quotation within the discussion of the "Rainbow" is introduced with a remark on the clouds being the place to which religion "finally" (*endlich*) transposes its holy realm. In this transposition, one can understand "*endlich*" in both temporal and historical terms, i.e., in the course of secularization, or in the absolute sense of "finite world": "Finally, religion transposes its holy realm into the clouds and its blessed realm into Paradise." As the metaphorical seat of the heavenly realm in the finite world, the iconographic clouds do, however, resemble those in nature. The two heterogeneous sets of clouds are linked by color and the imagination: "Thanks to color, the clouds are so close to the imagination" (VII.1/25). In this way, Benjamin's dialogue on the *Rainbow* sets in motion a kind of chain reaction among the interlocking concepts in which a series of close relationships eventually ends in an iconographic metaphor: from natural phenomena via color and the imagination to the heaven of painting. It consists of clouds, the seat of the saintly in the imagination. In another fragment, aphorisms on imagination and color, Benjamin describes the light and shade that emerge from the colors of a painting as an intermediate phenomenon between pure imagination and creation.

> On *painterly color*: it arises as a single phenomenon in the imagination, but its purity is vitiated by its relation to space and in this way light and shade emerge. These form something intermediate between *pure imagination* and *Creation*, and the painterly colors consist in them. (VI/109; SelWr 1.48)

This means that for Benjamin it is not the pictures or the art *as such* that form a sphere located between the imaginary and religion, but instead a specific use of colors in painting that gives rise to this median sphere.

In his "*Urgeschichte der Moderne*" the counterimages of such a movement recur—not as opposites but as images of a countervailing movement: in the sky and in the clouds in Charles Meryon's "etched views of Paris." Here, Benjamin is primarily interested in the views of the city that are presented, and thus also the themes of the images. In both "Central Park" and the sections on Baudelaire in the *Arcades Project* one finds countless short, scattered entries on Meryon's pictures, such as the question, "What's with the dilation of the sky in Meryon's engraving?" (Arcades 268). Or the observation, "Meryon's streets of Paris are chasms, high above which float the clouds" (V.I/344; Arcades 333). In a version of this note, the chasms have become abysses (Arcades 681), and "Meryon: the sea of houses, the ruins, the clouds, the majesty and decrepitude of Paris" (346). Benjamin uses Meryon's engravings as a way to discuss that phenomenon of modernity in which architecture and the cityscape of the metropolis appear to observers to be nature—precisely as a kind of "*Urgeschichte der Moderne*": "There is an effort to master the new experiences of the city within the framework of the old traditional experiences of nature. Hence the schemata of the primeval forest and the sea (Meryon und Ponson du Terrail)" (447). When the *holy realm* of religion has withdrawn from the heavens of painting, then the secularized clouds as the seat of the holy, magic, or transcendent in the imagination (of Modernity) are not all that remains for art. Images of nature, in whose wake all other things represented get involved, also remain. Even if they are artifacts and cultural products, they then seem to be part of the realm of nature.

Another entry states that Meryon "turned the tenements of Paris into monuments of modernity" (385), while Benjamin presumes that the criterion of a modern city is precisely the absence of monuments. Thus Meryon's *views* of the city stand quite literally for a *view* of modernity in which it is turned into a mythical or ancient scene. In his engravings, Benjamin thus discerns the very "Paris antiquity," or rather that "antiquated face of the city" that is at the heart of the *Arcades Project*: Paris, the capital city of Modernity, becomes the arena of the primordial history of Modernity, in which industrial epoch and classical antiquity are superimposed (SelWr 4.53). The guarantor for this view is none other than Baudelaire, whom Benjamin, in the third chapter on "Modernism" in the first version of his "The Paris of the Second Empire in Baudelaire" (1937/38), not only quotes but describes as someone with whom Meryon had an elective affinity:

Few of his prose works are a match for his short piece on Meryon. Dealing with Meryon, it is a homage to modernity, but it is a homage to the antique face of it. For in Meryon, too, there is an interpenetration of classical antiquity and modernity, also in him the form of this superimposition, the allegory, appears unmistakably. (I.2/591; SelWr 4.54)

The piece of prose to which Benjamin refers is the section on Meryon in the chapter on landscape painting in Baudelaire's *Salon 1859*. This culminates in a poetic image when Baudelaire says that Meryon painted "the black majesty of the most uncanny of all capital cities" (Baudelaire, 1989, 195). Taking this up, Benjamin (with Baudelaire) talks of the "poetic power" of Meryon's images. In his commentaries it becomes clear that not only are Baudelaire and Meryon close to each other, but thanks to the allegorical method, literature and art likewise have an elective affinity to each other. In this case, the pictures are not the prompt for a long-standing work on thought-images; nor do they function as art quotations in the above-mentioned sense. Rather, the images here are part of the material that Benjamin collected for his *Arcades Project* in order to assemble a phenomenological cultural history of modernity from the countless fragments. The images here are objects of a *studium*, which includes not only pictures but also texts, cultural practices, architecture, technologies, etc.

ILLUSTRATION 6: Charles Meryon, *Les nuits de mai* (1871), engraving

Charles Meryon, *Les nuits de mai*, 1871, Radierung; in *Charles Meryon, David Young Cameron, 3 avril–31 may 1981*, Cabinet des Estampes, Musée d'art et d'histoire (Ausstellungskatalog), Genf 1981, p. 84.

ILLUSTRATION 7: Gustave Courbet, *La vague* (1870), oil on canvas

Gustave Courbet, *La vague*, 1870, oil on canvas, National Gallery of the Berlin State Museums—Prussian Cultural Heritage Foundation.

In this context, Benjamin also studied the changes in artistic modes of representation that evolved against the backdrop of photography and the photographic eye. Here, the material properties of the artwork attracted his attention again when he engaged the "world of forms and structure" in painting. This world is the result of another kind of countermovement to the transposition of the holy realm into the clouds, namely, the transposition of the photographic eye into painting. Here, the meaning of art is once again looped back to its ground—in a quite concrete sense of the word. We can certainly take literally the insistence that art's meaning stems from the grounds of the *insignificant* (*das Unbedeutende*) as put forward in Benjamin's championing of a science of images emerging from the "spirit of true philology" as outlined in the previous chapter. The grounds are material, pigment, and structure, which though in themselves are insignificant and without meaning gain semantic properties when used in art.[14]

In the *Letter from Paris (II)* (1936), in which Benjamin discusses contemporary debates on the relationship of painting and photography, it is not a photographer but rather the painter Gustave Courbet to whom he ascribes the discovery of a photographic subject—in the latter's painting *La Vague* (1870):

The painting of the *juste milieu* had its adversary in Courbet; with him, the relationship between painter and photographer was temporarily reversed. His famous painting *La Vague* (The Wave) represents the discovery of a photographic subject through painting. In Courbet's age, both the enlarged photo and the snapshot were unknown. His painting showed them the way. It equipped an expedition to explore a world of forms and structures which were not captured on the photographic plate until a decade later. (III/503; SelWr 3.240ff.)

In this case, painting itself is the theme and object of analysis—as it was in the writings of the young Benjamin—but is now no longer discussed from the viewpoint of basic anthropological assumptions. Rather, he derives his reading from the observation of an actual Courbet painting. If Benjamin now reflects art-historical phenomena of modernity as regards the history of the media, then (as will be discussed in greater depth in Chapter 10) this has nothing to do with either a history of technological progress nor a "crisis in art" in the epoch of photography. He rather analyzes correspondences in the modes of representation in the process of changing me-

14. Cf. Monika Wagner's book on the material of art (Wagner 2001).

dia. The Courbet example shows that the artistic mode of representation by no means changes simply *following* in the wake of photography. Instead, modes of perception and representation interact as the artists create modes of seeing and perception that technology first has to catch up with.

For this reason, Benjamin does not identify the successors to Courbet among those photographers who raised their technology to the status of an art, as he claims that the "Surrealists' attempt to master photography by 'artistic' means" has failed (241). To Benjamin, Renger-Patzsch is another example of the failure of the attempt to elevate photography to art. He regards the title of Renger-Patzsch's famous photographic collection *Die Welt ist schön* (The World Is Beautiful) as simply being the petty-bourgeois creed of commercial photography that had missed the possible social significance of the medium. For him, it was Man Ray who acted as a counterpart to such a movement. With Ray, "photography succeeds in reproducing the style of the most modern painters" (242). This, however, is a topic for the next chapter.

## The Physiognomic Index of Knowledge

Whenever Benjamin addresses art itself, his attention also centers on expression, gesture, and pathos formulas in addition to color, structure, composition, and other aspects of representation in the history of art. Here, painting participates in physiognomic perception and a form of knowledge that derives its insights from a kind of physiognomic index of history. Often, images that are far apart in historical terms then appear in one and the same constellation. As with Expressionism and Medieval miniature in the *Trauerspiel* book, in the *Letter from Paris (II)* it is the major caricaturists of modern times and old artworks that take the stage together. What links them is the observation that they converted "social emotion" into "visual inspiration." Evidently, it is physiognomy that functions as the medium and material for this transformation of the social into the visual:

Such is the case with the great caricaturists, whose *political* knowledge permeates their *physiognomic* perception no less deeply than the experience of the sense of touch does to the perception of space. Masters like Bosch, Hogarth, Goya, and Daumier pointed the way. "Among the most important works of painting," wrote René Crevel, who died recently, "have always been those which, merely by pointing to corruption, indicted those responsible. From Grünewald to

Dali, from the putrid Christ to the rotten ass . . . painting has always been able to discover new truths which were not truths of painting alone." (III/506; SelWr 3.242ff.; emphasis S.W.)[15]

These are truths (or so we could continue in Benjamin's vein) that can best be expressed in the language of painting. If political knowledge and physiognomic perception blend in caricature, then this involves insights not prompted by theme or motif, but by the mode of representation. This corresponds to the following observation that the fascist censors felt attacked primarily by a specific way of seeing and less by the subject matter: "And it is usually the artists' style, not their subject matter, which brought the prohibition."

Alongside the doctrine of the insignificant, it is the physiognomic eye (and the latter is important for his entire oeuvre) that in Benjamin's way of writing and seeing is profoundly informed by art. The central meaning gestures and bodily expressions have in Benjamin's work already been described in the chapters on his commentaries on Brecht and Kafka. These authors' linguistic and dramaturgic gestures form a kind of literary counterpart to the pathos formulas in art history whose iconography Benjamin quotes at various points. Like his citation of Giotto's personification of *Ira*, referenced in the previous chapter,[16] in *One-Way Street* Benjamin quotes Andrea Pisano's allegory of the *Spes*. He characterizes it as a figure that expresses the synchronicity of helplessness and being winged: "She sits and helplessly raises her arms to grasp a fruit that remains out of reach. Yet she has wings. Nothing could be more true" (IV.1/125). In this allegory of hope, personified as an angel, the gesture described refers to a conventional meaning it embodies; that is to say, it is part of the coded repertoire of conventional iconography. To this extent, more interesting are the passages in

15. The "rotten ass" refers to Dali's painting "L'âne pourri" (1928), and the chapter with the same title in his *The Unvisible Woman* (1930) later expanded the analyses of the paranoiac-critical methods contained and published them in *Le Mythe tragique de l'Angélus de Millet* (Paris: Jean-Jacques Pauvert, 1963).

16. Benjamin had seen Giotto frescoes in Assisi, as he wrote in a letter to Scholem in November 1924. Instead of the Piero della Francesca frescoes, hardly visible in the darkness, he was able to "study Giotto's upper gallery all the better." The next sentence is more notable as it reveals what happens if the *studium* gains predominance: "Recently, given the solitude of my wanderings, I have set eyes upon too many pictures and yet had not enough time to concentrate on the architecture" (2/502).

ILLUSTRATION 8: *Wiener Genesis*, Fol. 14r (illustration 27)

*Wiener Genesis, folio 14r; in Barbara Zimmermann, Die Wiener Genesis im Rahmen der antiken Buchmalerei. Ikonographie, Darstellung, Illustrationsverfahren und Aussageintention*, Wiesbaden 2003, illus. 27.

ILLUSTRATION 9: *Wiener Genesis*, Fol. 15r (illustration 29)

*Wiener Genesis, folio 15r; in Barbara Zimmermann, Die Wiener Genesis im Rahmen der antiken Buchmalerei. Ikonographie, Darstellung, Illustrationsverfahren und Aussageintention*, Wiesbaden 2003, illus. 29.

which Benjamin's contemplation of the image concentrates on physiognomic gestures beyond the iconographical index. This is, for example, to be found in the passage on the *Vienna Genesis* in his essay on Karl Kraus.

Benjamin's knowledge of the late antique *Vienna Genesis* refers to an edition by Franz Wickhoff, who published the prints in 1895 together with Wilhelm von Hartel. Wickhoff also sparked a reinterpretation and reassessment of illuminated manuscripts. It concerns one of the oldest surviving Biblical codices after the Septuaginta, an illuminated manuscript presumably dating from sixth-century Syria. Forty-eight pages have survived, constituting a story that begins with the Fall and continues up to the death of Jacob, although the narratives do not match those in varying versions of the Bible.[17] In his review of the journal *Kunstwissenschaftliche Forschungen* (written two years after the Kraus essay), Benjamin indicates that he had "looked through Riegl and Wickhoff again" (4/260). From this point on, he was to repeatedly state his high esteem for these two representatives of the Vienna school of art history: for example in the passage from the 1935 artwork essay, in which Riegel and Wickhoff are mentioned as art scholars who took the historical determinacy of perception seriously and thus offered a reappraisal of Late Roman art. Thus in the Bachofen essay (1935, written in French), he considers Riegl and Wickhoff as Expressionists *avant la lettre*: "the other, Franz Wickhoff who—with his edition of the Viennese Genesis—draws attention to the first medieval miniatures which found a sizable voice in expressionism" (II.1/220; SelWr 3.11). Yet already in the Kraus essay, published in 1930–31, we find a lengthier passage on the *Vienna Genesis*, which unlike the other somewhat terse and dense quotations of artworks extends almost to an entire page.

Benjamin introduces *Vienna Genesis* in the second section of the Kraus essay, concerning the *Daemon*, in the context of the discussion of a feeling of guilt, "in which visibly the most private meets the historical consciousness"; for Benjamin, this meeting must inevitably lead to Expressionism. This is precisely why the *Vienna Genesis* is so important to him, because of the way the early medieval miniatures obviously influenced the Expressionists, an influence they themselves acknowledged. He was not interested in style or the developments of other art-historical

17. The assumption is that "the illustrations were not created following the Bible text but from Judaeo-Aramaic 'Bible novels,' which did not stick as rigorously as the Holy Scripture to the Hebrew ban on images" (Clausberg, 1984), 2.

criteria,[18] but rather in the expressive gestures. What follows in the text is an extended description of the "enigmatic" stances and gestures in the illustrations: "Yet if one considers its figures (taking the example of the Vienna Genesis), then one encounters something enigmatic not only in the wide opened eyes, the unfathomable folds of their robes, but in their entire expression" (II.I/351; SelWr 2.445). What he means by this is a posture of a "falling sickness" already mentioned in the previous chapter. Yet he interprets this quite literal physical bend as "only one, an as it were concave aspect of this matter," as a "gaze into the faces of the figures." The reverse side seems more important, namely the figures' backs: "How different the same phenomenon is for he who gazes at their backs." And he then describes the bowing backs of the figures as if they were geological formations in which the physical subjugation has ossified in the image:

These backs are staggered in the saints of the Adoration, in the knaves of the Gethsemane scene, in the eye witnesses of the entrance into Jerusalem to terraces of human necks, human shoulders that truly mount up to form steep steps, less to the heavens than downwards to and even to below the earth. Impossible to find an expression for their pathos that ignores this: [ . . . ] blocks of stone or roughly hewn steps. Whatever the powers were that fought the battle of ghosts on these shoulders, one of them enables us to state the name for the experience that we have been able to have of the state of defeated masses directly after the end of the war. (351; 445)

He then immediately identifies "that nameless power, toward which the backs of men bowed": it is guilt. In Benjamin's description, the illustration becomes an image for history, for dialectics at a standstill. When he cites the feelings of guilt that arise after World War I, which were given voice at the time by Expressionism, as the historical index of his considerations, then the constellation in which past and now emerge here together is condensed in the image of the bent backs. He interprets the gesture of the bent back as the expression of a guilt for which the contemporaries could find no other language.[19]

18. This is already clear from the fact that Benjamin always talks of early medieval manuscripts or miniatures, while Wickhoff focused precisely on a reappraisal of the art of late classical antiquity.

19. This approach is similar to Aby Warburg's in the interpretation of Renaissance painters who quoted the pathos formulae in gestures of antiquity in order to express affects and moods for which they couldn't find "words" in their Christian iconographic vocabulary.

A little later he returns to this trace in his work on the Kafka essay: "So it is the back on which it lies." Be it the hunchback, that "primordial image of defiguration" (II.2/432; SelWr 2.811), or the back of the guilty in "In the Penal Colony." From a consideration of the illuminations in a manuscript from Late Classical Antiquity, the motif runs from the "backs of the guilty" via Expressionism and Kraus through to Kafka's world, which Benjamin discusses as the venue of a disfigured, unredeemed world. If redemption appears there in the image of the Messiah, who will adjust the world only slightly, then this form of redemption is quite literally viewed in the final sentence of the Kafka essays as setting the back straight (*zurecht-rücken*),[20] as taking the burden off the distorted back: "if only the weight would be taken off his back" (438; 816). For Benjamin, the expressive gestures of the figures in the images, similar to Warburg's pathos formulas, are a part of a practice of linguistic and visual images in which *literalness* (which forms the basis of his thought on images) can appear both in image and text, either as the literal word or as the corporeality. His physiognomic perspective links art and literature, politics and religion, and the "has-been" and the now (*Jetztzeit*) in a gesture that he deciphers as the symptom of disfigurement (*Entstellung*) or, otherwise stated, as our distance from both Creation and redemption.

The concept of the image plays a central role in the epistemological reflections and theses in the *Arcades Project*. Since Benjamin there terms the image "dialectics at a standstill" or as "that wherein what has been comes together in a flash with the now to form a constellation" (Arcades, 463), then this concept of the image also includes the pictures of art history—to the extent that they are subjects of consideration and reading. However, the investigation of quotations from art, commentaries, and observations on pictures has shown that the artworks have a very special importance for him that stems from the specific epistemological properties of art, and without them Benjamin would not have been able to formulate his notion of the image. It is thus not the case that in working with an expanded, comprehensive concept of the image he includes different modes of linguistic, painted, imaginary, and other images; rather, his epistemic concept of the image is informed by works of visual art.

20.  Here the word *zurechtrücken* (adjust) also invokes the back (*Rücken*).

# 10

# Detail—Photographic and Cinematographic Images

*On the Significance of the History of Media
in Benjamin's Theory of Culture*

For a long time, the reception of Benjamin's writings on film and photography was shaped by the *topos* of reproducibility. Reduced to a far-too-simple formula, his media theory was banalized when turned into the thesis that with the introduction of the possibility for technical reproduction of the arts, they lost their aura. In fact, the relationship between aura and technology in Benjamin's studies on the history of media is much more complex and nuanced. It is not as significant that the reproduction of the arts forms the center of his engagement with media theory; but rather that he is fundamentally interested in those structural changes that occur in conceptions of images and time through the employment of apparatuses and the radically altered configuration between technical images and the physiologic-psychological activities of visual perception. Benjamin's writings dedicated to optical media are shaped by the fact that he invents the "technical question" for a theory of the image. This can be studied above all in the 1931 article "A Little History of Photography," which appeared in the *Literarische Welt* in three installments, and in the famous essay "Art in the Age of Mechanical Reproducibility" (1935), which remained unpublished in his lifetime and of which two versions exist. Since his stated goal is to involve photography in the "literalization of all conditions of life" (II.1/385), his approach concerns nothing less than the legibility of technically produced images. In the process, two terms come to the fore: the detail and shock. The *detail* emerges through photographic enlargement and allows the formulatibility (*Formulierbarkeit*) of minute image worlds not available to "normal" consciousness, while *shock* is its cinematographic, temporalized pendant, as it were. As a result, a theory of perception supported by psychoanalysis emerges, one that transcends the discourse of aesthetics in art criticism and leads to a dialectic of the histories of media and culture. Although Benjamin employs media theory's epistemological assumptions to reformulate the detail in light of photography (that is, *as* a media theory), the change in perception comes with modernity. That is to say, the optics of the detail (Detailoptik), shock, and haptic motor skills become the central structural elements of his cultural theory that bears the title "*Urgeschichte der Moderne.*"

## Epistemological Prologue: To Benjamin's Media Theory

Benjamin's *Paris Letters* on painting and photography, written in 1936 for the journal *Das Wort* (which was to be released in Moscow, but remained unpublished), contain a critical review of two publications concerning the debates of two contemporary artists' conferences—the Viennese and the Parisian[1]—in which the status of painting was negotiated, above all in terms of the *topos* of crisis. Benjamin in turn uses his review of these debates to articulate an underexposed aspect of contemporary art criticism and art theory, and from it derives his own argument about the so-called crisis in the relationship between painting and photography:

The present debate reached its height at the point where photography is included in the analysis and its relationship to painting is clarified. If this didn't happen in Venice, then Aragon made up for lost time in Paris. As he later recounted, it took some courage to do so. Of the painters present, some saw insult in undertaking to base thoughts on the history of painting on the history of photography. (III/499f)

Before he took the review of the artists' meetings as a point of departure for his own reflections on painting in the age of photography, thereby referring to a historiography of photography, the research on which began "eight to ten years before," Benjamin follows through with Louis Aragon's story: "'Just imagine,' concludes Aragon, 'a physicist who felt insulted be-

---

1. *Entretiens, L'art et la réalité. L'art et l'état*, with contributions by Mario Alvera, Daniel Baud-Bovy, Emilio Bodrero, et al. (Paris: Institut internationale de Coopération intellectuelle, 1935); *La querelle du réalisme. Deux débats par l'Association des peintures et sculptures de la maison de la culture*, with contributions by Lurçat, Granaire, et al. (Paris: Editions socialistes internationals, 1936).

cause someone spoke to him about chemistry'" (500). Whereas this comparison touches on a debate about the kinship or otherness between two related fields (on one hand, physics and chemistry, and on the other painting and photography), Benjamin's considerations bear on the historical and genealogical relationship between the two mediums here under consideration. His project, which seeks ground for his thoughts on painting in a history of another art that emerged in a later age and in addition deals with technical instruments and processes of reproduction, must have appeared scandalous from the perspective of painting as understood as an original art in the double sense of the term, that is to say as both originality and antecedence. For his project signifies a simultaneous reversal of hierarchy *and* genealogy, through which conventional historiographic narrations are transcended by abandoning the path of such developmental narratives that present the history of media within a model of progress determined by the advancement of its instruments, apparatuses, and technical practices.

Benjamin's commentary on Aragon's experience of the meeting raises associations to the reactions of contemporary academics who similarly feel that any attempt to ground the position of literature, culture, or the humanities in a history of new media is impertinence. One can effectively counter such resistance with Benjamin's arguments—not, however, if Benjamin's media theory is simply applied to the contemporary "crisis." If Benjamin's media theory is relevant in the present age of electronic media, then it is not in order to assert their current topicality or direct applicability. Instead, his specific work on a media theory is of interest today because of his investigation into technical phenomena and caesuras in the history of media and their effects on the cultural history of perception, writing systems, and the arts. Otherwise stated, the question of interest is which epistemological significance medial and technical phenomena receive in his theory of art and culture—since media *theory* in Benjamin's sense always also includes the *history* of media. If the topicality of Benjamin's media theory is open to debate, then it is certainly less as a question of how appropriate it is to the present and rather a question of an analysis that is concerned with the polarization of a matter of historical facts according to its "pre- and post history" (*Vor- und Nachgeschichte*), as Benjamin writes in Convolute N of the *Arcades Project*. This proposition requires several preliminary remarks on his specific historical method.

The "Little History of Photography" (1931) opens with the statement that "The fog that surrounds the beginnings of photography" (SelWr 2.507) is not as thick as that which obscures the beginnings of the printing press. After this observation, Benjamin immediately turns to these beginnings. The text is thus initiated by a reflection on the recognizability of the past by looking back. Benjamin will return to this image of fog when working on the "Work of Art" essay, where he explains his specific historical method as a stance of looking back, though the fog, as Benjamin writes in a letter to Kraft (October 28, 1935, 5/193) during his exile in Paris, has transformed into a fog of blood: "As for me, I try to focus my telescope through the fog of blood on a mirage of the 19th century that I attempt to depict according to those features that will reveal it in a coming state of the world liberated from magic. Of course, I must first build the telescope myself." Although here the telescope determines the view of the past, this optical dispositive moves to the images of history themselves in the epistemological chapter of the *Arcades Project* (one that also contains Convolute Y on photography), as a "telescoping of the past through the present" (Arcades 470). In this figure, the images of the past move directly toward the observer, so to speak. If the telescoping is also used as a dispositif for the history of photography and film, then object and method are linked to each other in the register of optical media. Thus for Benjamin media theory and epistemology cannot be separated.

As a dispositif of historical reflection, the telescope implies that certain citations, images, and scenes from the past become recognizable with amazing clarity out of the fog of beginnings. For instance, Benjamin cites the following passage from the painter Antoine Wiertz's article on the first special exhibition of photography at the 1855 World's Fair: "Some years ago, the glory of our age, a machine *has been born to us* which is the daily *amazement of our* mind and the *fright* of our eyes[. . . . ] Let no one suppose *that daguerreotype photography will be the death of art*" (II.I/384; SelWr 2.526; emphasis S.W.).[2] The quotation presents a remarkable rhetoric. In it, wonder over the new machine is bookended by propagation and prophecy. Between the sublime gesture of good news with which the advent of a new time is announced ("unto us a machine has been born") and a modi-

---

2. Wiertz's text is included in the anthology on the theory of photography edited by Wolfgang Kemp: *Theorie der Fotografie. Eine Anthologie* (Munich: Schirmer und Mosel, Bde. 1–3,1999; Bd. 4, 2000), I/96ff.

fication of Victor Hugo's famous dictum from *The Hunchback of Notre Dame* (that "the printing press will kill architecture") there are wondrous thoughts and scared eyes in the artist's text from one hundred years before that seem to jump out at the author, Benjamin. In his text we likewise find astonishment, in the form of "philosophical questions" (II.I/368), and shock that prefigure his media-theoretical reflections.

The consequence for today's readers of Benjamin's media theory is that we also find ourselves in a constellation that can be described as a correspondence or a telescoping between various threshold situations in the history of media. Although around 1930 Benjamin turned his eyes back to the beginnings of photography in the nineteenth century, the present readers of Benjamin, themselves positioned in a transitional period between analog and digital media (between technical and electronic images) turn their eyes back to a media-theoretical work that originated in the saddle period of photography and film. It is the era that, after the invention of sound films, saw cinema raised to the level of mass media, a situation from which Benjamin, for his part, looked back in order to study their effects on aesthetic and cultural phenomena.

## On the Interconnection of the "Technical Question" and the Concept of the Image

It is striking that in the extensive literature on Benjamin's media theory, many of the contributions rely on methodological principles that return to those formulated before Benjamin's. This is true for the long-standing captivation with the ideological-critical inheritance of the Frankfurt School's paradigm of *Kulturwarenindustrie*, as well as the fixation on the concepts of *aura* and *reproducibility*, predominantly understood as a simple opposition. This is also true for many recent works, especially when media is forced into the patterns of a history of genres or is faced with a conventional concept of art.[3] Benjamin had directly criticized both the

---

3. This is the case when, for example, Rolf H. Krauss, in his book on Benjamin and photography, investigated Benjamin's influence on discussions of photography in the 1960s and in the process found fault with the fact that Benjamin "shirked" the discussion of whether photography could also be art while Benjamin had explicitly dropped this question, one he saw as a dead end. *Walter Benjamin und der neue Blick auf die Photographie* (Ostfildern: Cantz, 1998), 34.

emergence and the discursive history of the question of whether "photography is art." He views it as a trap and instead shifted it to the much more productive question of how, in light of photography, the concept of art has changed and must be changed.

At least three methodological principles can be identified in Benjamin's analysis of media, whose disregard almost necessarily results in readings that go outside of its genuine arguments and specific approach, and thus miss the point of Benjamin's media theory:

1. The necessity of leaving behind the discourse on photography's status as art and the concomitant debate over the character of painting—that with the rise of photography painting has been on one hand restricted to a function of representation, yet on the other strengthened in its artistic character (beyond portraiture, evidence, realism, etc.)

2. The essential overcoming of the concepts of form and content with the help of the technical question: "The technical question liquidates the fruitless alternatives of form or content" (Fragment, 1934, VI/183)

3. The tearing down "of the barrier between writing and images," as Benjamin postulates with regard to photography in the 1934 speech "The Author as Producer" (II.2/693)

Only beyond a discourse on the character of art in terms of form and content and beyond the opposition of image to writing can the field of Benjamin's media theory begin.

·  ·  ·

In these principles, the "technical question" replaces his famous allegory of the stocking (in which the pocket and the gift within coincide), found in *Berlin Childhood Around 1900*. This project originates at the same time as the work on optical media, but the image (the allegory) goes back to the 1929 essay "On the Image of Proust." In *Berlin Childhood*, the image of a stocking conveys the lesson "that form and content, veil and what is veiled, are the same" (Childhood 97), while in the Proust essay a third concept is developed from the two, namely that of the image. Thus, for Benjamin the *image* replaces the traditional aesthetic binary categories of form and content. This image concerns, however, a concept in which it is thought of neither as the representation nor the opposite of writing;

it rather refers to a tradition whose ideas develop out of more than just the European history of art. When Norbert Bolz means to discover "analytic boundaries" of Benjamin's media aesthetic in the fact that it reduces these media to writing,[4] then one has to counter that Benjamin's reference to writing and legibility, including the legibility of technical images, is based rather on a complex history of writing systems that preceded the separation of images and writing. This is to say prior to a "migration," as it were, of the image out of the grapheme, to modify a phrase borrowed from Flusser's *Exodus of Numbers from the Alphanumeric Code*.[5] This concept of the image, one in which the pictographic character of scripts and the scriptorial character of images interact in various recording systems (*Aufschreibsysteme*), media, and arts,[6] must be considered an epistemic precondition of Benjamin's reflections on optical media in order to develop a sensible and fruitful discussion on it.

Benjamin had examined the scriptorial character of images before he turned to photography and film. We see this primarily in the book on the German baroque mourning play, and specifically in the section concerning allegorical fragmentation and its foundation in linguistic theory and grammatology. The transformation of things into "stirring writing," due to the allegorical gaze, had become the central focus of interest in the *Trauerspiel* book in figures such as the shard, ruin, fragment, torso, and detail. Among these figures, it is the detail that establishes the covert connection to the "Little History of Photography." Because of this, Hubertus von Amelunxen can with some justification point to the "allegorical intention" of photography in Benjamin's theory, although reservations must already be indicated here in respect to his reference 'intention.' I would like to object, however, when he writes that the chapters of the *Trauerspiel* book dedicated to melancholy and allegory "come closer to the essence of photogra-

4. Norbert Bolz and Willem van Reijen, *Walter Benjamin* (Frankfurt/M, New York: Campus Verlag, 1991), III.

5. Vilém Flusser, "Auswanderung der Zahlen aus dem alphanumerischen Code," in Dagmar Reichert, ed., *Räumliches Denken* (Zürich: Verlag der Fachvereine, 1996).

6. For more on this thought-image, see William J. Thomas Mitchell, "What is an Image?" in *New Literary History: A Journal of Theory and Interpretation*, vol. 15, no. 3 (Spring 1984): 503–537; on the tradition of pictorial scripts, see Sybille Krämer, "Kann das 'geistige Auge' sehen? Visualisierung und die Konstitution epistemischer Gegenstände," in Bettina Heintz and Jörg Huber (eds.), *Mit den Augen denken. Strategien der Sichtbarkeit in wissenschaftlichen und virtuellen Welten* (Zürich: Springer, 2002).

phy than the writings that concern the technical media itself."[7] Apart from this—that the question cannot be about the "essence of photography"—it will instead be shown in the following sections how Benjamin reconceptualizes the figure of the detail in the work on *Trauerspiel* for deployment in the history of photographic and cinematographic images and within the framework of a theory of media.

Alongside the reading of the "Little History of Photography" and several passages from the 1935 essay "The Work of Art in the Age of Mechanical Reproducibility," several steps from Benjamin's work on a theory of media will be reconstructed: (1) the birth of photography from the detail, (2) the introduction of the optical unconscious, (3) the temporalization of the detail through the concept of shock in the transition from photography to cinematography, and (4) the transformation of these media-theoretical reflections in an epistemological and cultural-historical dispositive.

## The Optical and the Messianic Sense of the Detail

As has been shown, it is the figure of the detail that establishes correspondences between the *Origin of the German Mourning Play* and the history of photography. This figure can be used to explore the moment when the "technical question" enters into media theory. Benjamin writes about "life of the detail" (Origins 182) in a section of the *Trauerspiel* book in which he counters the notion that science and art are opposed, just as he rejects the opposition of art and photography in the "Little History of Photography."

The philosophical basis for the importance Benjamin places on details is the concept of the *monad* in the "Epistemo-Critical Prologue" to the book on *Trauerspiel* (1927), or, more precisely, the reformulation of the idea of the monad that is carried out there: "The idea is a monad—that means briefly: every idea contains the image of the world. The purpose of the representation of the idea is nothing less than an abbreviated outline of this image of the world" (48). Although an *idea* is here no longer understood in the platonic sense as a mental image, but rather as a compressed representation of the whole, and indeed in the sense of the entire range of

---

7. Hubertus von Amelunxen, "Skiagraphia—Silberclorid und schwarze Galle. Zur Allegorischen Bestimmung des photographischen Bildes," in *Allegorie und Melancholie*, Willem van Reijen, ed. (Frankfurt/M: Suhrkamp, 1992), 96.

all extremes that are virtually possible, the interpretation of the *idea* approximates the concept of *structure* (47). On the other hand, structure (understood as a medium of scientific knowledge) corresponds to the *detail* (understood as a medium of artistic knowledge). Structure and detail must follow the same laws in order to accomplish the goal of uniting science and beauty, or of a "reciprocal interpenetration of art and science" (I.2/499; SelWr 4.265), as Benjamin will phrase it in the "Work of Art" essay. To counter the understanding that there is an opposition between art and science—illustrated by the statement that the landscape of the artist and that of the geologist or botanist have nothing to do with one and other—Benjamin invokes the interaction of structure and detail that leads him to the *topos* of allegorical fragmentation in the following step: "In the last analysis structure and detail are always historically charged" (Origins 182).

He understands the task of the philosophical critique as being the transfiguration of the historical material content that underlies each great work into its truth content—a process in which the decay of an effect based in contemporary stimuli is associated with the emergence of a rebirth "in which all ephemeral beauty is completely stripped off, and the work asserts itself as a ruin. In the allegorical construction of the baroque *Trauerspiel*, such ruin-like forms of the salvaged work of art always stood out clearly" (182). In this passage (one that organizes a conceptual exchange among structure, detail, ruins, and allegory), Benjamin develops his method of reading as a saving critique *in nuce*: as the gaze of a philosophical critique that perceives the historical charge in the detail and is able to decipher the traces of history in remnants or fragments. This view also presents itself as a scientific way of knowing that has passed through art and beauty. The allegorical fragmentation serves as its model. In this respect, the allegorist and his detail-obsessed readings becomes here the historical model for Benjamin's theory of the detail. It is not through the allegorical schema of *translatio* that things are transformed into writing, but rather through the gaze of the allegorist who contemplates the fragment.

Yet the allegorical process that Benjamin locates in various scenes of modernity must be distinguished from the quasi-melancholic version of allegorical fragmentation he discusses through the example of Baroque mourning plays. Whereas the Baroque's allegorical process occurs with figurative fragments, it is rather a temporal structure that underlies the allegorical procedure in "*Urgeschichte der Moderne.*" The allegorical procedure here consists in the breakout of single images from the continuum of history that has been informed by film—it concerns the fragmentation and dispersal that occurs during the succession of pictures. This *topos* constitutes the theoretical bridge to the historico-theoretical theses, one that enables a radical critique of the notion of progress as a basal concept for the theory of history to be articulated. The images from history, wrested from their context, are the historical details that are united with citations broken free from texts and images. In the gap between both models of allegory (Baroque and modern) the divine-demonic character of fragments also transforms itself. When Benjamin, in his *"Urgeschichte der Moderne,"* transfers the allegorical optics of the detail to a modern world of things and phenomena, this can no longer take place under the auspices of a dialectic of immanence and transcendence (as in the Baroque). The allegorical gaze directed at detail then refers to a radical immanence in the order of things. Correspondingly, modernity is described by Benjamin in the *Arcades Project* as the "time of hell" (Arcades 159). In the second part of his essay "Karl Kraus," he portrayed the appearance of the demonic's reign in modernity in terms of theory of language under the heading "Demon." Acting fully under the dominion of sign systems, comprehensible to anyone, this demonic position *in* history refers, through the figure of return, to a prehistorical order.

In order to describe the difference between his concept of history and the conception of time from a developmental paradigm in his historico-theoretical theses, Benjamin draws on an image from photography: just as the contours of a photographic image become visible in a developing bath, where one sees contours that remained invisible to its contemporaries become recognizable to the future generations; only in the gaze of the *Jetztzeit* do the latent traces become legible. Thus a historicized perspective is replaced by the perception of latent memory traces that becomes visible only in the developing bath of posteriority. From the obsession with details in the Baroque's allegorical practice that passed through modernity, a concept of reading has emerged that conceives of the remembered images and citations as the latency of a completed, whole history: "Of course only a redeemed mankind is granted the fullness of its past—which is to say, only for a redeemed mankind has its past become citable in all its moments" (SelWr 4.390).

## The Detail in Light of Photography

The detail visible in photographic images differs considerably from the melancholic version of allegorical fragmentation that Benjamin discusses by way of the Baroque mourning play. There, its significance is due in particular to the introduction of the issue of technique and in this way becomes the epistemo-theoretical armature for photography in general. However, the detail presents itself in Benjamin's theory of photography not only as a technical reconceptualization of the allegorical fragment but also as a reformulation of a traditional *topos* from the history of photographic theory. After the invention of the daguerreotype in the nineteenth century, the debate over the new medium was conducted under the auspices of one keyword: *the detail.*

The detail was, in this context, posed in opposition to the whole, total, or main subject and overwhelmingly thought of in a negative light. Discrimination against the detail naturally also summoned its defenders, such as John Ruskin or George Sand, onto the scene. At the time, the question of the detail was, as Wolfgang Kemp emphasizes in the foreword to the first volume of his edition (with historical texts) on the *Theory of Photography* (1980), "the most vexing" question.[8] The preference for painting over photography was mainly grounded in art's ability to represent the whole while disregarding the disruptive details: that is to say, sacrifice of the detail in deference to the whole—as per Baudelaire in 1846 or, similarly, Delacroix: "The great artist focuses interest by suppressing details that are useless or foolish."[9] During the proceedings of the Photographic Society of London (founded 1853), the illustrator John Leighton summarized the opposition established in the contemporary debates with these words: "In the highest and noblest form of art nature appears extremely conventionalized: the sum is given without the details. In photography it is reversed: the summary treatment is sacrificed for the detail." He equates this opposition to the one that exists between art and science, where the precision of details is an advantage for natural scientists, architects, and engineers, whereas artists are concerned with a general effect.[10]

8. Kemp, I/13.
9. Quoted in Kemp, I/14.
10. Leighton, quoted in Kemp, I/91.

This discourse is thus not only one of foolish and useless details, but also of the superfluous, talkative, wonderful, diminutive, and literal—against which the tools of photography itself are also deployed, as when, for example, the technical production of a blurry soft-focused image is proposed. With the qualification "too literal," however, the detail is inscribed into the traditional paradigmatic opposition of spirit to letter. Together with letters, the detail is then subject to a verdict that expresses hostility toward scripture—a hostility that is often the cover term of an anti-Semitic semiology.[11] The *detail* can thereby be regarded as a symptom of photographic theory at the advent of the medium,[12] one that is dominated by the opposition of spirit/art/the whole to letter/machine/detail.

## The Setting (*Schauplatz*) of the Optical Unconscious

Without recounting the debate at length: Benjamin refers to the detail and, in liberating it from its position within the ossified antagonistic paradigm, shifts it instead into a central epistemological position for his "Little History of Photography." This position is significant for cultural theories developed around 1900: "God is in the details." This shift in the handling of the detail is bound to reflections on new optics that commenced with the introduction of the category of the optical unconscious. With it, Benjamin attempts to grasp the effect the camera has on the status of the image:

For it is another nature which speaks to the camera rather than to the eye: other above all in the sense that a space permeated by human consciousness gives way to a space permeated with the unconscious. Whereas it is a commonplace that, for example, one gleans an impression of people's way of walking (if only in general terms), he certainly has no idea at all of their posture during the fraction of a second when a person actually takes a step. Photography, with its devices of slow motion and enlargement, reveals it to him. It is only through photography that he

11. On the history of enmity toward letters (*Buchstabenfeindschaft*), see Karl-Heinz Göttert's contribution, "Wider den toten Buchstaben. Zur Problemgeschichte eines Topos," to Friedrich Kittler, Thomas Macho, and Sigrid Weigel (eds.), *Zwischen Rauschen und Offenbarung. Zur Kultur- und Mediengeschichte der Stimme* (Berlin: Akademie-Verlag, 2002).

12. In addition to Kemp's volume, see the collection of texts compiled by Wilfried Wiegand, which, besides the theoretical contributions and numerous cultural and historical relics, contains, for example, letters that document the reactions to the new medium: *Die Wahrheit der Photographie. Klassische Bekenntnisse zu einer neueren Kunst* (Dresden: Fischer, 1981).

discovers the existence of this optical unconscious, just as he discovers the libidinal unconscious through psychoanalysis. (II.I/371; SelWr 2.511ff.)

This passage, an extremely condensed theoretical monad, contains a series of arguments that merit more extended consideration. Initially striking is the reference to slow motion, which does not exactly belong to the medium of photography, at least not in its early stages. It does, however, indicate the historical index of the analysis: it is retrospective, that is to say, written in light of a media-historical position that is informed by the advancement of the photographic into chronophotography (Marey, Muybridge, et al.) and cinema's moving pictures. Film's incognito presence in Benjamin's theory of photography here provides support for the development of the category of the *optical unconscious*. Theoretically, however, it is more significant that the comparison between the *unconscious* of psychoanalysis and that of the camera does not amount to the formation of a simple analogy between technical and psychological apparatuses, as can be observed in numerous conceptions of psycho-physiology from both the "nervous age" (around 1900) and the age of cybernetics. Benjamin instead argues beyond Freud's well-known clever *bon mot* that man is a "Prosthetic God," a remark based on the idea that technology is a projection of the functions of biological organs with which humans perfect their own bodies. Benjamin is explicit that, in his theory of photography, the camera does not substitute for the eye in order to improve its performance. Instead, a displacement of the "product" comes about through the camera. Only with the help of technology is knowledge that had before been literally inscrutable (because invisible) now somewhat accessible.[13] In Benjamin, however, the comparison operates on the episte-

13. In this way, the category of the optical unconscious takes the exact place where previously something inscrutable and unfathomable was occupied by the category of the unconscious, which was thought of as either purely technological-philosophical (Kapp) or without technology (Freud). Friedrich Kittler has called attention to the philosophy of technology of Ernst Kapp (1877), which, preceding Freud's discussion of the "prosthetic God," was based on the idea of the projection of organs. According to Kittler, however, the limits of the plausibility of his thesis—that the tools and technology emulate human organs (except, for example, the wheel)—lead Kapp to introduce a sort of unconscious that concerns the workings of physiology inscrutable for humans: "It is precisely this inscrutability that Kapp, in the spirit of Eduard von Hartmann, christens with the name, the unconscious." And precisely this inscrutability is made accessible to knowledge through media and named the *optical unconscious* by Benjamin: Friedrich Kittler, *Eine Kulturgeschichte der Kulturwissenschaft* (Munich: Wilhelm Fink, 2000), 209.

mological and conceptual registers, namely through the introduction of the category of the *optical unconscious*, a reference to the terminology of psychoanalysis. It functions differently from the unconscious within Freud's psychical apparatus, however, which is defined by its asynchronous relationship to the consciousness. As Freud writes in *Beyond the Pleasure Principle* in 1920: "Consciousness arises instead of a memory trace."[14] The optical unconscious, rather, opens the space for a triadic constellation of *camera*, *picture*, and *observer*. From this triad emerges an experience originating in the substitution of the camera for the eye and in the different relation of nature to the camera: the consciousness, as an entity or agent that structures time and space, is displaced through the optical unconscious.

When humans experience the optical unconscious through the technologies of photography, the medium itself is not the crucial element in this unconscious's existence as a product of technological development. Instead, human experience is characterized as an effect of the medium. This perspective makes a previously unavailable site accessible. What the observer would otherwise "certainly have no idea" of is now disclosed to him or her by photography, making visible what is not recognizable to the naked eye. On one hand, the category of the optical unconscious is based on the simple fact that apparatuses and technology have no consciousness; on the other hand, another type of knowledge is brought about through its effect in the image space. Inasmuch as the "other language" of the unconscious in psychoanalysis faces here another knowledge of photographic images, Benjamin's category of the optical unconscious is based on a theoretically plausible analogy.

### Enlargement and Virtuality: The Formulatability of Concealed Image Worlds

This other knowledge of photographic images is derived above all from the "device" of enlargement. In this way, the detail is reconceptualized through the deployment of the question of technology as a material structural element that first becomes visible in the photographic image:

*Structural consistency, cellular tissue,* with which technology and medicine are normally concerned—all this is, in its origins, more related to the camera than

14. Sigmund Freud, *Beyond the Pleasure Principle* (New York: Norton, 1990), 28.

the moody landscape or the soulful portrait. Yet at the same time, photography reveals in this material physiognomic aspects, *image worlds, which dwell in the smallest things*—meaningful yet covert enough to having found a hideout in waking dreams, but which, *enlarged and capable of formulation*, as they have become, make the difference between technology and magic visible as a thoroughly historical variable. (II.I/371; SelWr 2.512; emphasis S.W.)

Enlargement results in the dissolution of conventional systems of encoding and in a transformation of graphemic signs into scriptorial pictures.[15] In doing so, the technical processes of photography make a different legibility accessible: materiality, surface, and traces are readable instead of iconographic codes, and concealed dream images take the place of motifs. As in Warburg and Freud, the formulatibility of what is first visible and perceivable in the detail is therefore at stake.[16] The photographic detail, understood as a medium of recognizability (*Erkennbarkeit*), thereby opens access to a significance beyond consciousness or intention. Photography distinguishes itself from "allegorical intention" precisely with this visibility beyond intention, while at the same time creating the possibility to become fruitful for aesthetic practice. It is exactly this possibility that marks the limit of materialist concepts of media that are realized in a pure history of technology.

Benjamin's reference to an image world that is formulated in the photographic picture and yet otherwise concealed recalls the relationship between virtuality and the concept of art in his essay on Goethe's *Elective Affinities*. There, the "virtual possibility of formulating" described by the specific language of art cannot, as shown, be transferred into the discourse of art criticism. If photographic pictures now produce the effect of formulatibility for a concealed image world, then a genuine element of art has thereby been transferred to them and *virtuality* has traversed into technology. This is apparent, for example, when Benjamin paraphrases the legibility of photography with the vague word "something," which appears, for example, in the description of David Octavius Hill's "nameless pictures of humans, not portraits" such as the "New Haven fishwife." Benjamin's description of this photograph is structured and given rhythm through a threefold "something."

---

15. See Amelunxen, 101.

16. See my investigation of the detail in Warburg, Freud, and Benjamin in Weigel 2004.

With photography, however, we encounter *something* new and strange: in Hill's New Haven fishwife, her eyes cast down in such indolent, seductive modesty, there remains *something* that goes beyond testimony to the photographer Hill's art, *something* that cannot be silenced and provokes an unruly desire to know her name, she who was alive there and who even here is still real and will never consent to be wholly absorbed in "art." (II.I/370; SelWr 2.510; emphasis S.W.)

A little later, Roland Barthes will give this "something" the name "punctum," highlighting the element of photography in which it is not evidence of art, but rather a witness of what has been, the material trace of the moment that has passed and clings to the picture. It is this enduring trace of the shadow projected on the photographic plate that had so enamored the contemporaries of the daguerreotype. An example of the fascination at the time with the nearly sacred *aura*-ization of the shadow of the human body captured on the plate can be found in a letter from Elizabeth Barrett in 1843:

It is not merely the likeness which is precious in such cases—but the association and the sense of nearness involved in the thing [ . . . ] the fact of the very shadow of the person lying there fixed forever! It is the very sanctification of portraits I think—and it is not at all monstrous in me to say, what brothers cry out against so vehemently, that I would rather have such a memorial of one dearly loved, than the noblest artist's work ever produced.[17]

According to Benjamin, this material trace of photography is a residue that cannot enter into art. In this way, it is an a-semiotic *more-than-art* that constitutes the difference between photography and painting. It is not, however, the technical reproducibility of pictures that photography expels from art—as one legend within the reception of Benjamin's work would like. Neither does the destruction of aura automatically accompany technically reproducible pictures; this is instead described as an effect of a specific aesthetic practice, since photographic images are the first to "make the difference between technology and magic visible as a thoroughly historical variable" (SelWr 2.512). And so it is for many early photographs, that technique and technology produce a type of sur-

---

17. Elizabeth Barrett Browning, "On the Daguerreotype." Reprinted in *Illuminations: Women Writing on Photography from the 1850s to the Present*, eds. Liz Heron and Val Williams (Durham, NC: Duke UP, 1996).

plus, because "the most precise technology can give its products a magical value, such as a painted picture can never have for us again" (510). As regards the aura, Benjamin's examples encompass an arc that reaches from "technical determinedness of the auratic appearance" in the "incunabula of photography" (517) up until the destruction of aura in Atget's Paris photographs.

### The Viewing Space of Photography:
### Readings of Individual Photographies

For his "Little History of Photography," Benjamin was aided by the fact that a few books on the early days of photography had recently been published, "a number of works, mostly illustrated, on its beginnings and the early masters" (III/500). He also had available to him collections of photographic pictures in books by Karl Blossfeldt (1928), August Sander (1929), and Eugène Atget (1930). A comparison of Benjamin's text with the commentaries in the books about the beginning of photography that he references can illuminate his specific media-historical approach. It is the gesture of the *saving critique*, through which the "signature of the epoch" (SelWr 2.186) becomes discernable only at the moment of disappearance. Here, it concerns the early days of photography, "when Daguerre succeeded in fixing the images of the camera obscura" (514). Benjamin's method becomes evident in how he uses the split-second exposure of contemporary magazine photographs as a foil for his description the "viewing space (*Blickraum*) of photography" in which the cemetery, a shooting location motivated by technical concerns, is responsible for the temporal trademark of early photography, its duration:

In short, this art of portraiture owes its possibilities to the fact that photography had not yet come into contact with any contemporary relevance. Many of Hill's portraits were made in the Edinburgh Greyfriars cemetery—and nothing is more characteristic of this early period, except perhaps the way his subjects were at home there. And indeed the cemetery itself, in one of Hill's pictures, looks like an interior, a separate enclosed space where the gravestones propped against gable walls rise up from the grass, hollowed out like chimneypieces with inscriptions inside instead of flickering flames. But this locality could never have been so effective if it had not been chosen on technical grounds. The lower light-sensitivity of the early plates made prolonged exposure outdoors a necessity. This in turn made it desirable to take the subject to some out-of-the-way place where there was no obstacle to quiet concentration[. . . . ] The procedure itself caused the subjects to focus their life in the moment rather than hurrying on past it; during the considerable period of the exposure, the subject (as it were) grew into the picture[. . . . ] (II.I/372ff.; SelWr 2.512ff.)

The cemetery becomes recognizable as the ideal site of those "first people to be reproduced" (SelWr 2.512), whose posture was defined by duration; and the seclusion of the site corresponds to spaces such as the sewer system that are devoid of humanity, as one can see in Nadar's photographies. The location and time stamp of the early photography are marked by the cemetery and sewer, the s*cluded* (Ab*geschiedenheit*) and excreted (Aus*geschiedenes*), that is to say life's abjections.[18] As Benjamin stresses, they may also be seen as a type of paradisiac scene in which "a kind of biblical blessing" (515) seems to have likewise rested.

Along with the examples from Hill, collected in *The Masters of Photography*,[19] Benjamin discusses a series of earlier works, primarily those of Daguerre, Hill, Cameron, and Nadar, from the volume *Early Days of Photography 1840–70*, published in 1930.[20] Although the foreword of the book follows the conventional discourse on the question of a "photography with artistic value" and treats the definition of the epoch as the "early years" as a matter of finding the appropriate dates on the basis of particular technical innovations (printing on photographic paper, mass-produced dry plates, the invention of the curtain shutter, rolled film, interchangeable film cassettes),[21] for Benjamin the "incunabula of photography" is identified through the fact that the "photographer [ . . . ] was on a par with his instrument" (SelWr 2.514). What is decisive about the medium for Benjamin is the "relationship of photographers to their technology." In the early

18. To the concept of abject see Julia Kristeva, *Power of Horror: An Essay on Abjection* (New York: Columbia UP, 1982).

19. Heinrich Schwarz, *David Octavius Hill: Master of Photography* (New York: Viking Press, 1931).

20. Helmut Bossert and Heinrich Guttmann, eds., *Aus der Frühzeit der Photographie 1840–70. Ein Bildbuch nach 200 Originalen* (Frankfurt/M: Societas Verlag, 1930).

21. On the significance of these individual technical elements for the genesis of photography and film, see Friedrich Kittler, *Optische Medien. Berliner Vorlesung 1999* (Berlin: Merve, 2002), 155ff.

years, "object and technology" correspond to each other "just as sharply as they are separated in the subsequent period of decline" (II.I/376).

Conversely, when commenting on the photography of his contemporaries, he focuses on their position in the field of experimental practices beyond the division between the specialized spheres of art and science. In the forward to the publication of August Sander's socio-anthropological photography in his gallery of "deutscher Menschen," *Antlitz der Zeit*,[22] which Benjamin cites, Alfred Döblin dubs the book "a type of cultural history, better yet a sociology, of the last thirty years" in images. Döblin characterizes Sander's portraits as "comparative photography" and certifies them as "scientific standpoint superior to that of the photography of details." Yet at the same time he considers it "material" for the writing of history and thereby shifts its status to that of an ancillary science.[23] Contrarily, Benjamin links Sander's photo series to contemporary avant-garde filmmaking, writing that Sander's "physiognomic gallery" is "in no way inferior" to Einstein and Pudowkin, yet also ascribes the character of a scientific experiment to the photographs: "Sander's work is more than a picture book. It is a training atlas" (II.I/381ff.; SelWr 2.520). Regarded as an *atlas of images*, Benjamin positions the book within the field of methodologies of cultural studies developed around 1900,[24] methodologies that left behind the "territorial character" of existing scientific disciplines and in the same time integrated artistic, experimental process into the scientific archive—comparable to Aby Warburg's *Bilderatlas* (atlas of images).[25]

22. In 1934 the book was censored by the Nazis because Sander's "German People" ("deutsche Menschen") did not correspond to the Nazi's ideas about this "race"; cf. Roland Barthes, *Camera Lucida: Reflections on Photography* (New York: Macmillan, 1994), 37.

23. Alfred Döblin, introduction to August Sander, *Antlitz der Zeit. Sechzig Aufnahmen deutscher Menschen des 20. Jahrhunderts* (Munich: Transmare/Kurt Wolff, 1929), 13ff.; also appears in SelWr 2.520.

24. Kanichiro Omiya places Sander's cultural studies methodology of a "photographic catalog of people" in the context of his worthwhile analysis of photography as "reproduction technique of fraternity" and in-difference (*Gleich-Gültigkeit*): Kanichiro Omiya, *"Bruderlichkeit" des 20. Jahrhunderts. August Sanders fotografischer Menschenkatalog und Ryuzo Toriis Ethno-Fotografie* (unpublished manuscript, 2002). On Sander and Benjamin, see also Jochen Becker, "Passagen und Passanten. Zu Walter Benjamin und August Sander," in *Zeitschrift für Fotogeschichte 32*, 1989, 37–48.

25. On the genre of atlas, see Georges Didi-Huberman, ed., *Atlas: How to Carry the World on One's Back*. Exhibition catalogue (Madrid, Karlsruhe, Hamburg 2011).

Taking Eugène Atget's Paris photographs as an example, Benjamin then brings into the discussion the fact that the destruction of aura is not solely an effect of technology, but rather of a certain aesthetic approach that is informed by criminalistics. He describes Atget's works as a fore-runner of surrealist photography, characterizes it as devoid of mood, and provides commentary on the gesture with an image of demasking: just like an actor "who, disgusted with the business, wiped off the mask and then set about removing the makeup from reality too" (377; 518). The ab-sence of atmosphere and the emptiness thus become the characteristics by which Atget is exposed as the photographer who "initiates the emancipa-tion of object from aura" (SelWr 2.518). The emptiness—as distinguished from the technically determined seclusion of early photography—is here directed against an already established history of the medium as profes-sion and business. The turning away from photographic business turns into an attack on aura. The loss of aura is not (to refute once more one of the most serious misunderstandings of Benjamin's work) solely the work of reproducible pictures, but rather an effect of the interaction of photo-graphic and criminalistic optics: "It is no accident that Atget's photographs have been likened to those of a crime scene. But isn't every square inch of our cities a crime scene? Every passer-by a culprit?" (527). To continue with the comparison, Atget's Paris photographs become an allegory of that "*Urgeschichte der Moderne*" on whose threshold the "Little History of Pho-tography" stands in Benjamin's writings. The detail also plays a decisive role in Atget, in particular for the destruction of aura. When, Benjamin writes, avant-garde newspapers

show only details, here a piece of balustrade, [ . . . ] thus there is nothing but a literary refinement of motifs that Atget discovered. He looked for what was lost without trace and for the shifty (*das Verschollene und Verschlagene*), and in this way such pictures, too, work against the exotic, flaunty, and romantic sound of the cities' names; they suck the aura out of reality like water from a sinking ship. (II.I/378; SelWr 2.518)

Karl Blossfeldt's publication of enlarged microscopic pictures of plants, *Urformen der Kunst. Photographische Pflanzenbilder* (1928), serves as the best-known example of correspondences between photography in the nat-ural sciences and aesthetics. In his commentary on the book, which con-stitutes a type of *subscriptio* to the photographs, Benjamin demonstrates that formulatibility of a concealed image world which depends on enlargement. It thereby becomes clear that the historical variable introduced by photography into the relationship between magic and technology need not necessarily lead to the disappearance of magic; it can also do the opposite, and bring forth moments of only-now-visible similarities: "Thus Blossfeldt with his astonishing plant photographs reveals the forms of ancient columns in gorse willow, a bishop's crosier in the ostrich fern, totem poles in tenfold enlargements of chestnut and maple shoots, and gothic tracery in the fuller's thistle" (SelWr 2.512). Using Courbet's painting as an example, Benjamin will indicate in the second *Paris Letter* that the significance of the process of enlargement informed by optical media is not limited to photography, but can also be active in painting:

The painting of the *juste milieu* had its adversary in Courbet; with him the relationship between painter and photographer was temporarily reversed. His famous painting *La Vague* (The Wave) represents the discovery of a photographic subject through painting. In Courbet's age, both the enlarged photo and the snapshot were unknown. His painting showed them the way. It equipped an expedition to explore a world of forms and structures that were not captured on the photographic plate until a decade later. (III/503; SelWr 3.240ff.)

In this passage it becomes clear what Benjamin means when his desire "to base thoughts on the history of painting on the history of photography" (499) manifests itself. The formulatibility of a new image world that is carried out in photography makes another viewing space available to painting as well.

The detail thus plays a central role not only in the theoretical reflections but also within most of the photographs he discusses. In this way, the visualization of the covert and the literalization of the picture coincide to constitute a concept of a *legibility of images*. The destruction of mood and aura that produces a "new way of seeing" comes about through the "illumination of the detail" (SelWr 2.519). This "new optics," though itself due to the possibilities of the medium but realized only in a specific practice, establishes the legibility of images and thus becomes the guarantee of photography's participation in the literacy and "literalization of all conditions of life." As Benjamin remarks: "'The illiteracy of the future,' someone has said, 'will be ignorance not of reading or writing, but of photography'" (SelWr 2.527).

ILLUSTRATION 1: David Octavius Hill, *In Greyfriar Cemetery in Edinburgh*, 1843–1848
David Octavius Hill, *Auf dem Friedhof von Greyfriars in Edinburgh*, 1843–1848; in Heinrich Schwarz, *Der Meister der Photographie*, Leipzig 1931, illus. 57.

ILLUSTRATION 2: Félix Nadar, *The Paris Sewer*, around 1860

Félix Nadar, *Die Pariser Kanalisation, ca. 1860: Orte des Abjekts als ideale Schauplätze der frühen Photographie*; in Helmuth Th. Bossert, Heinrich Guttmann, *Aus der Frühzeit der Photographie 1840–70*, Frankfurt/M. 1930, illus. 185.

ILLUSTRATION 3: August Sander, *Catholic Cleric/Clergyman*, 1927
In August Sander's kulturanthropologischem Bilderatlas (1927), *Katholischer Geistlicher*, in August
Sander, *Antlitz der Zeit*, München 2003, illus. 28.

ILLUSTRATION 4:   Eugène Atget, *91 rue de Turenne,* 1911

Der Photograph als Detektiv städtischer Tatorte: Eugène Atget, *91 rue de Turenne,* 1911; in Eugène Atget, *Paris,* München 1998, illus. 57.

ILLUSTRATION 5: Karl Blossfeldt, *Ur-forms of Art, Tritonia crocosmiflora und Delphinuim*, 1928

Karl Blossfeldt's discovery of "Urformen der Kunst," from *Pflanzenbildern* (1928): *Tritonia crocosmiflara und Delphinium*, Fotografie; in Karl Blossfeldt, *Urformen der Kunst. Wundergarten der Natur. Das fotografische Werk in einem Band*, München 1994, p. 167.

## The Temporalization of the Detail in Shock:
## Re-Irruption of Fragmentation

The "illumination of the detail," however, has another side, one that Benjamin clearly wanted to keep separate from the discussion of photography. In a manuscript version of the photography essay, one comes across a variant of the "illumination of the detail," namely the "hell of the detail." Benjamin removed the passage: "our perception, to which the filmic close-up so perfectly complies. For photographers, however, it means entry into the unexplored monstrosity of the swarming hell of details" (II.3/1136). Although the suppression of filmic close-up is thematically consequential in the context of a theory of photography, it is by no means valid for the photographic blow-up. The image of hell could describe, for example, the process by which the visible contours and shapes of enlarged close-ups dissolve in the pure materiality of the surface or in the mere structures of light-and-darkness. It is precisely this moment in which the formulatability of the hidden image world capsizes in absolute unrecognizability and illegibility—exactly as Antonioni staged in *Blow Up*.[26]

Benjamin first articulates this fright of the detail in the final pages of the photography essay, and in fact does so with the concept that gains a central significance in his subsequent writings on modernity: *shock*. Here, shock marks the breach of a perspective that at the same time introduces the temporalization of the detail. Instead of enlargement, it is now the time intervals involved in perception that establish a new version of detail: "The camera is getting smaller and smaller, ever readier to capture fleeting and secret images whose shock effect paralyzes the associative mechanisms in the beholder" (SelWr 2.527). This is the only reference to shock in the photography essay, and comes at its end. The concept of shock thus marks the exact threshold between the "Little History of Photography" and film and the 1935 "Work of Art" essay, which, to a large extent, is dedicated to the economy of perception attendant in film. In addition to the "accentuation on hidden details" (SelWr 4.265) by the close-up, Benjamin here introduces the "dynamite of the split second": "With the close-up, space expands; with slow motion, movement is extended" (265). Whereas en-

26. See Peter Geimer's article, "Blow Up," in Wolfgang Schäffner, Sigrid Weigel, and Thomas Macho, eds., *"Der Liebe Gott steckt im Detail." Mikrostrukturen des Wissens* (Munich: Wilhelm Fink, 2003).

largement made "new structures of matter" visible, a completely unknown motif of movement becomes recognizable through slow motion—it is a sort of temporal enlargement.

Shock, however, is bound not just to the technique of slow motion but rather to the phenomenon of moving pictures in general, that is to say, to the cinematographic image that is manifoldly fragmented, its "parts being assembled according to a new law" (264). Filmic pictures represent in this way the temporal pendant to the detail and broken piece. Thus the effect of optics of the detail extends itself into the body:

Indeed, the progression of associations in the person contemplating these pictures is immediately interrupted by changes. This constitutes the shock effect of film, which, like all shock effects, is averted by means of heightened presence of mind (*Geistesgegenwart*). *By means of its technological structure, film has freed the physical shock effect—which Dadaism had kept wrapped, as it were, inside the moral shock effect—from this wrapping.* (I.2/503; SelWr 4.267)

A specific trait of film, the phenomenon is highlighted by Benjamin by way of a "most intensive penetration with the apparatus," producing "aspects of a reality free of apparatuses." The *optical unconscious* thus appears here in the fact that pictures are produced with the help of an apparatus in whose perception the requirement of their technical production disappears. Their medial structure, however, is at the same time inscribed into the physique. In this way, the optical unconscious of film (in the time interval of pictures) also provides access to the psychoanalytic unconscious. Cinematographic images' mode of operation points indeed beyond the still images of photography and produces the specific synthesis of immediacy and artificiality that is proper to film and until today has been the challenge to film theory—be it by means of a theory of apparatuses or Lacan's concept of the imaginary. In Benjamin's theory of the detail, shock not only occupies the vanishing point of *temporal*, *pictorial*, and *physical* fragmentations; in it, his category of the optical unconscious, grounded in the history of media, and the unconscious of psychoanalysis converge, the latter a version of trauma in which perception pierces the unconscious directly, without the protection of a defensive shield against stimuli. In contrast to the asynchrony and incompatibility that abides between the consciousness and unconscious in Freud's concept of memory, the consciousness is here situated in a position of a double asynchrony: asynchronous both to the psyche and to technology.

The complexity of the constellation outlined here runs through the entire Baudelaire book (1939) as a theoretical armature, whose project of a theory of culture in modernity arises from shock. In this way, shock can be regarded as a dispositif generated by media theory, one that arises with the study of optical media at the time of film's ascendancy, which in the "*Urgeschichte der Moderne*" is, however, projected back on the nineteenth century.

## The Haptic Shock of Modernity:
## Cultural History Based in Media Theory

The conceptual-theoretical introduction of the category of shock in the third chapter of "On Some Motifs in Baudelaire" famously takes place within a reading of Freud's concept of trauma in *Beyond the Pleasure Principle*, in the variant of Freud's description of memory that characterizes it as the mechanical workings of a psychical apparatus. This moment of fright that breaks through the protective shield is characterized as "absence of any preparedness for anxiety" (SelWr 4.317). From a discussion of Freudian theory, Benjamin derives his own distinction between two modes of experience: *Erfahrung* (experience that is structured by culturally transmitted tradition and meaning) and *Erlebnis* (actual, empirical experience). *Erlebnis* then becomes a phenomenon of a culture shaped through shock. It is significant in the context discussed here that in the subsequent passages the constellation of shock and shock defense (in the image of the duel) becomes the dialectic image for the stance of the artist in modernity. And on a detour through several sections dedicated to the condition of the individual in the crowd or masses, this image is brought together with the shock of optical media, as a marker of a culture shaped by tactile and optical shocks: "Thus technology has subjected the human sensorium to a complex kind of training." In this way, shock and shock defense are generalized, as they no longer condition only the stance of the artist but also mass culture in general. In order to again grasp this as an image, Benjamin goes back to the camera, or more precisely, the snapping action of photographers:

With regard to countless movements of switching, inserting, pressing, and the like, the "snapping" by the photographer had the greatest consequences. Henceforth a touch of the finger sufficed to fix an event for an unlimited period of time.

The camera gave the moment a posthumous shock, as it were. Haptic experiences of this kind were joined by optic ones, which are supplied by the advertising pages of a newspaper or the traffic of a big city. (I.2/630; SelWr 4.328)

His transferal and rewriting of the terms of Freud's psychoanalytic theory of trauma as a cultural-historical theory of shock is thus grounded in a history of media and apparatuses in which the camera plays a prominent role. Traffic, the telephone, film, and the assembly line are all phenomena of a culture that gains its rhythm through the movements of automata and produces "innervations in rapid succession" in the subject. In order to include the camera in this series of apparatuses, its significance as an optical medium at first recedes. Instead, it appears as an apparatus by means of which the haptic economy of a culture can be characterized as structured by reflective, involuntary movements and operations. In this way, the camera here became a mass medium and a dialectical image for the culture of modernity. Because of the position occupied by the camera in Benjamin's cultural history of modernity, Norbert Bolz distinguished the "metaphorical camera" present in the work on Baudelaire from "its technical-real counterpart" of "real photography." Whereas the latter expands the *mémoire volontaire*, the former serves as a topography for the search for lost time, that is to say, for self-images from the "darkroom of the lived moment."[27] The latter may apply to *Berlin Childhood*'s mode of writing, but it should be clear from the previous reading that the camera in the work on Baudelaire is more than a metaphor. One need only invert Bolz's title "Camera of knowledge (*Fotoapparat der Erkenntnis*)," in order to recognize the prominent place the photographic apparatus occupies in the Baudelaire book as an indicator of its epistemological role in the archaic history of modernity and its genesis in the history of media.

In the "Little History of Photography," the detail exhibits a double prehistory: first, and from an historical perspective, in the phototheoretical discourse of the nineteenth century, and second, in the genesis of Benjamin's writings, in fragments and allegorical writing of the *Trauerspiel* book. Similarly, in the context of Benjamin's remarks on memory in the Baudelaire book, the camera has multiple origins. The image here cited simultaneously responds to a manifold "forgotten." On one hand, Benjamin invents the medial and technical preconditions of both stimuli and

27. Norbert Bolz, "Der Fotoapparat der Erkenntnis," in *Zeitschrift für Fotogeschichte* 32, 1989, 22ff.

protective shield (not discussed by Freud) into the psychoanalytic concept
of memory and thereby enables the latter to become part of a cultural-historical perspective. On the other hand, however, the work on Baudelaire
takes up the trace that Benjamin still wanted to dismiss from his own early
essay on photography but now pushes to the foreground (by way of the
"Work of Art" essay and film), and leads to an altered image of the camera. It is not only the motion of snapping a photograph that is significant
for the description of a haptic culture of shock, but also the optics of photography, with which it fits into a culture of universal shock. The *mémoire
involontaire* is the connection to this element:

> If the distinctive feature of the images arising from *mémoire involontaire* is seen in
> the fact that they possess an aura, then photography participates decisively in the
> phenomenon of a "decline of the aura." What was inevitably felt to be inhuman—
> one might even say deadly—in daguerreotypy was the (incidentally enduring)
> looking into the camera, since the camera records our likeness without returning
> our gaze. (I.2/646; SelWr 4.338; emphasis S.W.)

This passage shows that with the inclusion of photography in the "*Urgeschichte der Moderne*," the infernal element Benjamin wanted to forget in
the "Little History of Photography" returns.

   This account was prepared by the entry of shock into the body (with
reference to film) in the "Work of Art" essay. Thus the swarming monsters
from the hell of the detail that Benjamin sacrificed in the final version of
his photographic theory of the detail return. As the infernal element of
modernity, they are entered into the dispositif of shock in the Baudelaire
book. This explains the note "'Modernity,' the time of hell" (V.2/676) that
is found in the *Arcades Project*. For the reconsideration of these infernal elements (also in photography), the temporalization of the detail for the concept of shock constitutes, however, an essential theoretical precondition,
namely, the transition from the visual and imagistic space of optical media
to the cultural-historical scene of theory.

   If one casts a sideways glance on the commentary on Brecht's *Mahagonny Songs* (written around the same time, in 1938) from this point of
view, from the standpoint of a technically determined hell of the detail,
the contrast between the texts dedicated to Brecht and those containing
Benjamin's own theoretical reflections becomes distinct once more. With
reference to Benjamin's assertion in the "Work of Art" essay that film by
means "of its technological structure [ . . . ] has freed the physical shock ef-

fect—which Dadaism had kept wrapped, as it were, inside the moral shock effect" (SelWr 4.267), the question must be asked once again: Why had the concept of modernity established in the history and theory of media that Benjamin had developed between the "Little History of Photography" (1931) and his work on Baudelaire (1938) not freed the image of hell that was morally packaged in Brecht's texts?

In summary, the relation between the theories of media and culture in Benjamin's writings takes the form of a dialectic figure. Although his cultural history of modernity is based on a history of media, this was initially developed through a technical reformulation of the detail as the dispositif of optical media while fading out certain cultural effects of the apparatus. With the introduction of the language of psychoanalysis to media theory, Benjamin found in the optical unconscious a category that served as the presupposition to inscribe the history of media into the psychoanalytical theory of memory both by temporalizing the detail as shock and by analyzing the effect of media on the unconscious. And only in this reciprocal inscription did he find his armature for the theory of modernity in which the elements of cultural and media theory are not, as is otherwise so common, mutually exclusive or discriminatory toward each other.

*Appendix*

*Documentation of the Correspondence on the Odyssey Taken
by Benjamin's* Trauerspiel *Book in the KBW
Extracts from the Letters*

Walter Benjamin's letters are published in the edition of *Gesammelte Briefe*; the other letters can be found in the Warburg Institute Archive (WIA) in London and in Scholem's literary estate in the manuscript department of the Hebrew University Jerusalem (HUJ). Panofsky's letters are published in the first volume of correspondence edited by Wuttke (Panofsky 2001).

12/22/1924: Walter Benjamin to Gershom Scholem (Correspondence 256)[1]
Now, after having completed the rough draft, a first-rate book has fallen into my hands whose title I will give you—and the Jewish National Library, should this still be pertinent. It is the last word on an incomparably fascinating area of research: Panofsky's and Saxl's Dürers *Melencholia I* (Berlin Leipzig, 1923; Studies of the Bibliothek Warburg). Don't miss it.

12/29/1928: Walter Benjamin to Gottfried Salomon-Delatour (2/517)
The work (as a rough draft) is finished, as far as I want to submit it in Frankfurt— namely, without the purely methodological introduction and conclusion[. . . .] In recent days I was slowed by "Dürer's *Melencholia I*" by Saxl and Panofsky, Leipzig 1922, which incomprehensibly escaped me, very good and very important.

10/30/1926: Walter Benjamin to Hugo von Hofmannsthal (3/206, 209ff.)
With each of your letters you renew the sense of support that I draw from the awareness that my work can count on you—in terms of content and externally[. . . .] And through you, it [the *Trauerspiel* book—S.W.] will concern, if not many, at least everyone it wants to affect and is allowed to do so. Perhaps later I may also, aside from the participation of [Walther—S.W.] Brecht, hope for Warburg's Hamburg circle's interest in me. In any case, it is most likely here, among its members (to whom I have no personal relation), that I would expect to find academically trained and sympathetic recipients; apart from that, I do not expect too much goodwill, especially from the official side of the academy.

---

1. Walter Benjamin, *The Correspondence of Walter Benjamin, 1910–1940* (Chicago: U of Chicago P, 1994).

10/20/1927: Fritz Saxl to Aby Warburg (WIA)
Dear good Professor!
Many Thanks for today's letter[. . . . ]
Scholem was here and spoke 300 words a minute for hours.

10/29/1927: Fritz Saxl to Aby Warburg (WIA)
Dear Professor!
In answer to the question:
Scholem can probably be described neither as totally good nor as bad; he comes from a west Jewish milieu in Berlin and is a Berliner patriot. At 15 he becomes interested in Judaism, learns Hebrew, and sets the goal for himself of combining Western science and Talmudic knowledge, a project that stems from the quite correct insight that either-or thinking only leads to incomplete results[. . . . ] Thus he found unknown documents from the early Middle Ages from which we know nothing[. . . . ] Yet what Scholem received from the West is the ambition to apply the methodology of philology within this limited circle and thereby he will certainly gain the essential knowledge. One only must hope that this tremendous energy and unrest buried in him will be channeled and resolved[. . . . ]

As soon as one asks him about a particular matter, he is bubbling over with information and concludes with the stereotypical phrase: I could give a very good lecture here about this.

11/24/1927: Walter Benjamin to Hugo von Hofmannsthal (3/308)
In your last letter you also remembered my desire to get in touch with the Warburg circle through my book. This is one of the few centers in which I may expect a friendly reception; above all, to which I feel obliged: I am certain that Panofsky will show understanding of my writing, especially if he receives your recommendation.

1/20/1928: Walter Benjamin to Alfred Cohn (3/320)
Naturally, I know nothing yet about the success of my book. In an almost unintelligible way, the Warburg Library circle seems to fail despite—or because of?—Hofmannsthal's mediation on my behalf.

1/26/1928: Clara Hertz (staff member at KBW) to the Rowohlt publishing house (WIA)
Honored Sir, Professor Warburg thanks you for the consignment of Walter Benjamin's book, *Ursprung des deutschen Trauerspiels*. On principle, the Professor does not accept samples that come with an obligation to write a review, although, however, the book interests him and fits within the framework of the library, he remits to you 12 Marks (postcheck enclosed), as payment for the copy.
With best regards, i/A

1/30/1928: Walter Benjamin to Gershom Scholem (Correspondence 324)

You will be interested to hear that Hofmannsthal, who knew I was interested in establishing a connection to the Warburg circle, sent the issue of the *Beiträge* containing the preview to Panofsky together with a letter, though perhaps somewhat prematurely. This kind act, meant to be of some use to me, has—*on ne peut plus*—*échoué* (gone awry, and how!). He sent me Panofsky's cool, resentment-laden response to his parcel. Can you make heads or tails of all this?

2/8/1928: Walter Benjamin to Hugo von Hofmannsthal (3/332)

I thank you for the delivery of Panofsky's disconcerting letter. I knew that he is, "by training" an art historian. I believed, however, based on the nature of his interest in iconography, that I could assume him to be cut from the same cloth, and, if not to the extent of Émile Mâle, to be one with an interest in essential things, even when they do not concern a discipline in its full extent. What now is left to me is to apologize for the timing of my request.

3/11/1928: Walter Benjamin to Gershom Scholem (3/346ff.)

The importance of Cassirer's vote would already be evident to me, but you will see, the way in which my cousin, William Stern, obviously glitters hostility toward me in Hamburg. So far, clouds surround Warburg, and nobody really knows what could break out of them. As soon as I learn what Cassirer thinks of me, I will let you know. I have tried, although whether successfully is doubtful—the only thing that is certain is that if it happens, it is done in a very wise manner that brings no harm to me.

4/4/1928: Hugo von Hofmannsthal to Judah Leon Magnes (VII.2/878ff.)

[Written recommendation to the chancellor of the Hebrew University, Jerusalem]

4/23/1928: Walter Benjamin to Gershom Scholem (3/369)

Quite wonderful, that you write or have written to Saxl.

5/24/1928: Gershom Scholem to Fritz Saxl (WIA; Panofsky 2001, 276)

Will the second edition of your *Melancholy* appear soon? A chapter on the problem of melancholy, which I believe to be very brilliant and quite obviously approaches your own purposes from a completely different angle, has just recently appeared in the significant work, *Ursprung des deutschen Trauerspiels* by W. Benjamin. Perhaps this suggestion is completely unnecessary (I have strongly recommended to the author to send a review copy to the Warburg library). But it is possible that this escapes your attention because of the seemingly unrelated title. The author of this book is my best friend and I regret very much that I did not tell you of him in Hamburg, because I believe that you seldom find many people who bring with them such an extraordinary understanding of the problems of history that concern the Warburg circle as this man does, who came upon you from such a completely different starting point.

6/4/1928: Clara Hertz to Fritz Saxl (WIA)
The book by Benjamin was sent to me a little while ago (probably urged by the author) from Rowohlt publishing house to be reviewed. We kept it without review and paid for it; it comes to you in this post.

6/4/1928: Title page from Benjamin's *The Origin of the German Mourning Play* with Warburg's dedication to Saxl (WIA):
To our (dear) Saxl / the K.B.W. / 4.Vi.1928

6/6/1928: Fritz Saxl to Aby Warburg (WIA)
Dear Professor!
Many thanks for the dedication in Benjamin's book. I was delighted by the fact of the dedication. To me, the book is too clever. Once again, as it so often happens to me, I am numbed by your power of divination in historical matters. This time it concerns your thesis that the problem of Medea is central. As you have often done before, this time you also graciously left to me the task of gathering up the stuff for it[. . . . ] I have come to realize, from all I am privy to here, that I have laid out the catalog too narrowly in the first two volumes. Through your atlas, it is indeed clearer to me that it does not work simply to leave this entire Medea thing, etc. out[. . . . ] I do not yet know how I still have the stamina for this undertaking, yet it does not interest you and the others. In a technical respect it is actually the case that these manuscripts always have hundreds of images.

6/17/1928: Fritz Saxl to Gershom Scholem (HUJ; WIA; 3/407; Panofsky 2001, 285)
My dear Doctor Scholem
Many thanks for the letter and book by Benjamin that I received a few days ago from Hamburg. It is incredible that Winter did not send you the volume. Today, I officially complained about it to the academy's secretary[. . . . ] Benjamin's book interested me very much, although it is actually not easy to read. But the man has something to say and knows his material. Today I again sent it back to Panofsky so that it can be incorporated into the second edition. Benjamin's material is particularly interesting for the late period, for which we have no material. I also sincerely hope to meet Mr. Benjamin in person sometime. Where does he live?

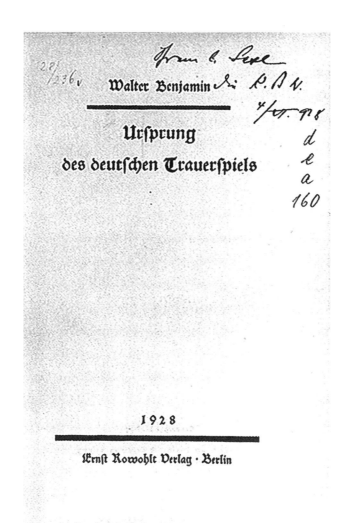

Walter Benjamin

**Ursprung**
**des deutschen Trauerspiels**

1928

Ernst Rowohlt Verlag · Berlin

Title page from Benjamin's *The Origin of the German Mourning Play*, with Warburg's dedication to Saxl (WIA)

Title page from Benjamin's *Ursprung des deutschen Trauerspiels* with Warburg's dedication to Saxl: "Ihrem (lieben) Saxl/ die K.B.W./ 4. Vi. 1928"; in Detlev Schöttker (ed.), *Schrift, Bilder, Denken. Walter Benjamin und die Künste*, Frankfurt/M. 2004, p. 124, illus. 7.

6/21/1928: Erwin Panofsky to Fritz Saxl (WIA; Panofsky 2001, 289)
My good old Saxl!
I have taken such joy from your long, lovely letter that I want to answer it straight-away, even though I know that it is not always pleasant to receive a letter in answer so quickly (because of the obligation for revenge that arises from it, but I, however, magnanimously release you from). First: I have already read the Benjamin book as well and also find it too clever, yet I nevertheless learned a great deal from it. The description of the 17th century baroque poet's melancholy is after all (though B. has not noticed) pretty much in accordance with Ripa: toss the cat in whatever manner you like, it always lands on its well-known iconographic hind legs. By the way, this Benjamin is, what is to me very embarrassing ex post, the same one about whom Hofmannsthal had then written to me (I believe I told you about that), and of whom, unaware of his book at that time, I wrote back that I did not know him and I am also not aware of having sent the proposal he received from me.

7/21/1928: Walter Benjamin to Sigfried Kracauer (3/400)
It [an article by Maria Altheim on Roman antiquity from the literature section of the *Frankfurter Zeitung*—S.W.] confirmed the assumption that the scholarly pub-lications that are most important for our perspective form more and more a group around the Warburg circle and therefore I am even more pleased that I recently received a message indirectly that Saxl shows an intense interest in my book.

8/1/1928: Walter Benjamin to Gershom Scholem (3/405)
With great joy comes your news of Saxl and Hofmannsthal's letter, for the details and refinements of which I must, however, await Dora's return.

8/9/1928: Gershom Scholem to Fritz Saxl (WIA)
[regrets that the article by him on the emergence of the Kabbalah will not be printed in *Lectures* of Warburg Library; S.W.]

1/28/1929: Fritz Saxl to Aby Warburg (WIA)
In the same post, I'm sending you yet another essay by Scholem that came to us in two copies, one for you and one for me. In my opinion, this essay is very important. It shows how the elder Kabbalah lays before us in two layers: first, the mythological layer that goes back to the Gnosis, and second, that layer which reworks Gnostic things by way of neo-Platonism. In this reading, I realized with discomfort that in establishing our program this year, we made the mistake of not including Jewish subjects. The entirety of Kabbalah clearly grounds in matters of Ascension and Scholem would certainly have been the right man to deliver such a lecture. Now the question is whether we should eventually ask him to contribute such a lecture for the printed volume? Your old friend, Saxl.

1/28/1929: Fritz Saxl to Gershom Scholem (WIA)

Lieber Herr Scholem!

I must say to you in all honesty that I find your work on the Kabbalah so good that I'm aggrieved that it has not appeared at our place. I don't believe a publisher can give a greater compliment to an author!

This year we have had lectures delivered about Ascension but unfortunately none on Jewish aspects. At present we do not have the resources to invite you to give a lecture. After reading your essay, however, I immediately sent an inquiry to Professor Warburg, who is currently in Rome, with the question as to whether he considers it possible, in principle, to print a talk of yours in this volume even if it was not actually delivered. I don't know what Warburg thinks about this, but I am naturally very curious what you think of a contribution on the theme of Ascension in Jewish thought. As you know, in the "Lectures" we do not skimp too severely on space and you could unfurl quite a bit of your material.

2/27/1929: Handwritten note/comment from Aby Warburg on a letter from Gershom Scholem to Fritz Saxl (WIA)

He should not give a lecture in the KBW; gladly publish him.

Cultural Memory | in the Present

Beate Rössler, ed., *Privacies: Philosophical Evaluations*

Bernard Faure, *Double Exposure: Cutting Across Buddhist and Western Discourses*

Alessia Ricciardi, *The Ends of Mourning: Psychoanalysis, Literature, Film*

Alain Badiou, *Saint Paul: The Foundation of Universalism*

Gil Anidjar, *The Jew, the Arab: A History of the Enemy*

Jonathan Culler and Kevin Lamb, eds., *Just Being Difficult? Academic Writing in the Public Arena*

Jean-Luc Nancy, *A Finite Thinking*, edited by Simon Sparks

Theodor W. Adorno, *Can One Live after Auschwitz? A Philosophical Reader*, edited by Rolf Tiedemann

Patricia Pisters, *The Matrix of Visual Culture: Working with Deleuze in Film Theory*

Andreas Huyssen, *Present Pasts: Urban Palimpsests and the Politics of Memory*

Talal Asad, *Formations of the Secular: Christianity, Islam, Modernity*

Dorothea von Mücke, *The Rise of the Fantastic Tale*

Marc Redfield, *The Politics of Aesthetics: Nationalism, Gender, Romanticism*

Emmanuel Levinas, *On Escape*

Dan Zahavi, *Husserl's Phenomenology*

Rodolphe Gasché, *The Idea of Form: Rethinking Kant's Aesthetics*

Michael Naas, *Taking on the Tradition: Jacques Derrida and the Legacies of Deconstruction*

Herlinde Pauer-Studer, ed., *Constructions of Practical Reason: Interviews on Moral and Political Philosophy*

Jean-Luc Marion, *Being Given That: Toward a Phenomenology of Givenness*

Theodor W. Adorno and Max Horkheimer, *Dialectic of Enlightenment*

Ian Balfour, *The Rhetoric of Romantic Prophecy*

Martin Stokhof, *World and Life as One: Ethics and Ontology in Wittgenstein's Early Thought*

Gianni Vattimo, *Nietzsche: An Introduction*

Jacques Derrida, *Negotiations: Interventions and Interviews, 1971–1998*, ed. Elizabeth Rottenberg

Brett Levinson, *The Ends of Literature: The Latin American "Boom" in the Neoliberal Marketplace*

Timothy J. Reiss, *Against Autonomy: Cultural Instruments, Mutualities, and the Fictive Imagination*

Hent de Vries and Samuel Weber, eds., *Religion and Media*

Niklas Luhmann, *Theories of Distinction: Re-Describing the Descriptions of Modernity*, ed. and introd. William Rasch

Johannes Fabian, *Anthropology with an Attitude: Critical Essays*

Michel Henry, *I Am the Truth: Toward a Philosophy of Christianity*

Gil Anidjar, *"Our Place in Al-Andalus": Kabbalah, Philosophy, Literature in Arab-Jewish Letters*

Hélène Cixous and Jacques Derrida, *Veils*

F. R. Ankersmit, *Historical Representation*

F. R. Ankersmit, *Political Representation*

Elissa Marder, *Dead Time: Temporal Disorders in the Wake of Modernity (Baudelaire and Flaubert)*

Reinhart Koselleck, *The Practice of Conceptual History: Timing History, Spacing Concepts*

Niklas Luhmann, *The Reality of the Mass Media*

Hubert Damisch, *A Theory of /Cloud/: Toward a History of Painting*

Jean-Luc Nancy, *The Speculative Remark: (One of Hegel's bon mots)*

Jean-François Lyotard, *Soundproof Room: Malraux's Anti-Aesthetics*

Jan Patočka, *Plato and Europe*

Hubert Damisch, *Skyline: The Narcissistic City*

Isabel Hoving, *In Praise of New Travelers: Reading Caribbean Migrant Women Writers*

Richard Rand, ed., *Futures: Of Jacques Derrida*

William Rasch, *Niklas Luhmann's Modernity: The Paradoxes of Differentiation*

Jacques Derrida and Anne Dufourmantelle, *Of Hospitality*

Jean-François Lyotard, *The Confession of Augustine*

Kaja Silverman, *World Spectators*

Samuel Weber, *Institution and Interpretation: Expanded Edition*

Jeffrey S. Librett, *The Rhetoric of Cultural Dialogue: Jews and Germans in the Epoch of Emancipation*

Ulrich Baer, *Remnants of Song: Trauma and the Experience of Modernity in Charles Baudelaire and Paul Celan*

Samuel C. Wheeler III, *Deconstruction as Analytic Philosophy*

David S. Ferris, *Silent Urns: Romanticism, Hellenism, Modernity*

Rodolphe Gasché, *Of Minimal Things: Studies on the Notion of Relation*